Setting the Table

M000247383

Letter from the Dean

This year marks a new approach to the way *Platform* is considered and produced. In the past, a faculty member collaborated with a team of students to devise an overall theme as a means of framing the work of the GSD from across its various disciplines and practices. With this volume, editorial responsibility shifted to the hands of three students—Esther Mira Bang, Lane Raffaldini Rubin, and Enrique Aureng Silva—who collaborated with the GSD's Office of Communications as well as three faculty advisors, Michael Hooper, Megan Panzano, and Robert Gerard Pietrusko. I am thankful to all of them for their contributions to this important document.

While both the former and the current models of production are based on collaboration across various fields and among individuals with different backgrounds, on this occasion the whole concept has special resonance as it is constructed through a student rather than a faculty perspective.

One distinguishing feature of this edition is its concern with what is placed on the table for consideration, both literally and metaphorically. The editors adopted the use of a series of "tables" as configurational devices for bringing together a diverse body of work. These themes, with headings such as "Conveyor Belt," "First Dates," or "Tabula Plena," enabled the editors to draw out a multiplicity of rereadings of the work. Each topic, conceived within a specific folder or pamphlet, contains further subheadings or strands. The method deployed here is rational-objective, yet the result is a poetic construct.

This strategy parallels the work and even more broadly the mission of the GSD, which lies at the intersection of imagination and implementation, of creativity and know-how. The capacity to conceive and realize complex design ideas and projects that can help enhance the built environment equally requires a range of negotiations and strategies between poiesis and praxis—a set of actions that exemplify the true art of making.

Mohsen Mostafavi
Dean and Alexander and Victoria Wiley Professor of Design

Letter from the Editors

To conceive of *Platform* as a means of framing people and objects, and to devise different relationships between them, is to approach the idea of a platform not as a neutral plane but as an active volume bringing together a multiplicity of conversations around it—literally and metaphorically as a table.

The table hosts a diverse body of topics from the witty banter of a first date to the weighty gravitas of a negotiation. Its materiality and temperament range from the cold sterility of a dissection to the adrenaline-pumping anxiety of an interrogation. Some guests are offered a seat at the table, some burst onto the scene uninvited, while still others must fight for their place.

The images by Adam DeTour on the following pages reveal a series of tables set within the context of the GSD, enabling us to overhear the different conversations taking place. "Sobremesas," named for the pause that follows a meal, shift the focus between pamphlets by looking at specific courses—each a kind of shared table for developing new forms of creativity and know-how.

After reading through hundreds of syllabi, event transcripts, project descriptions, research abstracts, and theses, we cut up these materials and collaged words and phrases that have special resonance for each table—shuffling them, reconfiguring them, juxtaposing them—ending up with a poetic construct:

a table of contents that draws out the true art of setting the table.

Esther Mira Bang
Lane Raffaldini Rubin
Enrique Aureng Silva
Editors

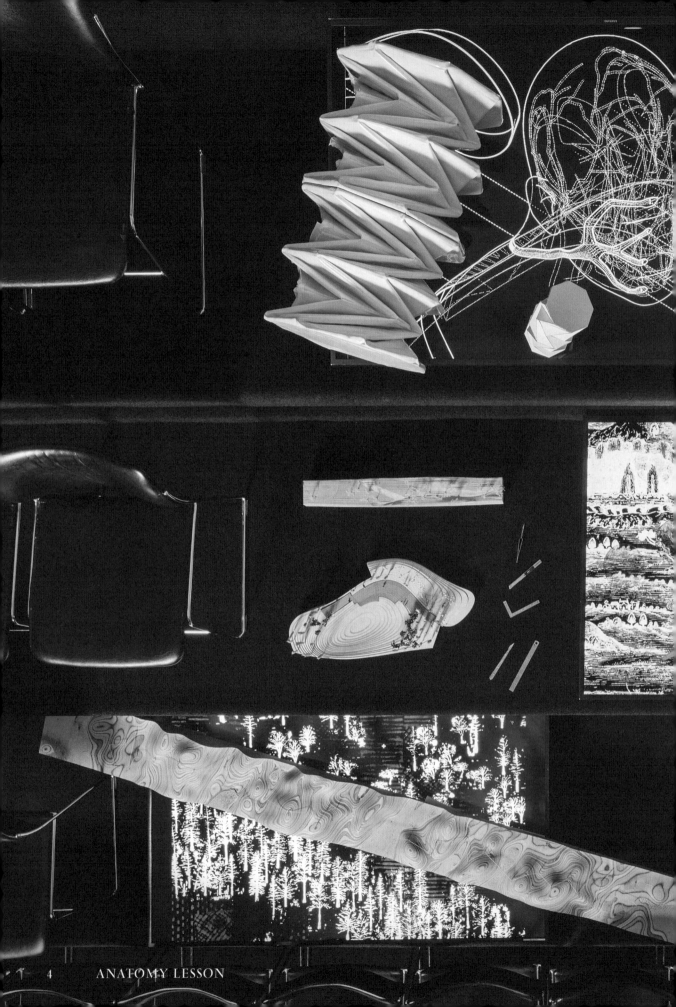

ANATOMY LESSON

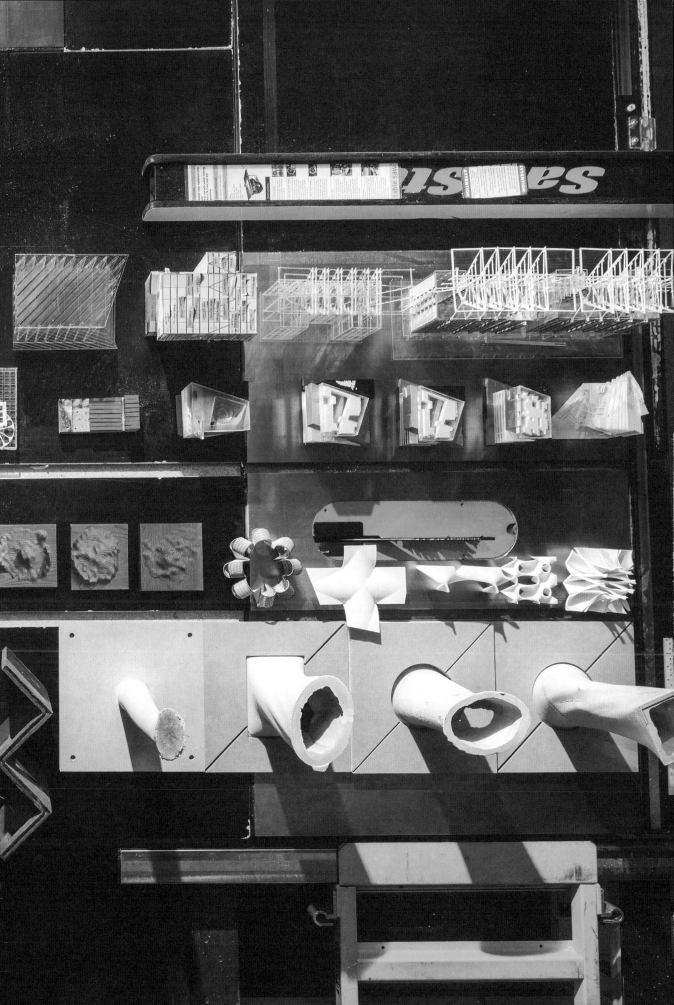

All writing is in fact cut-ups.

A collage of words read heard overheard.

What else?

William S. Burroughs

Leroi Jones, ed., *The Moderns: An Anthology of New Writing in America* (New York: Corinth Books, 1963), 347.

Anatomy Lesson

This poem is cut up from the following sources:
HIS 4490 Architecture and its Texts (1650–1800)
SCI 6141 Ecologies, Techniques, Technologies I
SCI 6465 Deployable Surfaces: Dynamic Performance
     through Multi-Material Architectures
STU 1112 Landscape Architecture Core Studio II
STU 1211 Landscape Architecture Core Studio III
STU 1231 Collaborative Design Engineering Studio I
STU 1402 The Anatomy of an Island
STU 1507 Urban Disobedience: 99 Provocations
     to Disrupt Injustice in St. Louis
ADV 9307 Design Studies Open Projects

Starting from atoms and molecules   24
across a long span of history
we come to define
a geography of intervention
more luminous than the rest.

A state of flux; a verb or a noun   29
the wonders of
        masking, sealing, surveying,
        dissecting, collecting, dredging.

Techniques as exploits,   33
points of astonishment
in forensic detail
under precise, digital control.

Out of these beginnings,   37
an explosion of interest.

Burgeoning space.   39

Anatomy Lesson: *a dissection table*

In the anatomical theater, a group of students looks upon the dissection
of various specimens laid out on a sterile table. Through incision, deconstruction, excavation, and analysis, the specimens' inner workings are
observed and studied.

        Piper Auditorium is a kind of anatomical theater, playing host to
pinups, reviews, and lectures in which the skeletal structure, geomorphol-
ogy, scalar relationships, textual origins, and core principles of projects
and ideas are probed.

        Anything and everything—not just the body—can be set out on
this panoramically visible table for scrutiny.

Remesys: Reanimating Emotional System

Saif Haobsh (MDE), Erin McLean (MDE)
Collaborative Design Engineering Studio I
Instructors: Jock Herron, Andrew Witt, Fawwaz Habbal (John A. Paulson School of Engineering and Applied Sciences), Peter Stark (John A. Paulson School of Engineering and Applied Sciences)

Aging in place requires distinct kinds of tools and provisions for mobility, many of which have ergonomic constraints or implications. For this project, design a prosthetic, broadly considered, that enhances mobility.

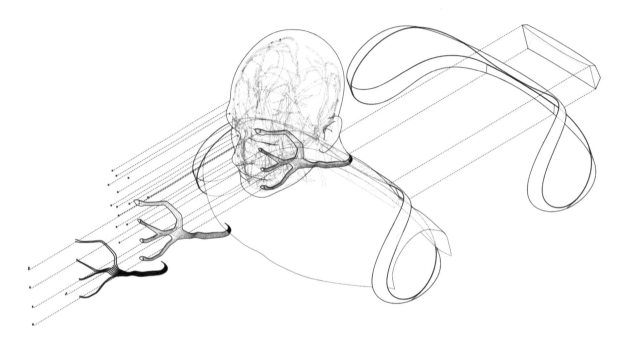

We looked specifically at the case of people affected by Bell's palsy, a temporary unilateral facial paralysis disease that has a high recovery rate within six to nine months. We designed a conceptual subdermal/wearable hybrid device that could reanimate the paralyzed side of a face based on muscle data from the nominal side. Our goal is for this device to be used to enable better emotional communication, as well as physical therapy treatment to prevent muscle degradation.

Communication
Health
Mobility
Prosthesis

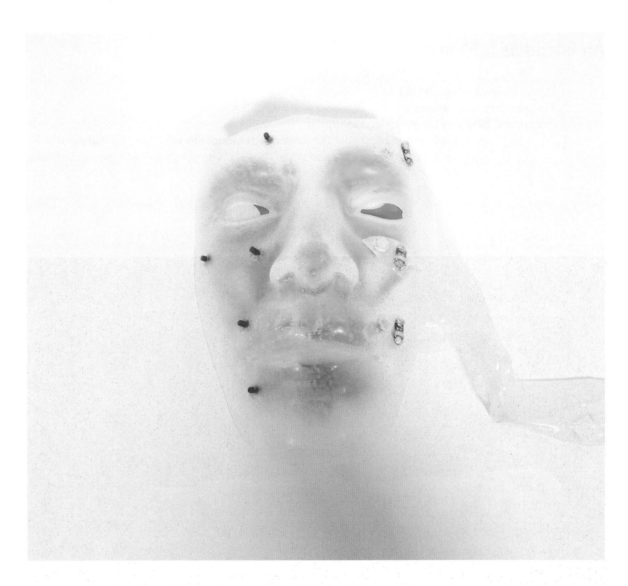

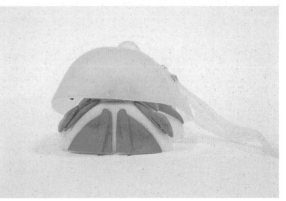

An Island as a Planet

Daniel Berdichevsky (MLA I AP)
The Anatomy of an Island
Instructors: Bridget Baines, Eelco Hooftman
      Explore and represent the anatomy of Mount Desert Island by means of a series of drawings, sections, and models. The research will focus specifically on representing geology and topography.

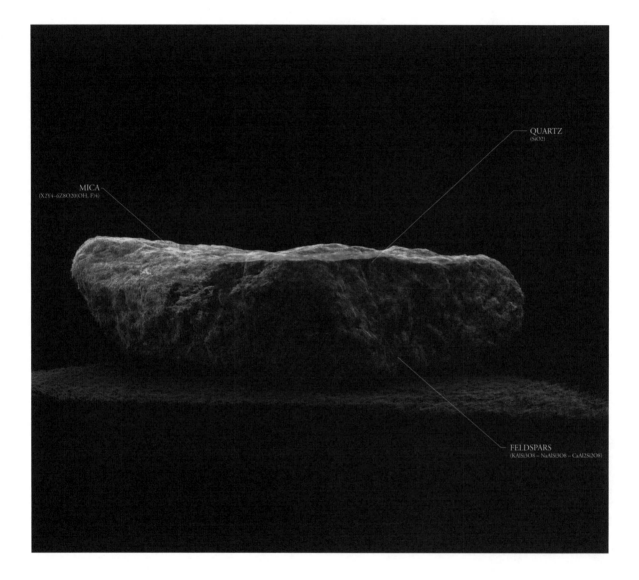

A set of three geological observatories were designed on the site, each looking at a different agent of erosion. The first one looks at the Geology by the Shore, where a rectangular pool is inserted on a granite head formation shaped by wave action. This makes the visitors feel the force that shaped this by bathing. The second one looks at the Geology by the Ice, where an observation platform shaped like a disk is built on the granite hillside. This makes the visitors look and walk on the cracks to reach the viewing platform. The third one looks at the Geology by Man, where an abandoned granite quarry is drained and further excavated to reveal the layers of the ground and utilizes a crane (like the ones that existed on the site) to bring visitors down to look at and experience the deep quarry.

Ecology
Geology
Representation

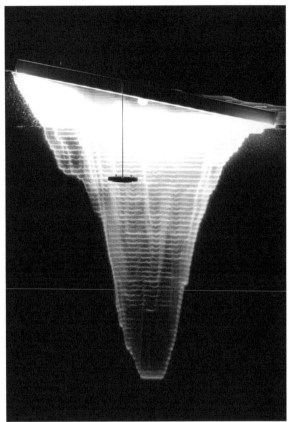

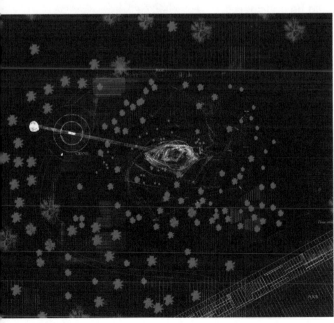

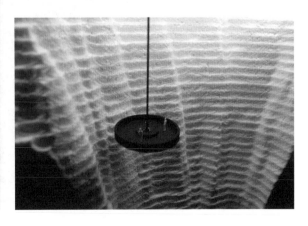

Provisionally Invisible: Depicting the Margins of the Known

Yara Saqfalhait (MDes HPD)
Design Studies Open Project
Advisor: John May

In his preface to the second volume of *Mundus Subterraneus* (1665), a 17th-century, two-volume atlas of the subterranean world, Athanasius Kircher promises his readers to make the most profound depths of the Earth visible "by means of a sharp penetration of the eyes."[1] Consequently, the following pages of the book are populated by lavishly illustrated depictions of natural phenomena that range from volcanic eruptions to underground springs and channels, in addition to machines and instruments that replicate natural processes that could not be directly observed otherwise, like the formation of metals and magnetic attraction. The German scholar's work was cast by some of his later biographers as an anachronism amidst the rising scientific empiricism of the 17th century, mainly due to the speculative nature of its claims and the irreproducibility of its experiments.

This thesis seeks to investigate the function of the pictorial representations employed by Kircher in *Mundus Subterraneus* in relation to the changing intellectual and institutional contexts, ways of seeing, belief systems, forms of knowledge, scientific practices, and colonial expansion of mid-17th-century Europe. Looking first at the wider economy of images circulating through the works of naturalists in 17th-century Europe, this thesis provides a reading of Kircher's illustrations against the backdrop of the epistemological status of scientific images of their time. It turns next to considering Kircher's investigation of the subterranean world—and other realms that reside beyond and below the threshold of unaided human vision—in light of the transformation of the relationship between vision and cognition instigated by the introduction of optical instruments like the telescope and the microscope at the beginning of the 17th century, and the ensuing change in the conception of scientific fact, evidence, and explanation. *Mundus Subterraneus* was deeply embedded within these changes and it is in connection to this that its ambitions and shortcomings should be considered.

1
Athanasius Kircher, *Mundus Subterraneus*, volume two in *XII Libros Digestus* (Amsterdam: Joannem Janssonium & Elizium Wegerstraten, 1665), ii.

more luminous than the rest.

Geology
History
Mapping
Representation

8Twist

Kevin Chong (MArch I), Elissavet Pertigkiozoglou (MDes Tech), Carla Saad (MDE),
Anne Stack (MArch I)

Deployable Surfaces: Dynamic Performance through Multi-Material Architectures
Instructors: Chuck Hoberman with Jonathan Grinham

Taken together, advances in the use of origami and inflatable, multi-material devices offer a new design paradigm for rapidly deployable structures. The critical next step is to bring these techniques up to the architectural scale.

The "8Twist" is a structural, inflatable, and modular system inspired by the origami Kresling pattern. It is designed to be compact and expandable while being efficiently and easily deployable. The module went through a series of interventions in order to progress from a vertical structure into an arching form. "Soft" zones were introduced by slicing the octagonal module at a specific angle, then mirroring it along its axis in order to induce the curvature.

Detail
Fabrication
Kinetic
Materials

Living Lighting

Pamela Cabrera (MDes EE), Aurora Jensen (MDes EE), Adam Kratch (MIT),
Peter Osborne (MDes EE)
Nano, Micro, Macro: Adaptive Materials Laboratory
Instructors: Salmaan Craig, Joanna Aizenberg (John A. Paulson School of Engineering and
Applied Sciences)

Braintrust: An arena for candid discussion that elicits ideas and insights and, over time, combines them into a single work of collective genius.
Mei-Mei: Milieu for extraordinary interactions of matter, energy, information.
Model: A substitute for what we are modeling. All models are wrong, but some are useful. We can regard a good model as the thing that interests us.

 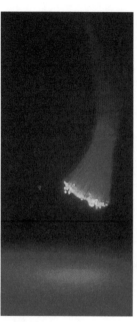  

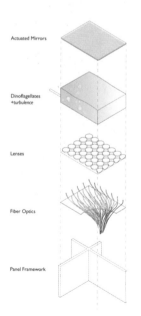

NIGHT

Actuated Mirrors

Dinoflagellates +turbulence

Lenses

Fiber Optics

DAY

Panel Framework

The goal of this system is to replace the use of artificial lights in interior spaces by extending existing fiber optic daylighting technology to also work during the night. Our proposed system leverages bioluminescent organisms, hydrogel actuated mirrors, fiber optics, and lenses in order to evolve existing technology into a fully diurnal solution.

Just City St. Louis Values

Urban Disobedience: 99 Provocations to Disrupt Injustice in St. Louis
Instructor: Toni L. Griffin

In concert with the frameworks of urban justice and design being developed by the Just City Lab at the GSD, the studio work examines and prototypes the ways in which design facilitates just outcomes, both spatial and social. St. Louis has 99 problems—but it also has 99 opportunities to eradicate divides, correct inequalities, and advance innovation and justice.

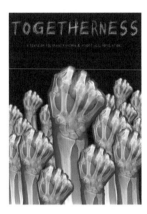

Left to right from top:
Ashutosh Singhal (MAUD)
Alice Hintermann (MUP)
Keunyoung Lim (MArch I)
Lena Ferguson (MUP)
Chaoran Wu (MAUD)
Carla Wijaya (MAUD)
Rose Florian Rodriguez (MAUD)
Juan Pablo Fuentes (MAUD)

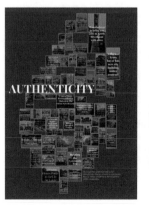
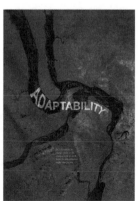

American City
Justice
Policy
Urbanism

Symbiotic Infrastructure

Aiysha Alsane (MLA I AP), Danica Liongson (MLA I, MDes ULE), Yifan Wang (MLA I)
Landscape Architecture Core Studio III
Instructor: Montserrat Bonvehi Rosich

Using landscape as a distinct starting point for the project of city making, this studio aims to conceptualize and articulate the adaptive city, the city in a state of flux as it responds to changing environmental, programmatic, market, and sociocultural conditions and circumstances. The studio asks students to amplify productive instabilities while inventing new types of urban and landscape form.

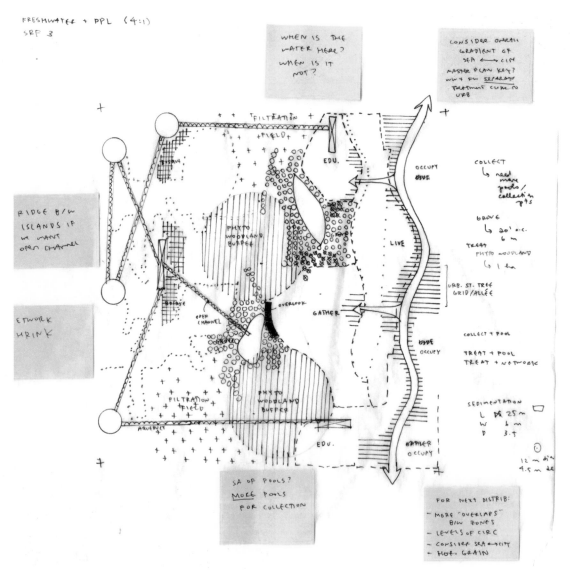

"Symbiotic Infrastructure" proposes a new model for urban living, where the interaction with water is more direct. Landform, vegetation, and buildings work together to collect, convey, and treat water. On a daily basis, at a human scale, the water infrastructure is revealed.

Strategy 1: Topographic Manipulation
Strategy 2: Strategic Planting
Strategy 3: Buildings as Aqueducts

Ecology
Infrastructure
Urbanism
Water

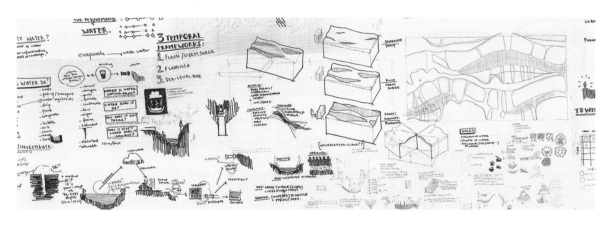

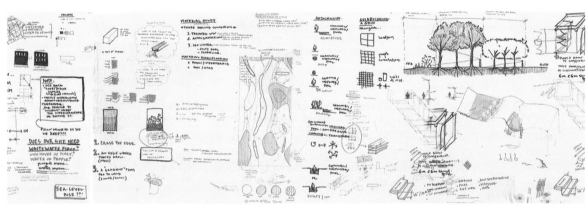

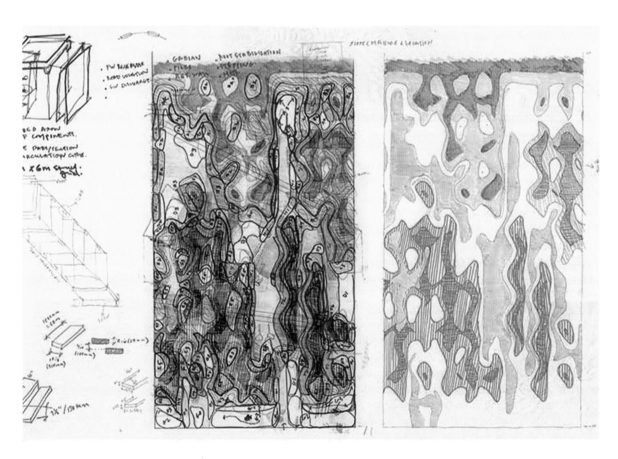

Flatbed

Phillip Denny (PhD)
Architecture and its Texts (1650–1800)
Instructor: Erika Naginski

Art historian Leo Steinberg introduced the concept of the flatbed picture plane in a lecture given at the Museum of Modern Art in 1968; it was published in *Artforum* in 1972 and appeared in an anthology of Steinberg's writing under the title *Other Criteria*.[1] The "flatbed" refers to his assertion that the essential verticality of the picture plane in painting had recently been substituted for a fundamental horizontality, like that of a flatbed printing press. For Steinberg, the flatbed picture plane is "any receptor surface on which objects are scattered, on which data is entered, on which information may be received, printed, impressed—whether coherently or in confusion." Importantly, Steinberg's "flatbed" is an abstract substrate, but it is also an irreducibly material one, that is, some *thing* onto which "objects are scattered" or "data entered." Steinberg's principal example is Robert Rauschenberg, whose screen-printed collages and combines evince a play of data that reconfigures the pictorial surface as an abstract window of sorts. This picture plane attains dual status as both abstract and real, a surface that is at once existing in actuality and as a conceptual ideal, like a geometric plane: a perfectly flat, featureless surface. Indeed, whereas Steinberg's deployment of the term "plane" is sometimes passive (e.g., "a receptor"), it is elsewhere rendered active:

> Rauschenberg's picture plane had to become a surface to which anything reachable-thinkable would adhere. It had to be whatever a billboard or dashboard is, and everything a projection screen is, with further affinities for anything that is flat and worked over—palimpsest, canceled plate, printer's proof, trial blank, chart, map, aerial view. Any flat documentary surface that tabulates information is a relevant analogue of his picture plane—radically different from the transparent projection plane with its optical correspondence to man's visual field.[2]

The inherent contradiction of the "flatbed picture plane" comes to the fore when Steinberg describes the "picture plane," a geometrical product of linear perspective, as if it were a material thing. The "picture plane" was just an "imaginary plane corresponding to the surface of a picture" before Steinberg's artists took hold of it, "to become a surface to which anything reachable-thinkable would adhere," like pasting bills to a wall.[3] This persistent contradiction suggests both the unresolved ontological status of the "picture plane" and the limited pliancy of the term as Steinberg resolved to stretch and to redefine it after 1968. But this ambiguous linguistic terrain arguably held the greatest import for architecture, and indeed, the question of "whatever a billboard or dashboard is" was also on the minds of Steven Izenour, Denise Scott Brown, Robert Venturi, and the Yale students they'd brought to Las Vegas that same year. Their task was twofold: an "open-minded and nonjudgmental investigation" of the strip and the invention of new graphic techniques to document it.[4] Their now-famous charts, diagrams, and collages of Las Vegas's abundant billboards, its neon signs, and "every written word seen from the road" suggest that some architects already had the flatbed in hand.

1
Leo Steinberg, "Other Criteria: The Flatbed Picture Plane," in *Other Criteria: Confrontations with Twentieth-Century Art* (New York: Oxford University Press, 1972).

2
Ibid., 88.

3
This definition of "picture plane" is taken from my nearest "reachable-thinkable" dictionary; see "picture plane" in *New Oxford American Dictionary* (3rd ed., 2017).

4
See Steven Izenour, Denise Scott Brown, and Robert Venturi, "Syllabus, Learning From Las Vegas Studio, Fall 1968," Yale School of Architecture, 1968. The first edition of *Learning from Las Vegas* was published in 1972 and a revised edition was issued in 1977.

An Index of Formation: Tree Life at Mount Auburn Cemetery

Ecologies, Techniques, Technologies I
Instructor: Rosetta S. Elkin

Morphology is the study of formation in plants. The pedagogic objective aims to transform observation into information, and information into knowledge.

Ecology
Plants
Representation

The Portrait of a Tree, Observations of Tree Growth

Ecologies, Techniques, Technologies I
Instructor: Rosetta S. Elkin

A drawing of a tree cannot be useful unless it depicts—in a convincing manner—the mechanisms that influence its form. While a sketch aspires to imitation, a diagrammatic depiction puts into action the causes by which certain effects are produced. Therefore, it is not sufficient to sketch the selected plant: the mere imitation of form is not instructive. This assignment requests a distinctly quantifiable observation, using formal comparison and fieldwork as the means for understanding tree formation.

Ecology
Plants
Representation

Orchard, Nursery, Public Park: Franklin Park's Next 100 Years

Kira Clingen (MLA I)
Landscape Architecture Core Studio II
Instructor: Kristin Frederickson

The drawing abstracts the location of street trees surrounding
Franklin Park, creating new potentials to structure the space
using tree canopy.

Ecology
Plants
Representation

TransVision: Exploring the State of the Visual Field

Jiabao Li (MDes Tech)
Design Studies Open Project
Awarded the Project Prize in Design Studies
Advisor: Panagiotis Michalatos

The three machines create:
Hyper-Sensitive Vision: a speculation on social media's ampli-
    fication effect and our filtered communication landscape.
Hyper-Focused Vision: an analogue version of the searching
    behavior on the Internet.
Hyper-Commoditized Vision: monetized vision that meditates
    on the omnipresent advertisement targeted all over our
    visual field.

Internet
Prosthesis
Responsive Environments

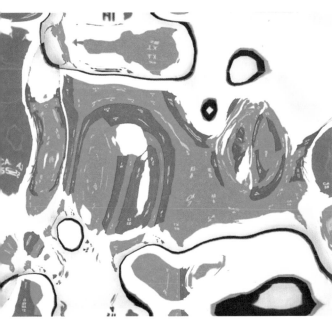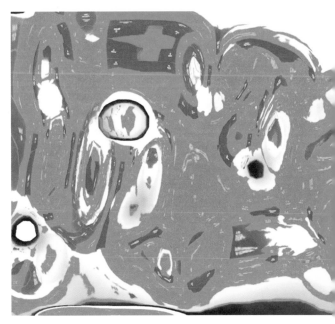

39   Burgeoning space.

Anatomy Lesson

Front

A–C Daniel Berdichevsky
D–F, H
    Kevin Chong
    Elissavet Pertigkiozoglou
    Carla Saad
    Anne Stack
G   Jiabao Li

Back

I   Zeqi Liu
J   Aiysha Alsane
    Danica Liongson
    Yifan Wang
K   Stacy Passmore

Also seen in
plan view (p. 4)

Kira Clingen
Saif Haobsh
Erin McLean
Yara Saqfalhait

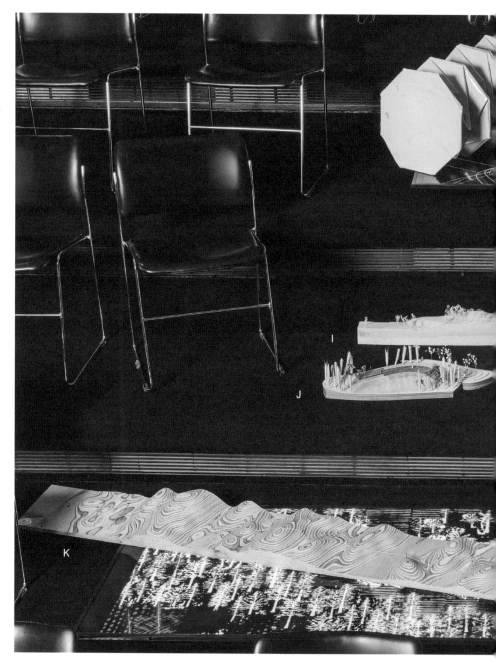

40

In the Round

Human landmarks   44
intended to outlive
the monument,
call into question
        the true,
        the false,
        and the indeterminate.

Innocent eyes   51
permute
mass, proportion, and tactility,
highly authored views
fully three-dimensional.

Autonomous   56
figural qualities
gesture
a neutral backdrop,
        common and mundane.

This poem is cut up from the following sources:
VIS 2141 Landscape Representation I
VIS 2224 Digital Media II
VIS 2482 Art, Design, and the Public Domain Proseminar
SCI 6322 Mapping: Geographic Representation and Speculation
STU 1101 Architecture Core Studio I: Project
STU 1102 Architecture Core Studio II: Situate
STU 1112 Landscape Architecture Core Studio II
STU 1201 Architecture Core Studio III: Integrate
STU 1211 Landscape Architecture Core Studio III
STU 1302 Tibet Contemporary: Building in the Himalayas
STU 1308 The Monument
STU 1313 ,Tri,3,Tre,
STU 1316 Root: Rediscovery of Jingdezhen Contemporary
STU 1318 In the Details: The Space between God and the Devil
ADV 9307 Design Studies Open Project
ADV 9342 Landscape Architecture Thesis
ADV 9382 Independent Design Engineering Project
Lecture   "FE_20180201," Sarah Oppenheimer

Between form and content,   61
obscured or distorted,
the domain of art
exchanges
the epic theater
of the public sphere
for a suspension of judgment,
          reorienting and clarifying,
          translated into permanence.

Links between the past and the future—   70

Andy Warhol   71
          god
The Mattress Factory
          tombs—

relevant enough to be remembered.   75

In the Round: *a pedestal for veneration*

At the center of Gund Hall we find the Donut: a kind of front desk, a
pedestal of sorts, a soapbox for open letters, a meeting point, a place
for pop-up events. We all know the Donut since we approach it from all
sides—we can't help but pass it by. It is the GSD's monument *par excellence* ("I'll meet you at the Donut!").

But the Donut itself is not much to write home about. Instead,
it is a neutral platform onto which objects of value are placed and around
which many people circulate. On this table we find sculptural architectures, unique and refined forms, and works that reinterpret memory and
history. Much like a doughnut, these projects are meant to be revered in
the round.

Memory-Go-Round

Hanna Kim (MDes ADPD), Eric Moed (MDes ADPD),
Andrew Connor Scheinman (MDes ADPD), Malinda Seu (MDes ADPD)
Art, Design, and the Public Domain Proseminar
Instructor: Krzysztof Wodiczko
Memory, Monument, Trauma

In August 2017, thousands of torch-bearing white nationalists descended on Charlottesville, Virginia, to protest the planned removal of a statue of Confederate General Robert E. Lee. This intensified a national moment of reckoning with the hundreds of Confederate statues that dot cities from Jacksonville, Florida, to Helena, Montana, leaving a stockpile of removed Confederate statues with nowhere to go and Americans with questions about what to do with them. Should these monuments be destroyed? Should they be relocated to museums or cemeteries?

Art Practices
History
Memory
Monument

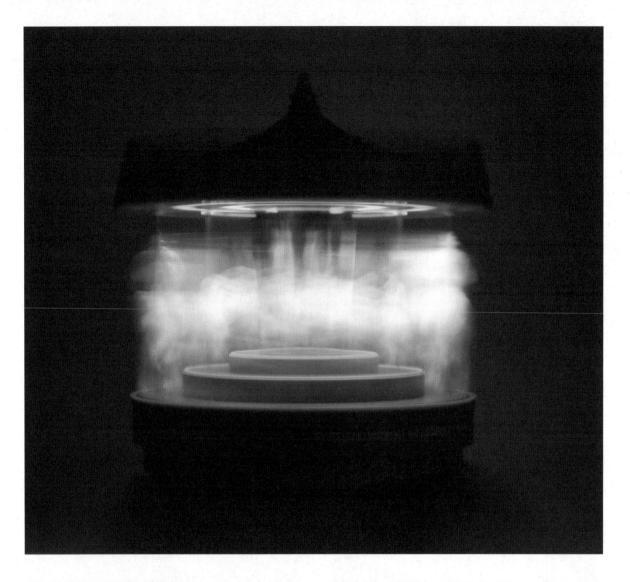

Enter the "Memory-Go-Round," a monumental carousel that confronts Civil War revisionism by tapping into a different sort of American nostalgia.

    Cyclical and nonhierarchical, the "Memory-Go-Round" confuses North and South, refusing to take sides or even acknowledge differences between mounted Civil War generals and the children riding with them. As a

monument to the removal of memorials from their pedestals, the "Memory-Go-Round" gives all Americans—Union or Confederate, past or present—equal footing.

What is a monument today? The aim of the studio is to design a contemporary version of a monument in a time when the collective, the expression of the public sphere, or, more politically speaking, the value of democracy are all called into question.

The tower is organized by the layering of various 20th-century American housing typologies that exemplify the social and economic structures of their time while evidencing the linear evolution of the house, constantly changing after every crisis. The balloon frame is taken as the epitome of American housing construction, utilizing its ephemeral aesthetic to address the fragility of an economic system that cannot again rely on the unstable foundation of the housing market.

Monument
Structure
Typology

Making a New City Image . . . or, An Eye for AI

Brian Ho (MDE)
Independent Design Engineering Project
Advisors: Robert Gerard Pietrusko, Krzysztof Z. Gajos (John A. Paulson School of Engineering and Applied Sciences)

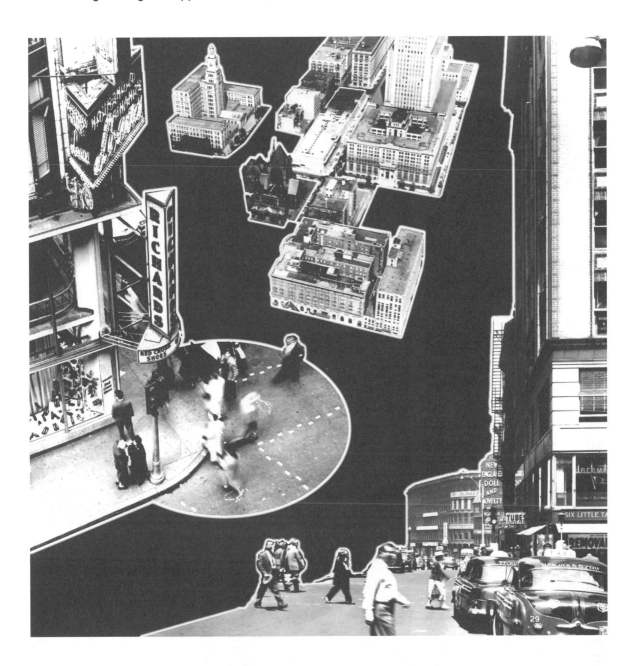

What might we learn about the city using computer vision, deep learning, and data science? How might the history, theory, and practice of urbanism—which has long viewed the city as a subject of measurement—inform modern applications of computation to cities? Most importantly, can we ensure that both disciplines understand the city as it is perceived by people? This thesis revisits Kevin Lynch's *Image of the City* (1960), applying machine-learning models to archival photographs and historical maps of Boston, and classifying from them Lynch's five elements of the city image. Together, these methods produce a new mode of analysis that balances a comprehensive perspective at the scale of the city with a focus on the texture, color, and details of urban life.

Computation
Mapping
Urbanism

The Boston Auction House

De Qian Huang (MArch I)
Architecture Core Studio II: Situate
Instructor: Jenny French

Design the facade between the city and the rooms. The facade should wrap the entire site, even though portions of the facade will not yet have rooms behind them.

  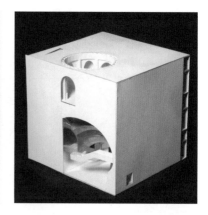

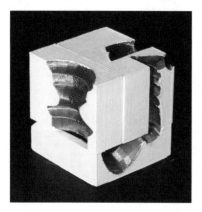 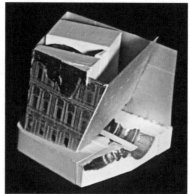 

 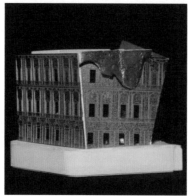 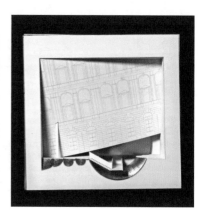

Facade
Ornament
Program

49   the false,

Stress Terrain

Anne Chen (MLA I AP), Yoeun Chung (MAUD), Shuo Zhao (MAUD)
Mapping: Geographic Representation and Speculation
Instructor: Robert Gerard Pietrusko

Maps do not represent reality; they create it. As a fundamental part of the design process, the act of mapping results in highly authored views of a site. By choosing which features, forces, and flows to highlight—and, implicitly, which to exclude—the designer first creates the reality into which their intervention will be situated and discussed.

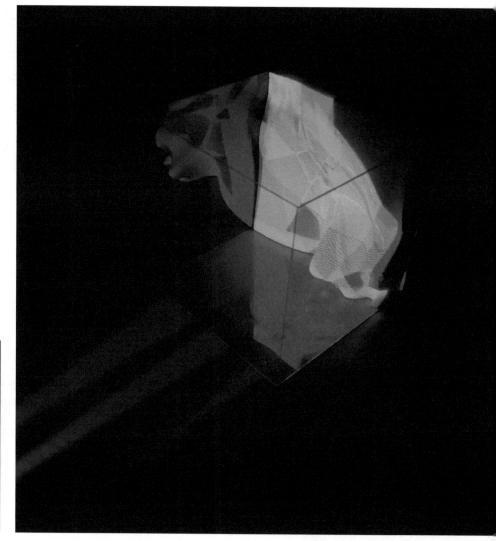

Our project examines human stress as a parameter to discover the new terrain of the city. By categorizing stress into two levels and reconnecting the points accordingly, a new region of stress is formed, largely related to the distance traveled by each person.

Borderhood: Reimagining the Canada–US Borderlands

Sonny Meng Qi Xu (MArch II, MLA I AP)
Landscape Architecture Thesis
Advisor: Sergio Lopez-Pineiro

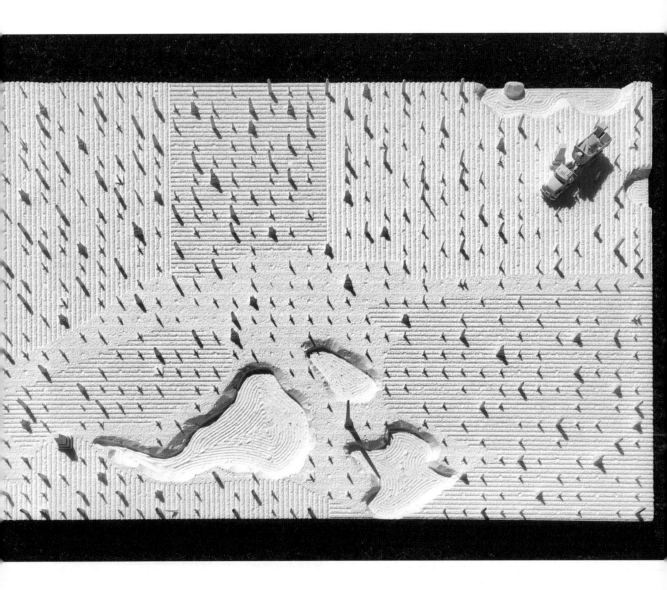

Through the mapping of the flows and "holes" along the border, this thesis aims to understand the different types of landscape conditions that the world's longest border crosses and creates. The thesis reimagines the Canada–US border as a cultural project that serves social, infrastructural, ecological, and recreational functions. At the same time, the thesis connects divided human and ecological communities and border towns. "Borderhood" aims to create a thick nationality gray zone between the two countries rather than the existing thin boundary line.

Borders
Infrastructure
Mapping

Jingdezhen Rekindled

Aaron Hill (MLA I), Caleb Marhoover (MArch I)
Root: Rediscovery of Jingdezhen Contemporary
Instructor: Zhu Pei

In Jingdezhen, we can rediscover the roots of human settlement and architecture, which are deeply connected to Jingdezhen's nature, culture, and history. We will undertake the challenge of designing around 6,000 square meters of the Blue and White Porcelain Museum at the Yuan Dynasty kiln relic site.

A pavilion sits above grade, spanning two of the dormant brick chimneys. It transitions visitors from the bustle of the rejuvenated factory floor toward the archaeological sites, where exposed relics emerge from the slope. Below ground, a relic gallery connects the two excavations, exhibiting unearthed porcelain from the three dynasties of production represented at the site.

Journey

Wilson Harkhono (MArch I AP), Yina Moore (MArch I)
Root: Rediscovery of Jingdezhen Contemporary
Instructor: Zhu Pei

This project, a museum of porcelain, discovers and relates to the local attitude toward working and living. It creates an intimate public place that allows visitors to explore the history and the contemporary urban culture through fluid movement between indoor and outdoor spaces.

Perceiving

Han Cheol Yi (MArch I AP)
Landscape Representation I
Instructor: Emily Wettstein

fully three-dimensional.

Shadowboxer

Jonathan Gregurick (MArch I)
Architecture Core Studio I: Project
Instructor: Sean Canty

The hidden room requires the exploration of the techniques by which spatial and organizational paradigms become formalized.

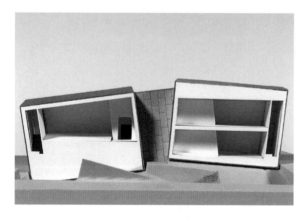

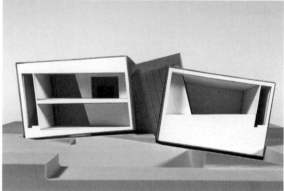

The occupant has arrived at an identical room directly below the first room in the first box. Perhaps this formal system would make the occupant feel as if they have arrived in the same room where they began, creating the illusion of a hidden room.

Circulation
Interior

Blurred Lines

Andreea Vasile Hoxha (MLA I)
Landscape Architecture Core Studio II
Instructor: Belinda Tato

This studio is focused on a paradigmatic typology of the urban landscape: the large public park, examining issues of space through measure, circulation, sequence, topographic form, canopy, and climatic influence.

Landform
Program
Public Space

A Summer Retreat for Lindsey Vonn

Caroline Chao (MArch I)
,Tri,3,Tre,
Instructor: Mack Scogin

Structured around the exploration of the liberating suspension of judgment found in an architecture born of ternary logic. A logic composed of three values: the true, the false, and the indeterminate. A kind of "architectural triptych" of the completely incomplete that can sustain innocent eyes, irritate the anxious and guessing, and free the vulnerable and innocent.

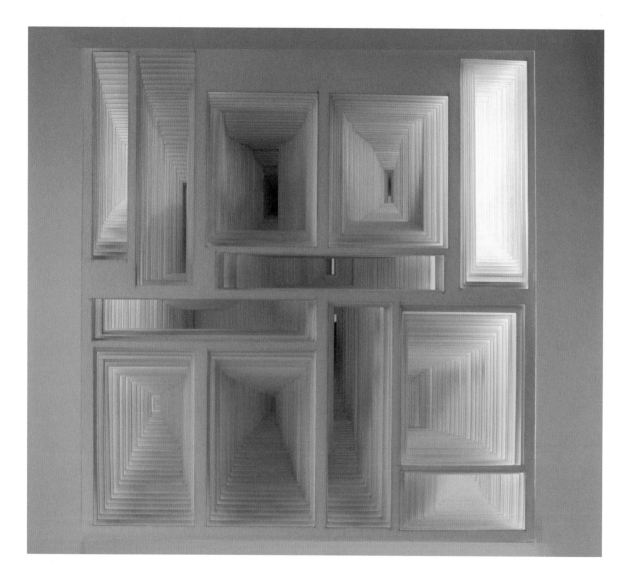

The world we inhabit is intrinsically connected to our mental operations and our instinctual understanding of space. It is influenced by physical space, but perhaps more dependent on our subjective understanding of that space. This project examines the way we see and perceive—personal space, belongings, and memorabilia become a personal language—the only thing that defines us from each other. These relationships are the remnants of ourselves—perhaps the only things we leave behind.

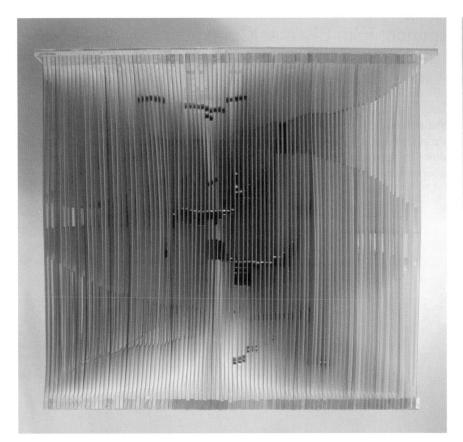

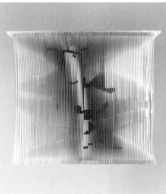

"A Summer Retreat for Lindsey Vonn" allows her to experience this continuity as it breaks down. It is a physical condition that would never exist within her typical understanding of space. It is a freezing of time and space—a suspension in resonance— where the pace is neither fast nor slow. Frames appear to be a timeline, but instead, time breaks down and another world appears. Here there is no beginning and no end, no start marker and no finish line. There is only infinity.

Converging Divergence: Film Shed as Cinematic Device

George Zhang (MArch I, MLA I)
Architecture Core Studio II: Situate
Instructor: Sean Canty

We will study the manifold relationships between the enclosure and the experience of a building and its activity. Beginning with its span and scaling down to occupation and ground, architecture will be used as the means of addressing varying environment and site.

Sited on the water's edge in Boston's Seaport District, this film studio aims to bring together the shed typology and types of perspectives as a cinematic device. The disposition of four film sheds between land and water is connected to produce a continuous figure. Optical devices of the film still and panoramic are internalized within the architecture through the serial repetition of a spatial bay and the profile of the film shed in the spaces between soundstage volumes, allowing for multiple vantage points to be on display across an interior void. The gradually transitioning, discrete, framed openings in the transition areas render the surrounding site and city as a backdrop, externalizing the idea of a film setting to the urban fabric.

Film
Program
Structure

common and mundane.

"FE_20180201"

Sarah Oppenheimer
Rouse Visiting Artist Lecture
February 1, 2018

Sarah Oppenheimer: When it comes to the building in motion, drafting conventions are largely limited to the representation of a pivoting door. The turning of a door is drawn as an arc in plan. This arc represents the total possible positions of a door, the door at all times—360-degree rotation extends the arc into a circle. When the trace of this movement is viewed in elevation or at eye level, the circular path appears as a line.

While developing *S-28*, the studio began to study the orientation of this rotational axis. The geometry of the glass volume in this early mechanized prototype is based on the insulated glass unit, also known as an IGU. Two layers of glass are separated by two aluminum bars. A volume of air is sandwiched between the glass planes.

By orienting the axis at 45 degrees, the rectangular element rotates from vertical to horizontal. This reorientation of the axis of rotation transforms the apparent path of motion from a circle to an ellipse in both elevation and plan. The representational convention of multiple viewing planes, naturalized in the four view ports of computer-aided drafting systems, became an essential conceptual guide and methodological tool in the project's development. The point of view in a representational system became inextricably linked to the point of viewing in processional space.

The orientation of objects and the position of bodies developed relationally. Not only does the glass boundary plane rotate around this central axis, but each internal mechanical component also rotates around this axis.

In order to develop these moving parts, the studio constructed multiple reference frames within our digital and physical models. Coordinate systems allowed for rapid translation between the world's vertical axis and each object's primary reference frame. These new frames of reference allowed us to study the relational transformation of each component throughout its rotational path and to predict potential interference between the multiplicity of moving parts.

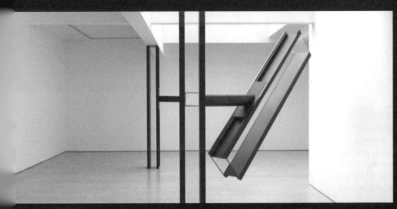 

Sarah Oppenheimer, *S-010100*, 2017, aluminum, glass, and architecture, variable.

Outside/In_Between

Morgan Starkey (MArch I)
Tibet Contemporary: Building in the Himalayas
Instructor: Zhang Ke

Tibet is facing the social-environmental pressure of rapidly expanding tourism, high-speed urbanization, and, more fundamentally, a dilemma of identity as it examines what it means to be traditional and/or to be contemporary.

Museums represent permanence, a crystallization of singular moments in history and humanity's advances through the accumulation of knowledge. Simultaneously, they also represent the cyclical nature of things. We connect with the past in order to read the timeless human condition in any artifact. Museums, like Tibet at large, serve as an in-between state: between singular permanence and the cyclical.

Materials
Memory
Museum

obscured or distorted,

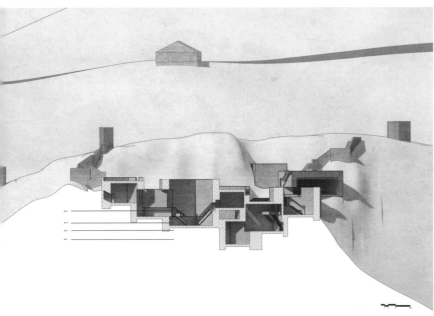

Adaptive Bipartite Staircase

Ian Miley (MArch I AP), Peteris Lazovskis (MArch I)
Digital Media II
Instructor: Andrew Witt

These logical investigations of modeling will cultivate a certain objective approach to form, both external and internal, that explores the application of parametric approaches that are both deductive (e.g., plan and spatial partitioning, topological classifications, surface characteristics, and pattern logics) and empirical (e.g., material deformation, generative detailing, optimization methods, and dynamic relaxation).

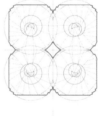

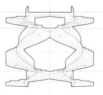

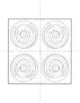

Computation
Fabrication
Geometry
Representation

Nested Twist

Zhixin Lin (MArch I AP), Yina Moore (MArch I)
Digital Media II
Instructor: Andrew Witt

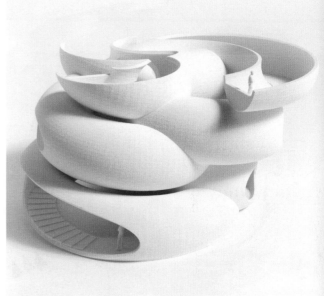

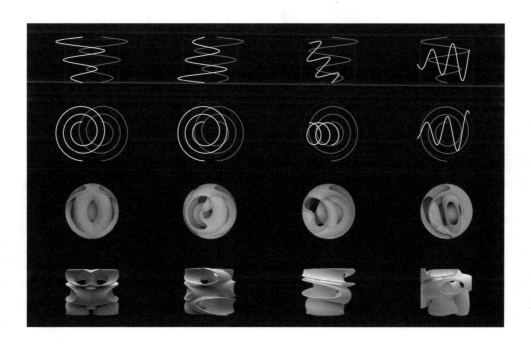

Circulation
Computation
Geometry
Representation

The Stair Core Theater

Alfred Chun Hin Pun (MArch I AP)
Architecture Core Studio III: Integrate
Instructor: Kiel Moe

Buildings are embedded within their built, cultural, and climatological contexts, which inevitably inform the design, construction, and operation of the building. Urban architecture acknowledges its participation within the larger framework of the city.

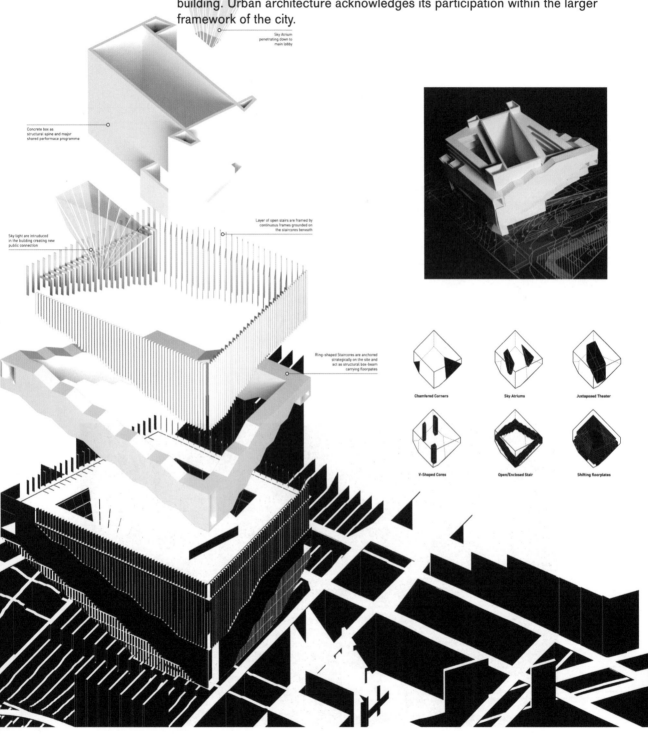

Sky Atrium penetrating down to main lobby

Concrete box as structural spine and major shared performance programme

Layer of open stairs are framed by continuous frames grounded on the staircores beneath

Sky light are introduced in the building creating new public connection

Ring-shaped Staircores are anchored strategically on the site and act as structural box-beam carrying floorpates

Chamfered Corners

Sky Atriums

Justaposed Theater

V-Shaped Cores

Open/Enclosed Stair

Shifting floorplates

Circulation
Infrastructure
Theater
Typology

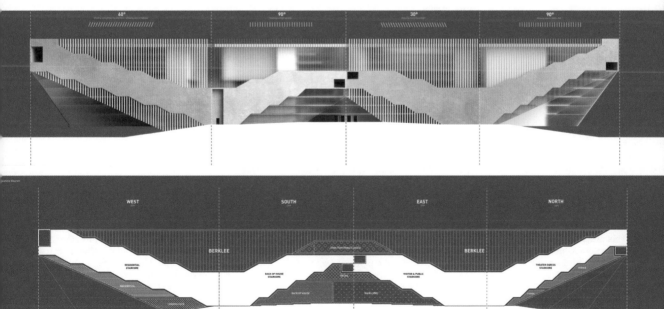

for a suspension of judgment,

Cryosphere

Keith Hartwig (MDes ADPD)
Design Studies Open Project
Advisors: Silvia Benedito, Krzysztof Wodiczko

>On Mar 18, 2018, at 10:25, Hartwig, Keith <keith_hartwig@gsd.harvard.edu> wrote:
>
> Hello Mr. Twickler:
>
> My name is Keith Hartwig. I am a graduate student at the Harvard Graduate School of Design, enrolled in my final semester of the Master in Design Studies program.
>
> Last semester, during thesis preparation, I conducted research on human technological and social relationships to the cryosphere. This semester, and with the project component of my work, I am zeroing in on the ways that refrigeration technologies, utilized in climate archives and research laboratories, are involved in preserving and researching the frozen environment—in the form of ice cores and other material proxies.
>
> My final project proposal is the creation of a public exhibition featuring a de-accessioned ice core from the NSF-ICF. The plan is to exhibit the ice core inside of a refrigerated shipping container on the grounds of Harvard University in Cambridge, Massachusetts. By modulating the temperature of the refrigerated shipping container, the ice core will be allowed to slowly melt. The project is meant to evoke two things, 1) the complicated relationship between the natural cryosphere and human technologies for producing cold and 2) the means by which information is extracted from the ice cores, often involving the transformation of matter and the loss of the ice core itself.
>
> At minimum the exhibition would require four linear feet of ice core and at maximum twelve linear feet. The exhibition is scheduled from May 4—11.
>
> I have provided a brief description of my thesis project; it elaborates a bit more on my position and outlines my objectives. Please let me know if you can accommodate my request to visit the facilities and to retrieve a de-accessioned ice core. If possible, I would need to do so within the next five weeks.
>
> I look forward to hearing back from you.
>
> Sincerely-
> Keith Hartwig

>On Mar 19, 2018, at 08:49, Twickler, Mark <twicklerm@unh.edu> wrote:
>
>Dear Keith,
Thanks for your interest in ice cores. We might be able to accommodate this. First, please go to https://icecores.org/. And fill out the "SAMPLE REQUEST/FACILITY USE FORM".
>
>A suggestion: As the ice core melts, it would be good to collect the meltwater and pass it on to a lab who does isotopic measurements. The melted water makes a great negative value of oxygen and hydrogen.
>
>Thanks
>Mark

>Dear Mark:
>
>Attached you will find the SAMPLE REQUEST/FACILITY USE FORM for the described project. Please let me know if additional information is needed or if the form needs revision.
>
>Sincerely-
>Keith

This project will reveal the entanglement of cold-producing technologies and the climate/environment. It will highlight the precarious nature and absurdity of trying to preserve the cryosphere within "Arks of the Apocalypse" by bringing people into closer dialogue with the substance of the cryosphere itself: ice (Malia Wollan, "Arks of the Apocalypse," *New York Times*, July 13, 2017, www.nytimes.com/2017/07/13/magazine/seed-vault-extinction-banks-arks-of-the-apocalypse.html). On May 8—10, 2018, a de-accessed ice core from the NSF-ICF will be publicly exhibited in Cambridge, Massachusetts. During the exhibition, the ice, disconnected from its life-support system, will slowly melt. Following NSF protocol, meltwater from the core will be saved as an oxygen/hydrogen analytical standard.

69   translated into permanence.

Offcut: A Museum in Los Angeles

Morgan Starkey (MArch I), Alexandru Vilcu (MArch I AP)
In the Details: The Space Between God and the Devil
Instructors: Dwayne Oyler, Jenny Wu

While it's been legitimately debated, Mies is commonly credited with having uttered the phrase, "God is in the details." Well, for anyone with a deep concern for the enduring impact of the built environment, and its role in shaping human experience across all scales, you may also want to keep in mind the equally common phrase, "The devil is in the details."

Computation
Fabrication
Ornament

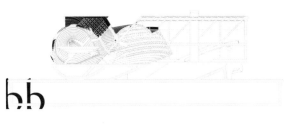

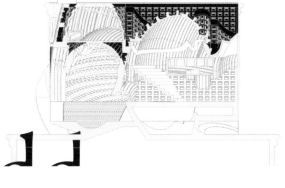

bb

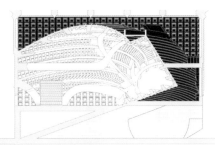

r.b

ee

two fou

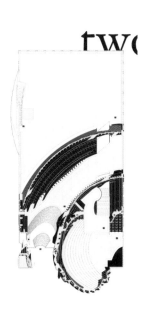

Death, Divorce, Downsizing, Dislocation, and (Now) Display

Hyojin Kwon (MArch I)
Architecture Thesis
Advisors: John May, Andrew Witt

Materialistic culture encourages self-identification with objects. Today, storage finds itself compartmentalized into two categories: visible and invisible. However, in response to excess due to overconsumption, self-storage centers—one of the fastest-growing industries in the United States—provide users with an invisible alternative to hide a multitude of belongings. This image of the tightly packed storage room is not a new phenomenon. Sixteenth-century cabinets of curiosities contained enormous quantities of possessions that were curated and exhibited as archives of knowledge. Can cabinets of curiosities trigger a new typology of architecture for the contemporary self-storage center? Can such an establishment blur the distinctions between storage space, personal collection, and cultural museum?

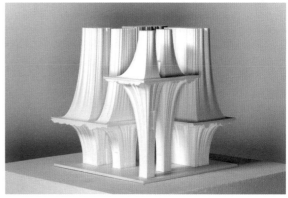
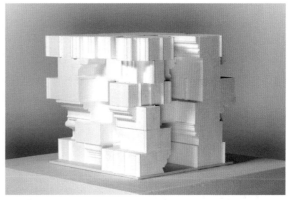

Center Stage

Adam Sherman (MArch I)
Architecture Core Studio III: Integrate
Instructor: Kiel Moe

Sited in Boston's Back Bay, this performing arts center provides a new home for the conglomerate of the Boston Lyric Opera, Berklee College of Music, and Boston Conservatory. The program demands a flexible theater design, housing performances that range from small student productions to large operas. To accommodate the diverse needs in capacity, the building's theater contains six pods—four raked and two flat—that connect to a central stage and fly tower. Acoustic wall panels can be raised and lowered in the fly tower, opening the stage up to a variety of configurations, from a small proscenium arrangement to a large theater in the round. This centripetal organization radiates throughout the entire building, which cantilevers over the Massachusetts Turnpike and assumes a distinct urban figure as a gateway to the city.

Facade
Theater
Typology

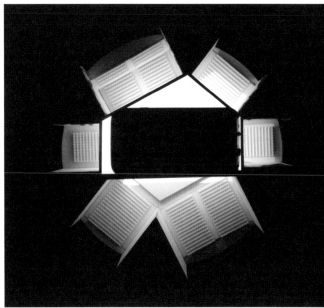

relevant enough to be remembered.

In the Round

Sharing Recipes

Experiments in Computer Graphics
Instructor: Zeina Koreitem

Over the past three decades, the architectural process has been drastically reorganized by what historian Jonathan Crary calls "a transformation in the nature of visuality probably more profound than the break that separates medieval imagery from Renaissance perspective."[1] Architecture's previously stable graphical conventions have dissolved and been replaced by an ever-expanding repertoire of computational mediums.

If we acknowledge that architecture has for centuries produced new ideas and forms by treating representation as a space of exploration, how might techniques that belong to computational media—which so often seem to prioritize "workflow optimization" at the expense of representational experimentation—be made to serve this same experimental function? Any such inquiry would entail imagining and testing methods by which computational image making—or what Friedrich A. Kittler calls computer graphics—might be used to disrupt the smooth workflows that presently define digital fabrication culture.

The course will first address the difference between two forms of representation that have historically defined architecture's relationship to culture—the documentary and the experimental—through a set of historical-theoretical texts. Second, students will be exposed to a diverse set of precedents in computer graphics, ranging from early video-art practices to more recent experiments in compression aesthetics. These case studies will be paired with multi-week design exercises that explore specific technical processes extracted from those precedents. The objective is to catalog a range of technical processes as a way of gaining fluency in media practices that have generally been regarded as lying outside the domain of architectural practice, but which might now be used profitably as a way of opening up and expanding architecture's own digital culture.

1
Jonathan Crary, *Techniques of the Observer: On Vision and Modernity in the Nineteenth Century* (Cambridge, MA: MIT Press, 1990), 1.

Computation
Fabrication
Materials
Precedent
Representation

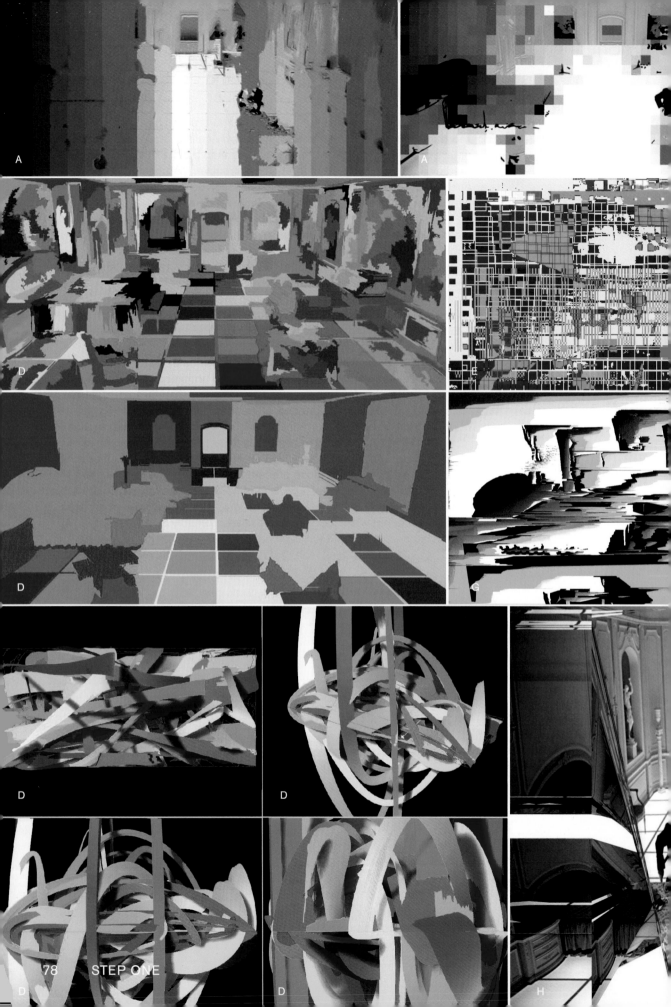

STEP ONE

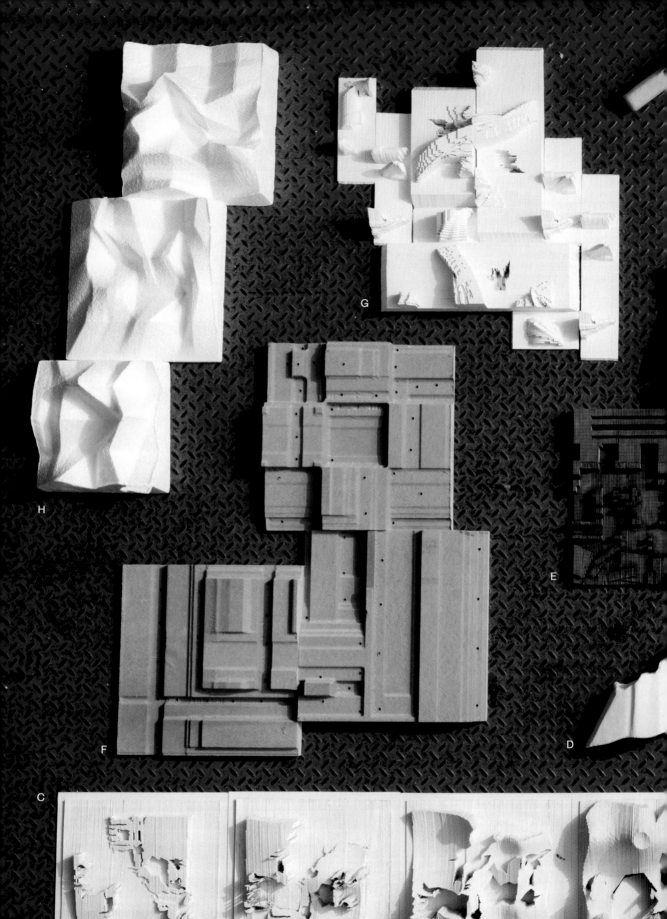

G

H

E

F

C

D

STEP TWO

G

F

E

F

D

STEP THREE

A   Stratton Coffman (MIT)
     Aaron Powers (MIT)
B   Madeline Eggink Lenaburg (MArch I)
C   Alexander Searle Porter (MArch I)
D   Dalma Földesi (MIT)
     Jung In Seo (MIT)
E   Kai Liao (MArch II)
     Julia Roberts (MArch I)
F   Bradley Silling (MArch I AP)
     Alexandru Vilcu (MArch I AP)
G   Esther Mira Bang (MArch I)
H   Borislav Angelov (MIT)
     Igsung So (MArch I AP)
I   Je Sung Lee (MDes ADPD)

Step One:

Blurring, Blending, Eroding, Mish-Mashing, Pixel Sorting,
Polar Gridding, Segmenting, Reordering, Threading,
Grasshoppering a Snippet of *2001: A Space Odyssey* (1968)

Step Three:

Vacuum-Form the Leftovers

Step Four:

Dig In!

Step Two:

Build a Never-Fail Mold by Hand or with a Toolpath,
One Layer at a Time

All You Can Eat

This poem is cut up from the following sources:
VIS 2142 Landscape Representation II
SCI 6463 Hybrid Formations: In Pursuit of Novel Forms
STU 1102 Architecture Core Studio II: Situate
STU 1211 Landscape Architecture Core Studio III
STU 1319 Museum Island
STU 1504 Zhengzhou: Designing Critical Nodes for the Urban Grids
STU 1506 Extreme Urbanism V: Exploring Hybrid Housing
         Typologies, Elphinstone Estate, Mumbai
STU 1601 Robots In & Out of Buildings
ADV 9301 Architecture Thesis
Exhibition Portman's America & Other Speculations
Lecture   "Insert Complicated Title Here," Virgil Abloh

An assembly of   88
elaborate baroque embellishment,
taken to an extreme
    4 million . . . almost 9 million . . . to 2.5 million—

such a large amount.   92

Extend a list   93
    in the largest
    with the least
traditionally served
with an autonomous fork
which has grown
plot by plot,
in and out.

A state of massive   101
shortage,
no less profound.

All You Can Eat: *a table of plenty*

This table has a lot to offer! With so many options, how does one choose? When does one stop?

Here we find a surfeit of picks and a glut of choices meant to be sampled and heaped onto one's plate. The projects at this feast cater to our desires for abundance, the ordinary and the extraordinary, lush vegetation, bespoke housing, endless arcades, and hyperspace.

Will you have room for seconds?

Almost, But Not Quite, Entirely Unlike a Supermarket

Shaina Kim (MArch I)
Architecture Thesis
Advisor: Preston Scott Cohen

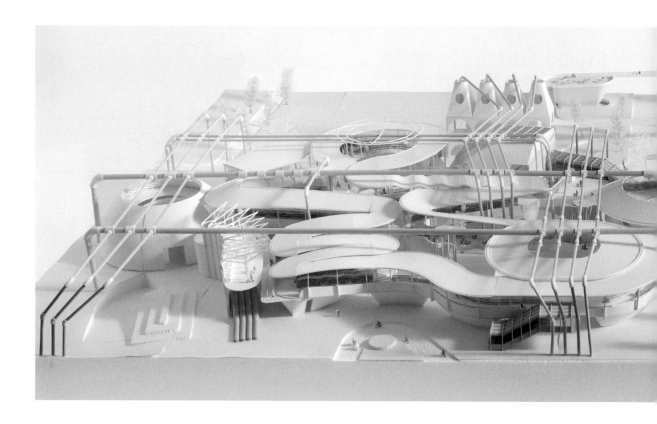

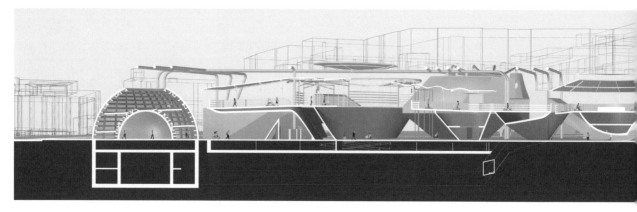

An assembly of

Food
Literature
Program
Typology

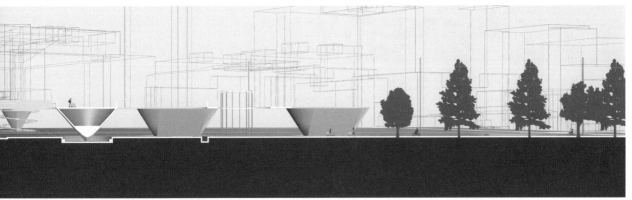

This thesis proposes an architectural typology of the supermarket. By extracting formal representations of the habitual rituals that we go through on a regular basis, architecture becomes a cognitive system that defamiliarizes the familiar. My interest in redefining the ordinary started with a towel, which features in the novel *The Hitchhiker's Guide to the Galaxy* (1979) as a multifunctional device in circumstances across the universe. An object as banal as a towel suddenly obtains new meaning by taking it out of its ordinary context. The spectacle is not rendered by never-before-seen novelties, but through the reinterpretation of banal things.

elaborate baroque embellishment,

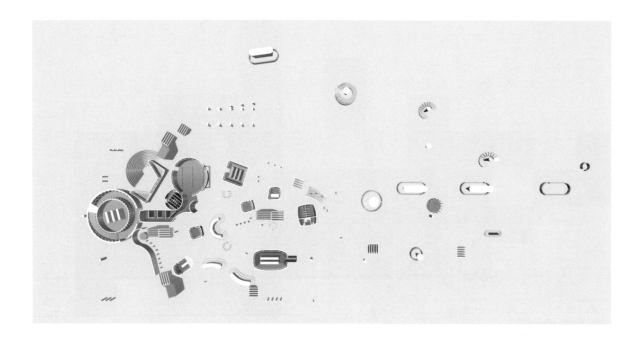

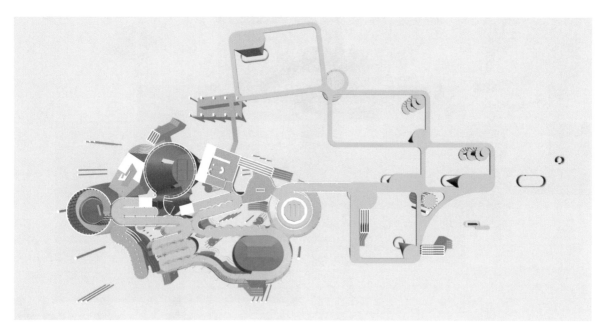

taken to an extreme

4 million . . . almost 9 million . . . to 2.5 million—

Tin Whiskers, or The Ghost in the Machine Part II

Matthew Gehm (MArch II), Jonathan Gregurick (MArch I)
Hybrid Formations: In Pursuit of Novel Forms
Instructor: Volkan Alkanoglu

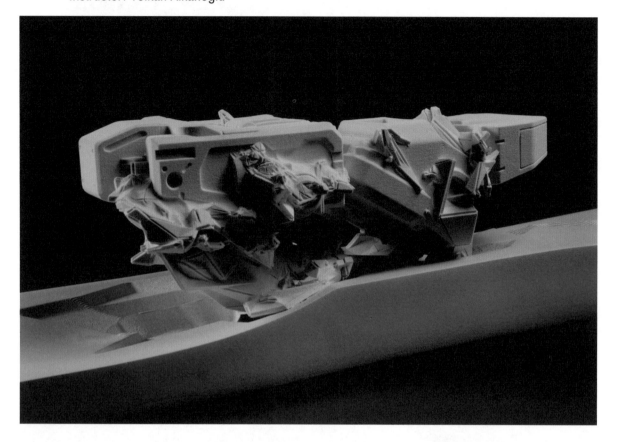

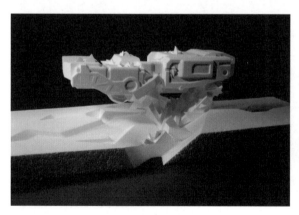
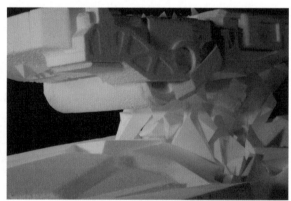

The machine is an entity in motion (the ceaseless turning of gears, belts, pulleys, or hydraulics) that becomes "trapped" or frozen by its own formal corruption: the introduction of an algorithm that builds new geometries from its existing vertices and faces in a seemingly chaotic yet highly controlled mechanism. As "tin whiskers" preclude the inevitable functional destruction of the machine, so too does the algorithm formally deconstruct the machine, like a geometric virus. The project is a conceptual hybrid of motion and stasis that blurs the lines between control and chaos, structure and fenestration, and machines and technics.

Computation
Fabrication
Ornament

such a large amount.

Tectonic Construction

Landscape Representation II
Instructor: Emily Wettstein

Create something physical that engages with the materiality of the site. Get dirty with the physicality of its making and leave the traces of your process on the piece.

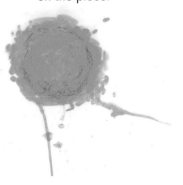

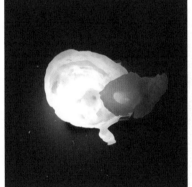

Xingyue Huang (MLA I)

Andreea Vasile Hoxha (MLA I)

Ecology
Materials
Representation

Hyperbolic Embrace

Brayton Gregory (MArch I)
Architecture Core Studio II: Situate
Instructor: Jeffry Burchard

The shed is entirely servant—the served are transient and the space is designed to lease. In this sense, the building is simultaneously physical mediator, social condenser, and protagonist in every production. It is a location, offering not only facility but place, full of atmosphere and promise. The shed is in itself cinematic, not foreground but background, a machine but also a theater, a sign and a busy small town in itself, and a landscape too, all at the same time and constantly changing.

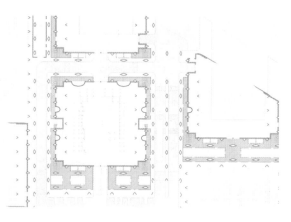

The structural module is composed of three hyperbolic paraboloids stitched along tangencies and scaled vertically, mimicking typical planar truss systems. This acts as the main structure while also creating modular spaces of inhabitation above each film studio. The module creates a covered arcade surrounding each film studio, producing a layered system of public and private spaces.

Geometry
Structure

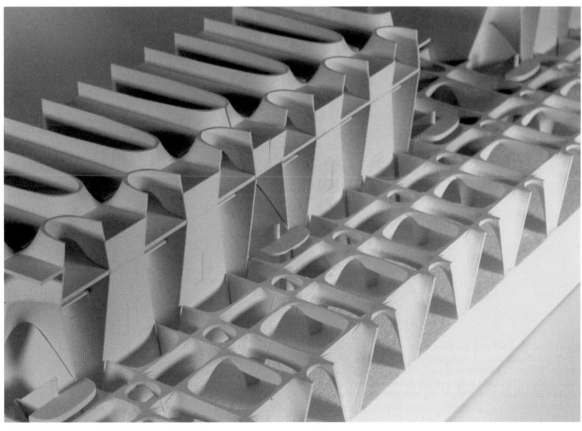

Anthropic Infrastructure

Yoeun Chung (MAUD), Luke Tan (MAUD)
Zhengzhou: Designing Critical Nodes for the Urban Grids
Instructor: Joan Busquets

Design priority will be given to public transportation integral nodes (PTIN) as hierarchical points of urban centralities. The study of a few "critical nodes" may give room to understand how the maxi-grid can allow development by enclaves where the development of mixed-use program and new forms of housing may be possible.

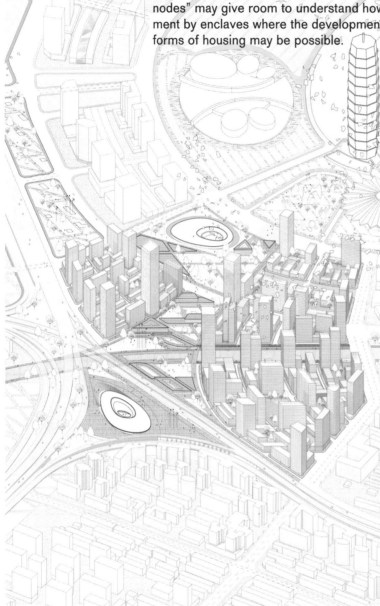

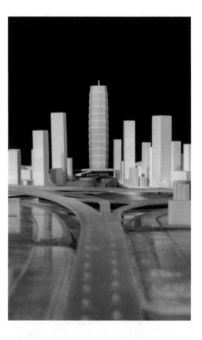

The project aims to bring the site's confluent forces into a synergistic relationship in three operations: first, by reconfiguring the interchange to liberate its previously inaccessible residual areas; second, by introducing a programmed green spine to increase access and influence of the adjacent metro station while preserving the city's symbolic axis; finally, by gridding the adjacent regions to enhance connectivity for densification.

Portman's America & Other Speculations

Exhibition in Frances Loeb Library
August 28–October 25, 2017

Portman's America & Other Speculations takes an unconventional and speculative approach toward the understanding and future potentials of the work of one of the world's most creative, controversial, daring, and prolific architects. The exhibition features materials from the 2017 book of the same title edited by Mohsen Mostafavi, with new photos by Iwan Baan, copublished by Lars Müller Publishers and the GSD.

 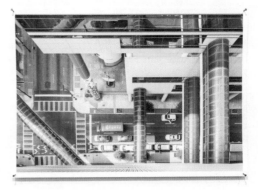

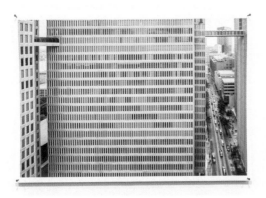 

American City
Photography
Typology
Urbanism

Stable/Unstable Grounds

Sarah Diamond (MLA I), Wan Fung Lee (MLA I AP), Matthew Macchietto (MLA II)
Landscape Architecture Core Studio III
Instructor: Sergio Lopez-Pineiro

Prototyping emphasizes the experimental and the speculative while encouraging open-ended explorations of multiple rather than singular outcomes. It deliberately resists totalizing visions across large territories, focusing more on specific interactions and interrelationships at smaller scales.

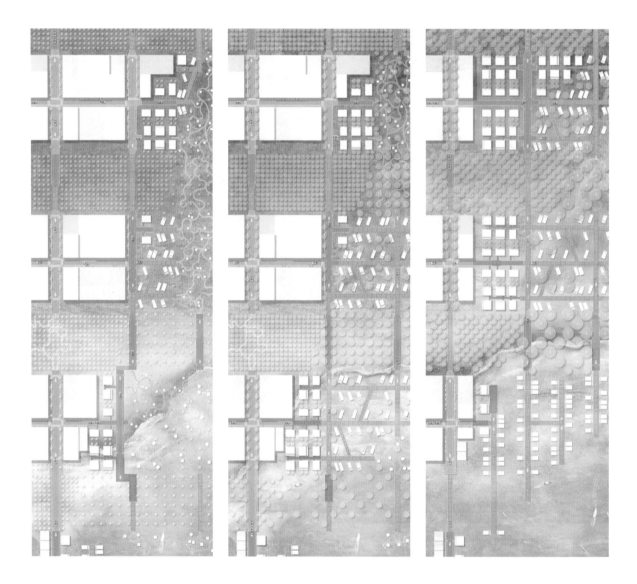

Our project is an exploration of the relationships between materials—organic and inorganic, living and dead—of various longevities and their inherent levels of stability. The layering of materials and their various life cycles yields a diverse and flexible urban fabric and allows us to reimagine the way that a city is organized.

Ecology
Labor
Urbanism
Water

plot by plot,

Form-Based Coding

Evan Shieh (MAUD)
Extreme Urbanism V: Exploring Hybrid Housing Typologies, Elphinstone Estate, Mumbai
Instructor: Rahul Mehrotra

The studio will be focused on developing typologies for affordable housing on high-value land in Mumbai. Questions of hybridity, mixed use, and high density will be among the issues that the studio will grapple with in the condition of extreme urbanism in the context of Mumbai.

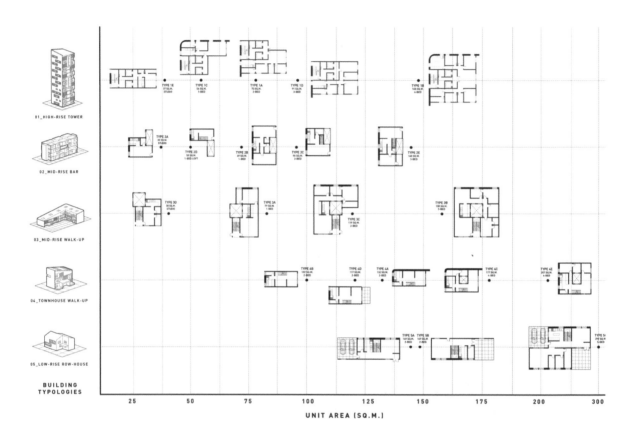

BUILDING
TYPOLOGIES

UNIT AREA (SQ.M.)

A gradient of building typologies, from the tower to the single-family home, can successfully coexist on the same parcel of land while dually ensuring that a wide range of unit sizes can accommodate household incomes of all ranges.

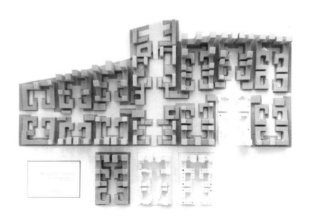

Housing
Social Equity
Typology
Urbanism

Islands in Islands

Eduardo Martinez-Mediero Rubio (MArch II)
Museum Island
Instructors: Sharon Johnston, Mark Lee

In the design of museums, the planning of isolated and singular buildings often approximates a form of proto-urbanism. This studio attempts to forge new understandings of urban islands as city models as much as museum models.

The art depot is internally structured by a 15' × 15' chain-link grid that organizes the warehouse in nonhierarchical rooms where art is stored and exposed, allowing for unexpected cross-relations and dialogue between the various pieces of artwork that belong to the Menil Foundation.

Futurism 2.O

Nicolas Turchi (MArch II)
Robots In & Out of Buildings
Instructors: Greg Lynn, Jeffrey Schnapp

The project aims to address the question of why and how
autonomous vehicles should integrate with architecture
(specifically in an office-building typology). The project is
also informed by the feeling of fascination with technology
and progress that has always intrigued humans and produced
accompanying utopic and dystopic literatures.

Responsive Environments
Robotics
Transportation
Work

"Insert Complicated Title Here"

Virgil Abloh
Core Studio Public Lecture
October 26, 2017

Virgil Abloh: I'm going to turn off my WhatsApp before it starts annoy-
ing you. All right. That introduction was serious. Thanks, Oana. Thanks to
Harvard for allowing me to come and share random things on my laptop.
That's what this is about to be. First and foremost, I identify with you guys. I
feel like I'm a perpetual kid at school. I wish that when I was a student, one
person would have given me one ounce of advice that wasn't: *The rest of
your career will be an uphill battle.* But instead: *There are all these shortcuts
that you can take.* That's what this whole presentation is about. It's about
shortcuts that I've learned through studying super practical things like engineering and architecture.

In the outside world, there are all these caveats that you can use to
find your career path that are not delineated by a single major. My work is
by nature cross-disciplinary. It lives outside the walls of architecture, but it
follows the same line of thinking that I learned in school.

So that's the premise of my talk. I'm going to flip through and
showcase different things that Instagram doesn't have the capability to show.
I'm going to share every project that I'm working on that I would never
Instagram—like Ikea, Nike stuff. I'll probably get in trouble with some corpo-
ration in two seconds, but let's do it.

All You Can Eat

Front

1 Yoeun Chung
  Luke Tan
2 Eduardo Martinez-
  Mediero Rubio
3 Evan Shieh

Back

4 Sarah Diamond
  Wan Fung Lee
  Matthew Macchietto
5 Brayton Gregory
6 Shaina Kim

Turntable

Turntable: *a table for reworking and remaking*

Flipped on its head, the turntable reshuffles the [un]known. At this table
we reconfigure, recombine, fake it until we make it, rouse, juxtapose, remix
the old and new. Why reinvent the wheel when we've got all this material
to cut up and reassemble?

> Don't start from scratch when you can begin by scratching.

This poem is cut up from the following sources:
HIS 4382 Andrea Palladio: Innovative Learning Experience
STU 1202 Architecture Core Studio IV: Relate
STU 1303 A Bank for Burbank and Other L.A. Stories
STU 1310 The Frugal Palazzo
STU 1401 Retooling Metropolis II: L.A.!
STU 1405 Broadway Shuffle II: Performance/Space
STU 1503 Quito and the Elasticity of the Spanish-American Block
ADV 9301 Architecture Thesis
ADV 9342 Landscape Architecture Thesis
DES 3368 It's a Wild World: Future Scenarios for Feral Landscapes
Event   Harvard HouseZero Typology Symposium
Lecture   Gamma, Kahlil Joseph

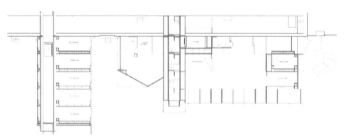

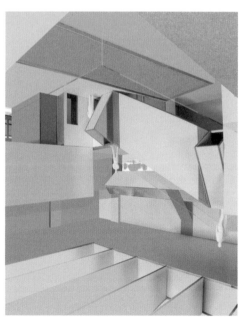

A Bank in a Bank

Taylor Halamka (MArch I), Julia Roberts (MArch I)
A Bank for Burbank and Other L.A. Stories
Instructors: Andrew Atwood, Anna Neimark

Design a bank—a commonplace monument—alongside several other buildings at an L.A. intersection. A building set beyond the background, composed of unlikely juxtapositions of materials, forms, and organizational systems at three architectural scales.

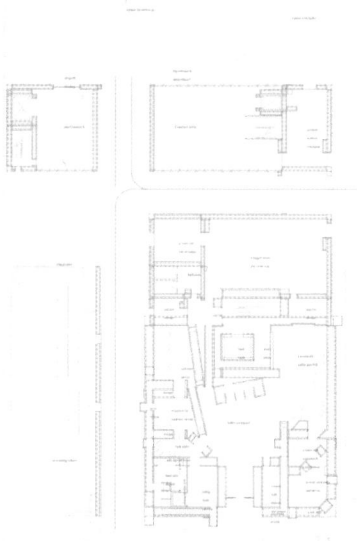

A bank for Burbank demands a purposefully plain and solid structure to house its flimsy program. A bank for Burbank is a bank in a Bank; a Sullivanian structure reconstituted with dumbed-down materials, flickering between conception as model and construction as building. This is discovered by the driver, by the pedestrian, by the patron. This bank is a pile of anxieties over what a bank should be.

The Paradox

Je Sung Lee (MDes ADPD)

It's a Wild World: Future Scenarios for Feral Landscapes
Instructor: Jill Desimini

The word "wild" alone is explained most clearly by antonyms, defined by a series of "uns": uncultivated, untamed, uncontrolled, undomesticated, and uninhabited. The wild is seen as other, and the urban wild, itself, is an oxymoron. A succinct definition of the "urban wild" has been difficult to achieve. Yet, the wild is fundamental to the urban experience.

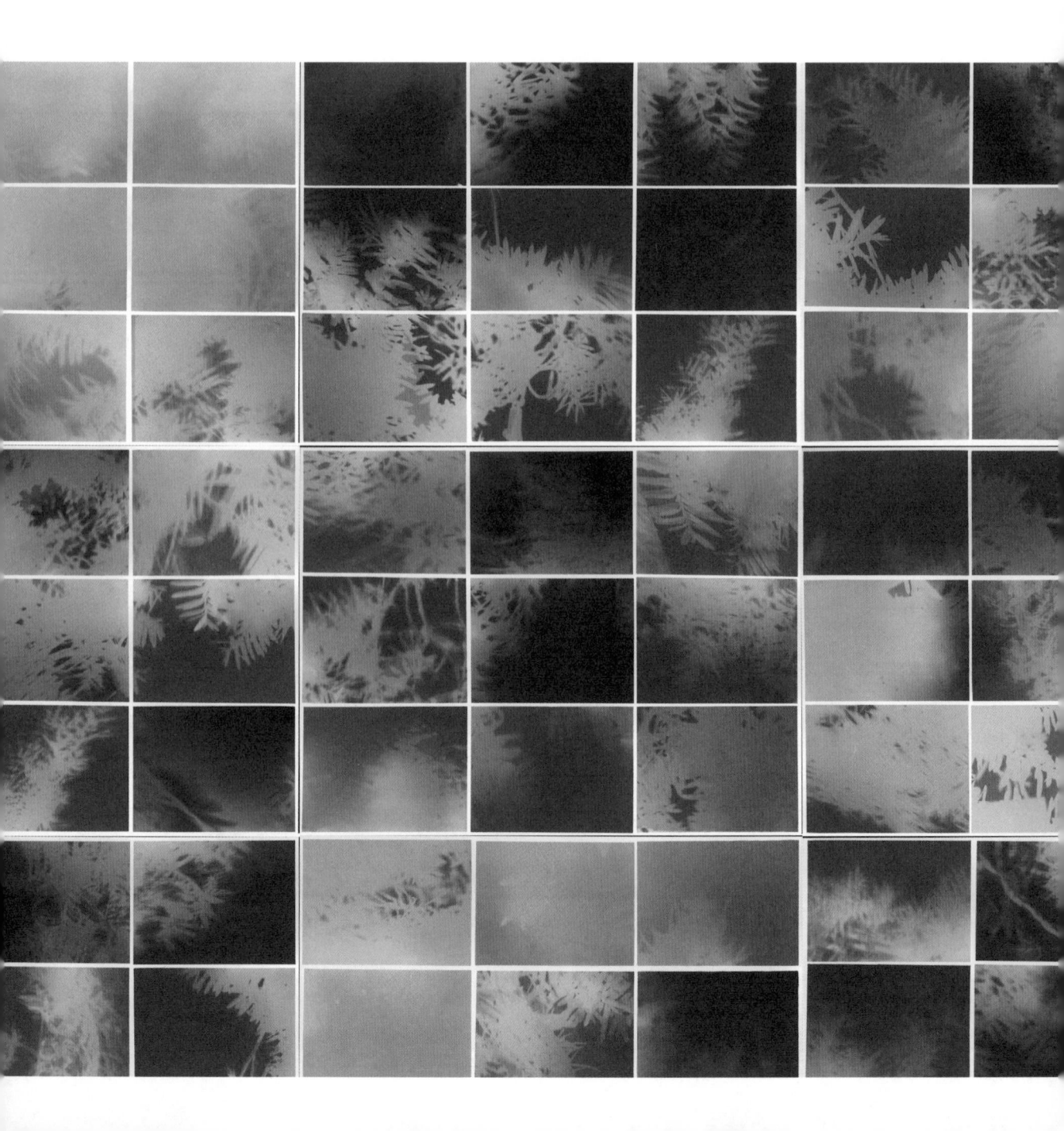

Thickened Symbolism

Scarlet Ziwei Song (MArch II)
Architecture Thesis
Awarded the James Templeton Kelley Prize
Advisor: Megan Panzano

China has adopted and integrated Western architectural education and design languages for more than 60 years. Recent
architecture in China, however, is exhibiting a prevailing trend
of the use of cultural and symbolic elements: large buildings
whose forms are oversimplified, scaled-up cultural symbols, or
accompanied by historical appliqué on the facade. This thesis
proposes replacing the oversimplified symbol-as-architecture
of today's global developer with a thickened symbolism,
integrating experiential culture and craft culture in hyper-local
vernacularism.

Nomadic Permanence

Kaoru Lovett (MArch I)
Architecture Core Studio IV: Relate
Instructor: Elizabeth Whittaker

Imagine an inside-out urbanism that reconsiders the fundamentals and takes an aggressive re-look at shared urban and domestic program—all deep within the city block—to consider an expanded architecture that creates an extension of the city within the city.

The project acts as a subversion of conventional housing arrangements. The private introspective program is placed along the street front, acting as porous shield for the expressive community behind. In doing so, the housing project produces an interior life—a shared community between the two ways of living. The dichotomy of the two housing forms acts as commentary on the typical housing types.

Excavated Extrusions

Huma Sahin (MArch II)
Quito and the Elasticity of the Spanish-American Block
Instructor: Felipe Correa

This studio will investigate the historic evolution and current state of the Spanish-American colonial city. The strategies will aim to provide Quito's historic core with a new lease on life by creating a framework for mixed-use residential spaces that could bring residents back to the city center.

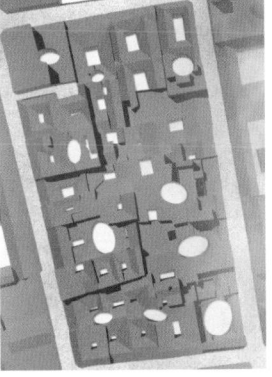

A patio design investigating the elasticity of the Spanish-American grid with the goal of adapting the physical and social environment to contemporary life, serving as a new scale of collective space rethinking the use and publicness of the zaguan.

A play on optical corrections, the "PostGuild, GuildHouse" becomes a paradox in the appearance versus the authentic treatment of the palaces, while located at the northern intersection of Denny's Triangle in Seattle. The triangular site acts as the perceived part of the articulated whole, as the palazzo becomes a play between the illusion of the formal city block and the diagrammatic cut of its informal housing. A duality of scales, the formal appearance of its exaggerated facade performs as the assimilated veneer toward the city, as its informal counterpart strives to reveal the hidden everyday occupation typically unseen within palaces, a reveal between the superficial encounter of perimeter within palaces and the occupied, inner contents of its infilled skin.

PostGuild, Guild House

Farnoosh Rafaie (MArch II)
The Frugal Palazzo
Instructors: Kersten Geers, David Van Severen

Today, the American city is fragmented by the implementation of a varied set of mutated and again imported ideas. Perhaps this particularly stressed context provides the unlikely opportunity for a revival of the gigantic palace, this time not for the bourgeoisie, but rather as a housing hypothesis for the hard-working, mobile, and active new urban middle class. A palace without decadence, a co-working environment with shared grandeur.

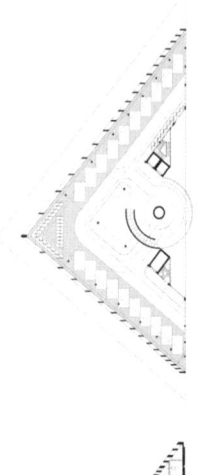

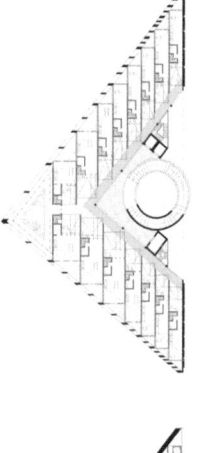

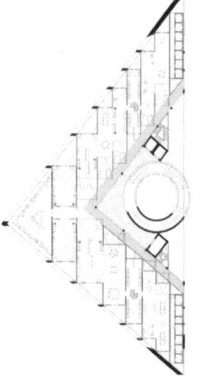

Water Assemblage: A New Politics for the Mekong River Collective

Tam Banh (MArch II, MLA I AP)
Landscape Architecture Thesis
Advisor: Robert Gerard Pietrusko

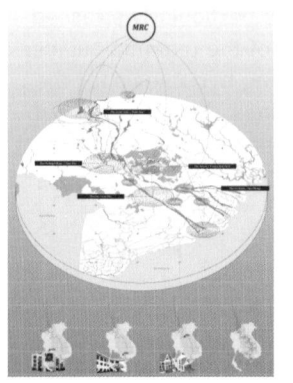
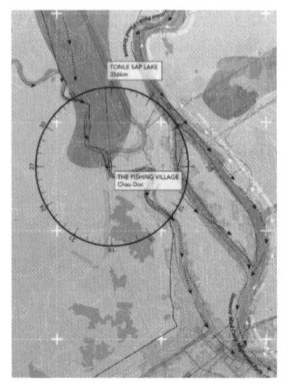

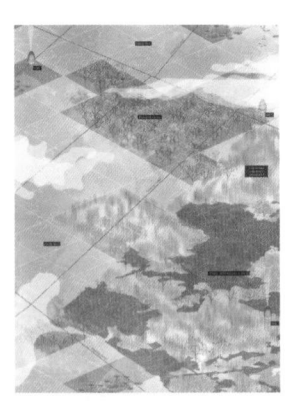

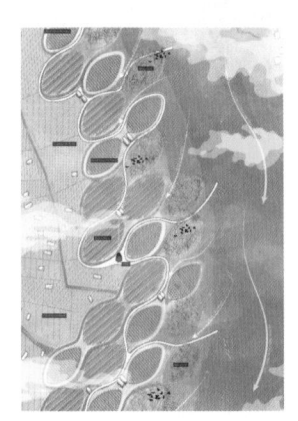
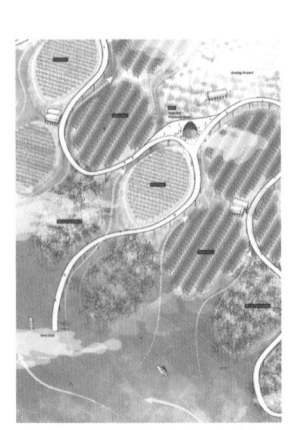

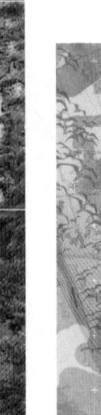

Flowing for 4,630 kilometers through the heart of Southeast Asia, the Mekong River is the lifeblood of countless wildlife species and tens of millions of people across six countries. But the enduring legacy of hydropower developments that devastate its landscape and plunder the natural resources it supports is jeopardizing the Mekong's gifts and the survival of those who depend on it. This project explores a new working and living dynamic between the Mekong and its inhabitants by redesigning the Mekong River Commission, an intergovernmental body responsible for water resource management and development in the Mekong Basin. Sited in the Mekong Delta in southwestern Vietnam, this project examines both the institution's form and its operational structure.

Gamma

Kahlil Joseph
Rouse Visiting Artist Lecture
February 22, 2018

Screening in Piper Auditorium of *Process* (2017), directed by Kahlil Joseph.

"A true Renaissance man, Kahlil Joseph is a writer, a director, an artist. He works principally in film. Born in L.A. in 1981, Joseph's work reveals a talent that is at the height—but not the peak—of its superpowers. There are even greater things to come for this Grammy and Emmy Awards nominee, whose remarkable *Until the Quiet Comes* (2012)—a collaboration with Flying Lotus—won the Sundance Film Festival's Short Film Special Jury Award in 2013.

Watching any of his films feels both celebratory and cathartic. For example, the shooting death at the heart of *Until The Quiet Comes* becomes a moment of uplifting celebration—a sinuous, jaw-dropping march to the afterlife. Joseph manages to juxtapose tragedy and exhilaration in a manner that mimics real life, especially among people of color in America and elsewhere. It is gratifying to see that captured with such a vivid eye, energy, and imagination on film.

Rumble, young man, rumble!"

Tau Tavengwa (Loeb Fellow)

Harvard HouseZero Typology Symposium

Harvard Center for Green Buildings and Cities
April 3, 2018

The Harvard Center for Green Buildings and Cities at the GSD is retrofitting its headquarters in a pre-1940s, stick-built house to demonstrate how to transform this challenging building stock into a prototype of ultra-efficiency that will use no HVAC system, no electric light during the day, 100-percent natural ventilation, and almost zero energy, and produce zero carbon emissions, including embodied energy of materials. Drew Faust, President of Harvard University, remarked that HouseZero is "something more than a house"—it's a laboratory.

Whose Digital Property

Wendy Fok (DDes)
Doctoral Dissertation
Committee: Martin Bechthold, Antoine Picon, William W. Fisher (Harvard Law School)

The innovation and development of the Internet since 1989 have allowed the digital practice of architecture to eschew the traditional limitations of physical space and professional hierarchy: architecture depends increasingly on collaboration in digital spaces. Online collaboration across industries has allowed innumerable advances within global manufacturing, including architecture, and has thus facilitated electronic file distribution, allowing for borderless information exchange; however, online collaboration also makes vulnerable the creators and innovators, as they are not protected by the myriad of possibilities for duplication, non-permitted file-sharing, and high speeds of transfer.

How do we regulate the various dimensions of applying creative measures into the role of ownership and authorship within design?

Architecture's exponential growth and migration into the digital realm have increased the need to evaluate the balance between ethical and equitable forms of design practice, as the two are often in conflict. Because the architecture, engineering, and construction (AEC) industry is tradition-ally underwritten as a service-based industry, the product is driven by client needs. As design assets and cross-platform and international collaborative models between the client and the designers become increasingly digitized in the AEC industry, categories become more difficult to define. Soon actors in the field will become mutual creators and partners for creative solutions, rather than relying on a top-down, single-solution designer who creates tangible end products. Often these solutions and products are derived from an intangible good in the form of digital goods with multi-user developments.

Professional codes of conduct and legal regulations become a means to an end in the development of design, as digital barriers lift much of the necessary precautions that are required for the authentication of the construction and fabrication of three-dimensional, computer-aided design files. The Digital Millennium Copyright Act covers much of the intellectual property issues within the dissemination of technological devices or ser-vices, such as broadcasting, radio, and software, while the Digital Rights Management maintains the protection and ethical use of digital technologies by hardware manufacturers, publishers, copyright holders, and after-sale use of digital content, commonly used for music and software. Architecture, on the other hand, has not adopted similar practices and the discipline has the difficulty of maintaining critical control over the global practice within the built environment, from duplication, copycats, and faux reproductions.

This theoretical body of research addresses the very core of archi-tecture's identity: the relationship between the creators and the consumers, the state of design ethics and intellectual property pertaining to architectural production, and the combinatory methods and mechanisms that employ these technologies, such as the Traceable Geometries project, based on early concepts of the Blockchain systems, which explores offering mone-tary compensation and preventative measures for creators to protect and disseminate their designs.

The Four Ecologies 2.0

Suthata Jiranuntarat (MArch I), Sonny Meng Qi Xu (MArch II, MLA I AP)
Retooling Metropolis II: L.A.!
Instructor: Chris Reed

Retooling examines possibilities for cultivating new landscape occupations and new forms of nascent urbanism. Initial investigations will examine the forces at play across the wider metropolitan territory to establish a baseline of understanding and research across the studio.

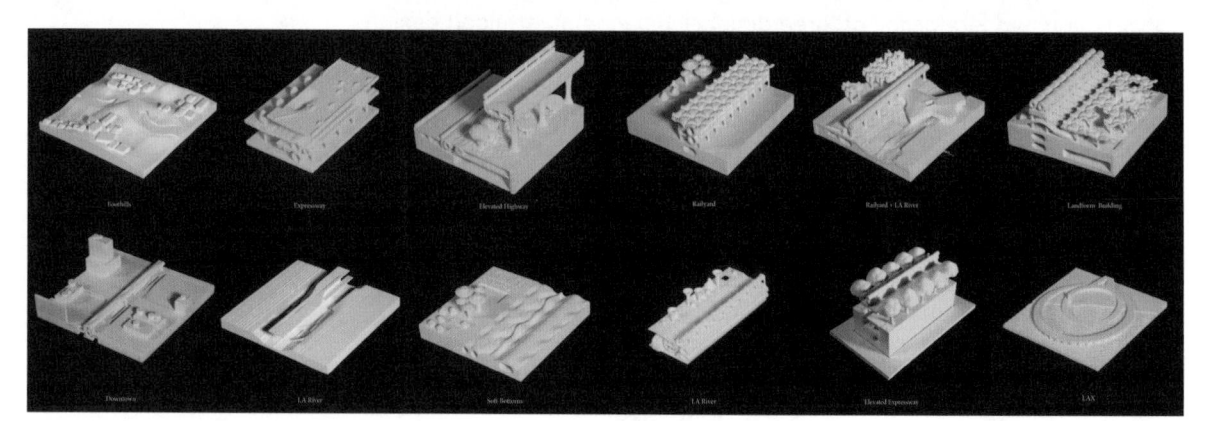

"The Four Ecologies 2.0" confronts Los Angeles's aging, derelict, and underutilized infrastructure and lack of public spaces and reconceptualizes potentials and experiences of multifunctional, productive, and performative infrastructure and urban realms. The project reimagines Reyner Banham's *Los Angeles: The Architecture of Four Ecologies* (1971) for the 21st century. "The Four Ecologies 2.0" proposes a new language of movement and civic life for Los Angeles—one that not only serves mobility, but integrates social, cultural, economic, and ecological functions to create hybrid systems for the future.

Faking Palladio

Andrea Palladio: Innovative Learning Experience
Instructors: Guido Beltramini, Howard Burns
    The creation of a fake requires in-depth knowledge of the qualities of the item
    to be copied and the cultural background in which it was [originally] produced.

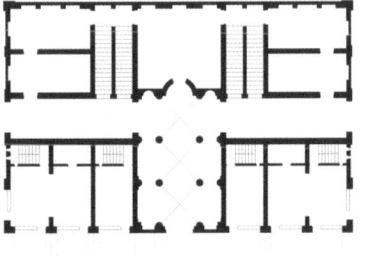

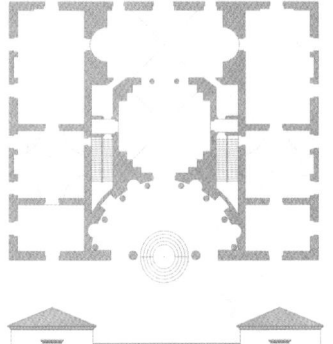

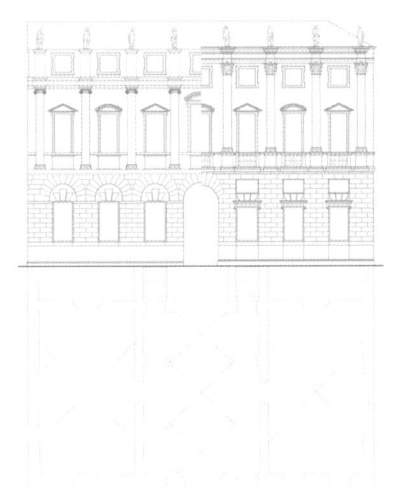

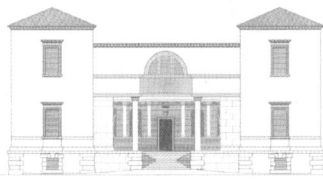

Farnoosh Rafaie (MArch II)

Christopher Grenga (MArch I)
Alexandru Vilcu (MArch I AP)

Taylor Halamka (MArch I)
Lane Raffaldini Rubin (MArch I, MLA I AP)

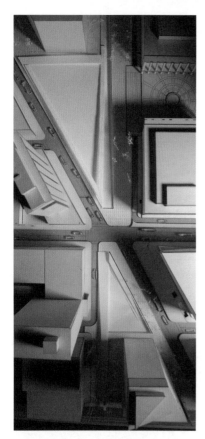

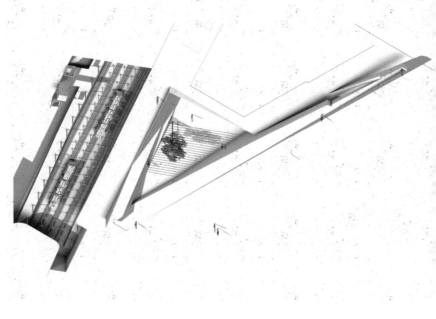

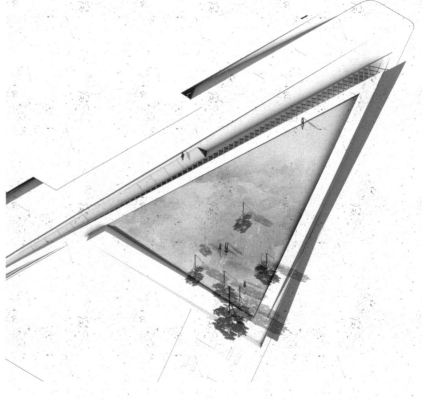

cannot begin—or end—

Ungrid

Boxiang Yu (MLA II, MLAUD)
Broadway Shuffle II: Performance/Space
Instructor: Gary Hilderbrand

We reject any presupposition that the city's surface cannot be biological, and we aim for a permeable, vegetal city that brings benefits to public accommodation and ecosystem health. Through these combined agendas, the studio will thoroughly reimagine the intersection of Broadway and Columbus Avenue at Lincoln Center.

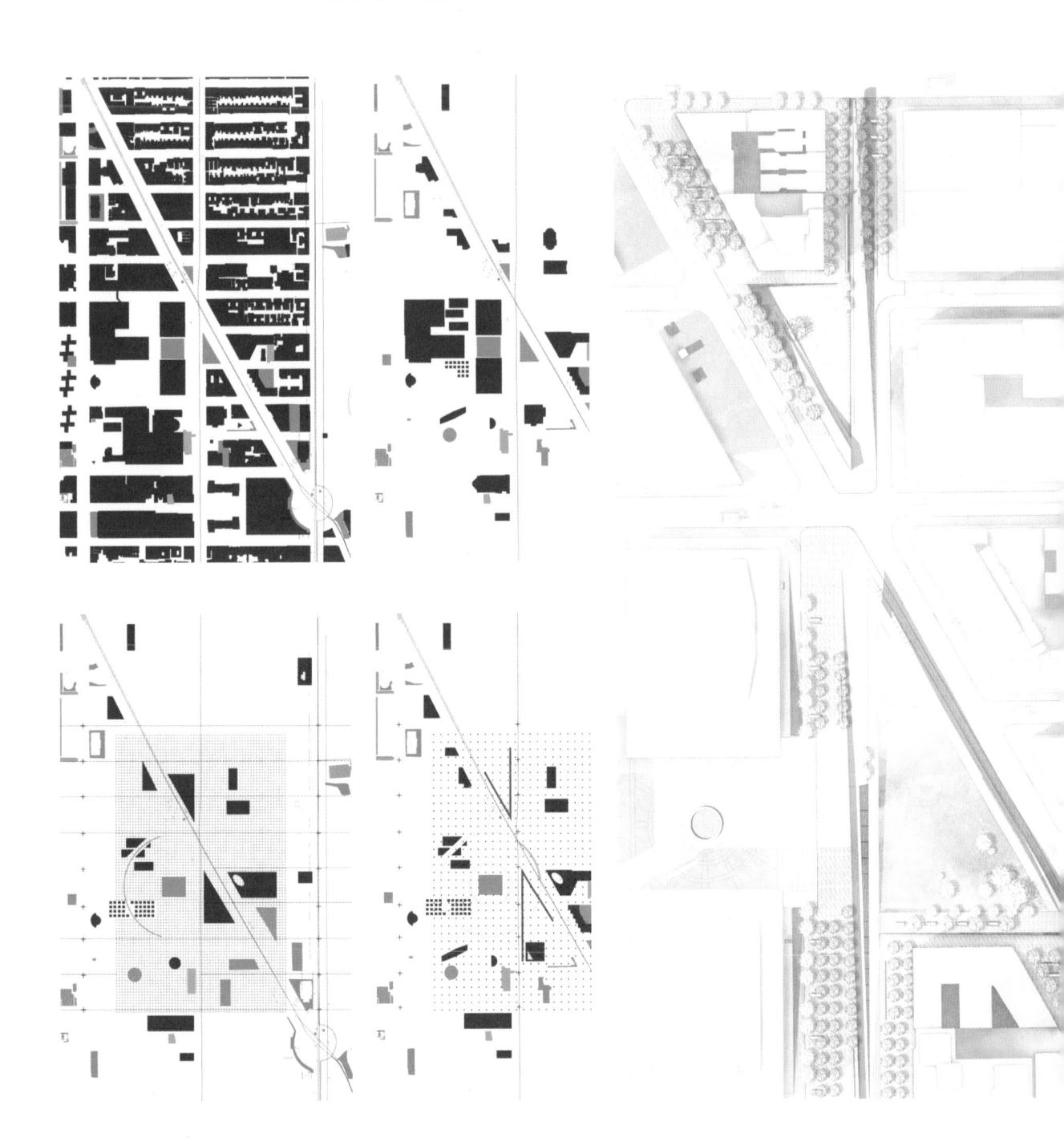

Turntable

Out in the Field

Field Methods & Living Collections
Instructor: Rosetta S. Elkin with William Ned Friedman
(Arnold Arboretum of Harvard University)

The aim of the class is to put theory to work and think in the field. In other words, too much design research is predicated on thinking "here" and doing "there," thus not enough attention is paid to our insistence on separating things and thoughts. So, we are interested in the relationship between "things" and how we name them.

For instance: *plant*. Here, naming gets in the way of our perception. We spend time with rosy cheeks and warm tea reading to each other in depth and we go outside with a mind full of concepts that are confusing and tough to apply. The students are encouraged to get muddled and put words to what they are thinking and feeling and not able to easily name. We hope this gives rise to more critique and to the task of taking a position.

So, it is a methods class, whereby the students develop their own unique approach to engaged research, such that the final assignment acts as a means to describe the method.

We use the Arnold Arboretum as a "site" in order to question what site means in the field, since it offers a proxy of many dynamics that the students are developing in their thesis or studio work. One of the most gratifying lectures this past semester was on plant evolutionary theory, during which Ned Friedman and I were disagreeing. Of course, this not only is healthy, but forced my thought, and in turn I believe it forced his.

This is the tension between the sciences and design, manifest in almost everything we do now. Yet, the sciences learn by making propositions, and failing. Design insists on solving and succeeding. Different methods raise the question of how to synthesize scientific speculation in real time.

Ecology
Mapping
Photography
Plants
Representation

ACER ASSEMBLAGE

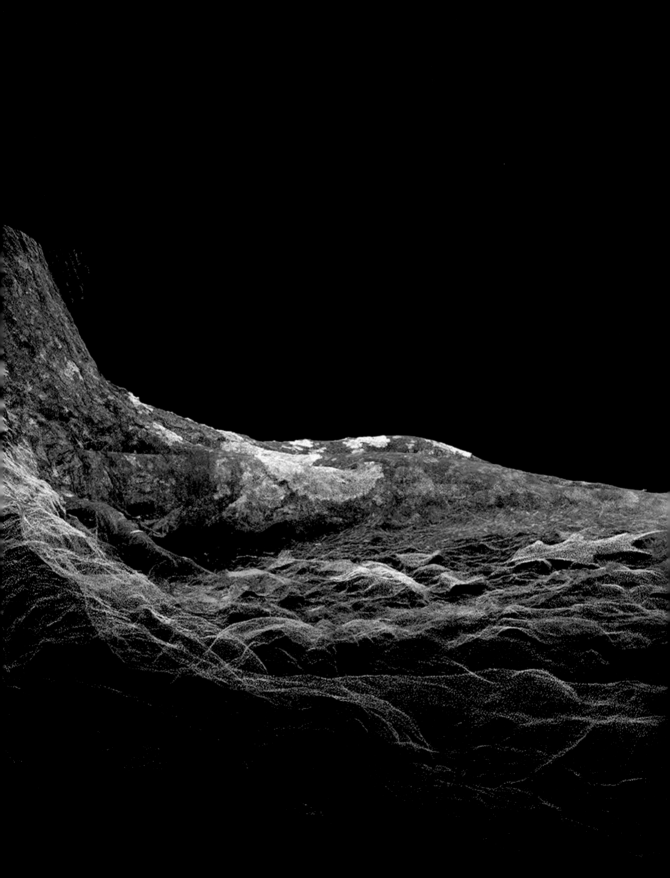

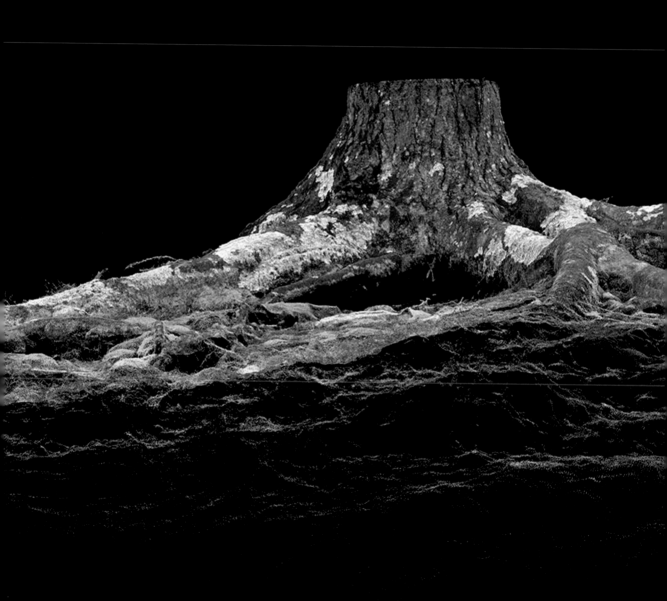

Root to Shoot / Shoot to Root

Emily Drury (MLA I)
Stacy Passmore (MLA I AP)

We identified two adjacent research areas within the Arnold Arboretum beech collection: a station on a slope of dense suckering American beech, and a station on the same slope where the weeping branches of the European beech *tortuosa* graze a mown and maintained lawn.

Our research evolved through close observation and description of these stations as we made measured drawings, collected herbaria samples, and photographed and examined the root-to-shoot suckering form of the American beech and the shoot-to-root propagation and spread of the European beech *tortuosa*. Our fieldwork provided us with insight into the distinct ways that two related species have evolved to move—albeit with radical slowness—and to claim and create ground, producing micro-topographies that over time become visible and measurable within scales more familiar to designers.

Acer Assemblage

Pablo Escudero (MDes ULE)
Keith Hartwig (MDes ADPD)
Naomi Woods (MDes RR)

Our group set out to investigate the organismic assemblages located within a 200-square-foot area of the Arnold Arboretum. Using this relatively small and manageable site within the *Acer* collection, we tasked ourselves with unpacking the biological and ecological relationships between the accessioned plant specimens, spontaneous and successional plant growth, and the site they collectively inhabit.

We developed a research methodology to document and describe the growth habits of these organisms—to visually express how the behavior they exhibit above ground relates to what is happening within the soil itself. Conversely, we attempted to describe how the conditions of the site (such as soil composition and topography) relate to these various topologies (such as rhizomatic growth or seed-dispersed progeny). On a theoretical level, the work served to demystify the assemblage itself.

The Gravity of the Loss of a Single Beech Tree

Madeleine Aronson (MLA I)
Maclean Sarbah (MDes RR)

Has this tree been loved to death? We speculate that when humans stab trees, they provide a way in for pathogens—an opening in the cambium. Beetles and scales seize this opportunity as a space to cultivate their symbiotic fungus—which in turn creates disease that spreads and is visible through sap crying on the beech tree's bark.

Soon this tree, with all its vitality and interwoven histories, will be gone. How can we convey the gravity of this loss?

Through representation, we are seeking to convey this tree's character, its aura, and the interrelationships that have merged onto its trunk. Through photographic mapping, we are unraveling and representing the tree's trunk up to 10 feet in height. By gathering textural impressions of the tree's scars and bark through rubbings and clay imprints, we bring to discussion its tactile and emotional qualities.

Indeterminacy on Hemlock Hill

Daniel Berdichevsky (MLA I AP)
Ernest Haines (MLA I)
Yanick Lay (MLA I)

On Hemlock Hill we ask the following questions: Do we keep repeating failed or failing systems? Do we accept the failure of past systems? How is our influence accelerating the pace of environmental change? How does its history set the conditions for our influence over the landscape? How are plants and the environment changing through time, and how are they changing us?

Future 1: Lenta Hill/Succession: The Arboretum stops curing for woolly adelgid, all hemlocks are cut down. *Betula lenta* and other complementary organisms succeed Hemlock Hill, causing it to be renamed.

Future 2: Hemlock Hill/Preservation: The Arboretum routinely replants hemlocks and treats species for woolly adelgid. Hemlock Hill becomes one of the few locations on the East Coast where hemlocks still grow.

Tabula
Plena

This poem is cut up from the following sources:

HIS 4475   Conservation, Destruction, and Curating
           Impermanence
STU 1111   Landscape Architecture Core Studio I
STU 1305   Northern Light
STU 1312   Tokyo Study Abroad Option Studio: Transforming
           Omishima into a Beautiful Japanese Garden
STU 1314   Model as Building—Building as Model
STU 1315   After the Storm: Restructuring an Island Ecosystem
STU 1403   Excavating Space and Nature in Tokyo
STU 1503   Quito and the Elasticity of the Spanish-American Block
STU 1603   Manila: Future Habitations
STU 1604   Between Earth and Sky: A Building for the
           HafenCity, Hamburg
ADV 9147   Beyond Reconstruction: Mexico and the
           2017 Earthquakes
ADV 9307   Design Studies Open Projects
ADV 9342   Landscape Architecture Thesis
Lecture   Reclaiming Space: Riwaq's 50-Village Project in
           Rural Palestine, Suad Amiry
Lecture   Trying to Remember, Jennifer Roberts

Written, erased, and rewritten,   136
echoes
of extraordinary history,
    natural and man-made
    ephemeral and stable.

Trying to remember   141
historic skeletons, hidden and forgotten,
changing over time.

A point of departure   144
at the very heart,
    a new lease on life.

Remnants once masterpieces   147
go beyond
the myth of permanence.

A canvas   150
of what has always been.

Tabula Plena: *history and context define this table*

AFTERMATH – BROWNFIELDS – BULLDOZING – COEXISTENCE
– CONSERVATION – CONTEMPORARY – CONTINUITY –
CURRENT STATE – DECLINE – DIALOGUE – ERASING – EROSION
– ESSENCE – EXCAVATION – FULL – GROUND – HERITAGE –
ICONOCLASM – IDENTITIES – LAYERS – MEMORY – NATURE AND
CULTURE – OBSOLETE – OLD CITY – OVERWRITE – PALIMPSEST
– PREEXISTING – REFORMATION – RENEWAL – RESILIENCE –
REUSE – REVIVAL – REWRITING – ROOTED – SILHOUETTE – SITE-
SPECIFIC – STRUCTURES OF THE PAST – TIME – TOPOGRAPHY
– TRACES – TRADITION – TRANSFORMATION – UPDATE – URBAN
FABRIC – VACANT LOTS – VEGETATION – WASHING OF SINS
    from the Tabula Plena, a table that, unlike a tabula rasa, bears the
    inscription of all the marks and erasures of its lifetime.

Old and New Narratives

Beining Chen (MArch I AP), Rodrigo Solé (MUP), Matthew Wong (MLA I)
Tokyo Study Abroad Option Studio: Transforming Omishima into a Beautiful Japanese Garden
Instructor: Toyo Ito

The Toyo Ito Museum of Architecture, Imabari, opened among the orange orchards of Omishima in 2011. Rapidly declining birth rates and an aging population resulted in the decreasing of orange orchards. The approaching path to the shrine, the "Sando," has also become desolate. This studio pursues small architectural projects at vacant lots, reconsidering the landscape adjacent to Furusato Ikoi-no-ie for the Sando's revival.

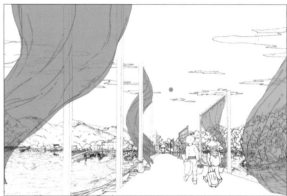

The Shimanami Kaido expressway linking Hiroshima to the islands of Ehime Prefecture drastically improved the connectivity between the city of Tokyo and the Seto Islands. However, the improvements in transportation efficiency have also changed the way people approach historic shrines. This project aims to illustrate the historic significance of the Sando along seven key moments while at the same time depicting new potentials to help revitalize this historic approach.

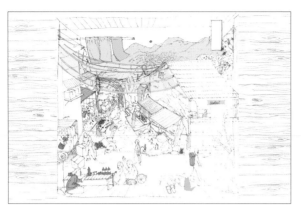

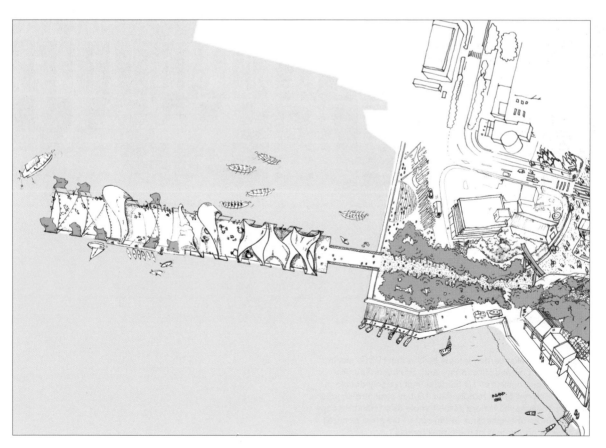

Temple of Decision

Jungchan Yee (MArch I)
Model as Building—Building as Model
Instructor: George L. Legendre

The phenomenon of "Model as Building—Building as Model" isn't about making buildings in the traditional sense; rather, it is about making 1:1 models. Is the process of making and distributing buildings and models integral to their identity? The studio will look for ways in which off-site manufacturing can be creatively applied to select programs, some existing and some speculative.

A Greek Revivalist garden temple built in the 1950s sits in ruin atop the Lomond Hills in Falkland, Scotland. The proposed design consists of 13 modules that roughly double the existing footprint of the temple. The 13-bay structure simultaneously engages the history of the temple as a miniature copy of the Temple of Hephaestus in Athens, as the shed restores the original proportions of the Greek temple.

Under One Roof

Stacy Passmore (MLA I AP)
After the Storm: Restructuring an Island Ecosystem
Instructors: Jeanne Gang with Claire Cahan

Climate change is already making significant impacts on island environments and their diverse populations, and unfortunately, these impacts will only continue to grow. Toward exploring how architecture can help address the unfolding challenges faced by island dwellers, this studio will employ research and design to respond to the specific needs of a community in the Caribbean in the aftermath of Hurricanes Irma and Maria of 2017.

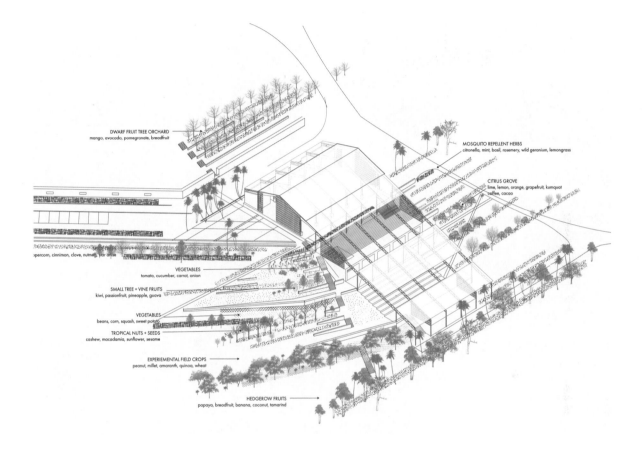

DWARF FRUIT TREE ORCHARD
mango, avocado, pomegranate, breadfruit

MOSQUITO REPELLENT HERBS
citronella, mint, basil, rosemary, wild geranium, lemongrass

CITRUS GROVE
lime, lemon, orange, grapefruit, kumquat
coffee, cacao

ppercorn, cinnimon, clove, nutmeg, star anise

VEGETABLES
tomato, cucumber, carrot, onion

SMALL TREE + VINE FRUITS
kiwi, passionfruit, pineapple, guava

VEGETABLES
beans, corn, squash, sweet potato

TROPICAL NUTS + SEEDS
cashew, macadamia, sunflower, sesame

EXPERIMENTAL FIELD CROPS
peanut, millet, amaranth, quinoa, wheat

HEDGEROW FRUITS
papaya, breadfruit, banana, coconut, tamarind

The new design extends the existing market roof over the hillside, expanding its function as a dynamic community center. New indoor and outdoor terraces and structures provide space for an expanded market, an amphitheater, orchards, gardens, workshops, storage, and the production of value-added goods.

Climate Change
Community
Plants
Reconstruction

Trying to Remember

Jennifer Roberts (Faculty of Arts and Sciences)
On Monuments: Place, Time, and Memory
February 27, 2018

Spencer Finch, *Trying to Remember the Color of the Sky on That September Morning*, 2014, watercolor on Fabriano paper, National September 11 Memorial & Museum, New York. Photo: Allan Buxton.

Jennifer Roberts: Traditional monuments, as we've come to know them, are permanent, massive, elevated, and usually figurative. Over the past 40 years, the development of counter-monumental practices has seen each of these qualities challenged and often literally overturned. There is one way, however, in which these counter-monuments share the language of their antithetical forebears, and that is that their critique of monumental form is generally pursued using the same monochromatic material palette. This evening, I want to focus on an exception—a monument made out of dazzling color—and explore the implications of inserting color at the center of the discourse of memory and community.

Color cannot be explained by its objective status as a measurable wavelength of visible light. Color is impossible to capture precisely in words. It is near impossible to reproduce faithfully. For all of these reasons, color is a highly unreliable tool of visual and cultural memory.

The artist Spencer Finch has spent his entire career wrestling with the implications of precisely this. In 2014, Finch was commissioned to design a memorial for the World Trade Center dead at the National September 11 Memorial & Museum. The work is a grid almost 40 feet high, made up of 2,983 individual squares of Fabriano Italian paper. And its title is *Trying to Remember the Color of the Sky On That September Morning*. Each of the paper squares is hand-painted in watercolor in a different shade of blue. Each is made in the memory of one person killed at the towers, both during the 9/11 and 1993 World Trade Center attacks. They're unframed and simply hung on a wire armature. Finch's squares bring luminous sky blues down into the subterranean gloom of the museum. The watercolor is protected by its entombment in the grave-like dim, preserved by the conditions of destruction that occasioned it. So, although this is not at all a traditional stone monument, the delicate watercolor relies on its massive bedrock encasement. I like to think of it as a rock-and-paper monument.

The hope for Finch is that these colors and their elemental ineffability will reject fixation, preclude didacticism, and prevent fascist identification.

Art Practices
Color
Memory
Monument

Reclaiming Space: Riwaq's 50-Village Project in Rural Palestine

Suad Amiry
Aga Khan Program Lecture
March 20, 2018

Suad Amiry: For whom do we preserve and why do we preserve? What is the role of a conservation architect? Are we the ones who decide what will happen to our historic cities or historic buildings? Or most importantly, what is our relationship to the people who live in these places? Who are the users that we want to bring back? Are they the same users?

Trying to protect cultural heritage is not one of the easiest fields. And in Palestine, the challenges are even greater. However, the most demanding part for us at Riwaq [the organization founded by Amiry] is how to deal with the community.

If you recall, [Ariel] Sharon, the former Prime Minister of Israel, made the decision in the year 2000 that he did not want any Palestinian workers working in Israel. As a result, 150,000 Palestinians from Gaza and the West Bank found themselves without jobs, which meant that one-third of the population in Palestine woke up one day jobless.

We at Riwaq felt a responsibility to contribute to the creation of jobs, so we created a program called "Job Creation Through Conservation," where conservation was not really about the technical aspect, but rather about the number of people that could be hired in each project. So that's the only time when villagers started feeling like they were putting a buck in their pockets at the end of the day. Before, we used to go and work with the community and tell them about our history, about our identity, and about why it is important to keep these buildings. And they would yawn, not really interested in any of it.

That is when the 50-Village Project came to life. We decided that if we protected 50 villages in Palestine in Gaza and the West Bank, we would be protecting 50 percent of our cultural heritage. So instead of putting $150,000 into one building, we started putting $150,000 into preventive conservation—that is, stopping the buildings from deteriorating in such a way that if we came in 15 or 20 years, we would still find them standing, improving also the quality of life in the village.

Conservation
Memory

The Woven Edge

Elizabeth Savrann (MLA I)
Excavating Space and Nature in Tokyo
Instructors: Toru Mitani with Manabu Chiba

Facing the heavy construction in the city, consider the possibilities of open-space design that excavates the history and nature behind the urban fabric.

The excavation between the existing subterranean infrastructure and the Kanda River creates room for an active waterfront, dual rivers, and a functional edge condition. The river's edge is rethought as an interface for viewing and experiencing the woven nature of riverside infrastructure in Tokyo.

Infrastructure
Landform
Water

Reimagining Hamburg's Skyline

Ece Comert (MArch II), Benjamin Hayes (MArch I)
Between Earth and Sky: A Building for the HafenCity, Hamburg
Instructor: Eric Parry

Hamburg is a city that works and plays hard: the ground offers opportunity to provide a site for both. The tower will offer the opportunity to debate questions of use, priorities, and the particular technologies and construction associated with taller buildings.

Initial urban design with
Oorvi Sharma (MArch II)

Facade
Program
Urbanism

Ascending and Descending Planes

Andreea Vasile Hoxha (MLA I)
Landscape Architecture Core Studio I
Instructor: Gareth Doherty

> Understood as an open courtyard/plaza, the site will articulate different levels in the city through sculpting. Tactical and precise, the reimagining of the surface through landform (with cut and fill) will be at the center of this project.

Through a series of ascending and descending planes, the plaza emerges from Cambridge Street through the City Hall courtyard, creating a series of unique experiences emphasized by the relationship between the surface and the canopy.

In Between Pitched Roof and Modernist Slab

Francisco Ramos (MArch II)
Quito and the Elasticity of the Spanish-American Block
Instructor: Felipe Correa

Using the city of Quito as a laboratory, this studio examines the urban legacy, current decline, and future opportunities of the Spanish-American colonial grid. It will specifically focus on the typological tropes and morphological elasticity of the Spanish-American block as a point of departure to imagine new urban development in the context of a historically charged site.

A contemporary building is proposed to set the stage for restoration and preservation of the entire block. Two new pitched-roof houses negotiate the insertion of the project in context and intertwine with a modernist bar that holds residential units and offers the promise of transparency.

Grid
Housing
Typology

A City of Extraordinary Extremes

Manila: Future Habitations
Instructors: Rok Oman, David Rubin, Špela Videčnik

The studio reconsiders existing dwellings and the connective tissue of neighborhoods—from informal, spontaneous settlements to the Spanish-informed architecture of the historical core and residual landscapes of fortification—to find potential for new prototypes that merge architecture and landscape. These new developments will connect form with space and interiors with landscapes, consider climate, vegetation, and sea level rise, and create sustainable, ecologically sensitive habitations that consider technologies focusing on material reuse.

"Manila: Future Habitations" final review.

a new lease on life.

Climate Change
Ecology
Infrastructure
Materials

The Flak Towers of Germany: A Case Study

Rebecca Han (MArch I)
Conservation, Destruction, and Curating Impermanence
Instructor: Natalia Escobar Castrillón

This seminar on critical conservation aims to develop concepts and strategies able to describe and curate the transitory and dynamic nature of architecture, landscapes, and cities.

Paul Ricœur writes of the problematic of forgetting as a disturbing threat that may be countered by appeasements of memory. The art of forgetting, he argues in this respect, remains a delusion, as there is simply an impossibility embedded within the active process of forgetting. Inevitably, the "underpinning of memory . . . is to some considerable extent a nationalist effort premised on the need to construct a desirable loyalty to the insider's understanding of one's country, tradition, and faith."[1] The long-standing towers of Nazi Germany are thus unavoidably towers of memory and history. Each form of forgetting remains relevant to the discussion of how memories play a role in influencing the narrative regarding contemporary topics, particularly in the case of the Holocaust and its consequential effects on the relics of Nazi Germany.

Of particular importance is how these forms of forgetting may range in type: memories can be effaced or destroyed; things can be forgotten yet kept in reserve; or they may undergo a physical transformation by being altered, manipulated, or obligated. Specifically, the uses and abuses of memory range in typology between blocked memory, manipulated memory, and obligated memory, which translates to a similar taxonomy of forgetting or measures of erasure in actual practice. The contemporary methods of appropriation embodied in various forms by the Flak towers can thus be studied through a taxonomy of practices by which monuments have been destroyed, hidden, refashioned, or reappropriated throughout the years.

In the analogy that memory is a material trace of something—similar to the way the brain retains cortical traces or in the same way the documentary traces an event—Ricœur defines forgetting in the sense of a "context of dysfunction of mnestic operations, along the uncertain border between the normal and the pathological."[2] As a subjective representation of the past, there is the "central problematic of the memory-image, namely, the dialectic of presence, absence, and the distance that inaugurated, accompanied and tormented our investigation."[3] Ricoeur goes as far as to venture that the stability of a healthy brain can be labeled through forgetting in the realm of knowledge within which the border between what is "normal" and what is "pathological" can be categorically defined.

Thus, utter destruction is one way by which memory can be entirely obliterated both from the mind and in physical form. Just as the obliteration of existing synaptic connections of neurons in our brains may effectively erase memories by way of physical deletion, destruction in the object-world may operate similarly by the demolition or complete razing of the tower, in effect producing the same results.

1
Paul Ricœur, *Memory, History, Forgetting* (Chicago: University of Chicago Press, 2004), 242.

2
Ibid., 418.

3
Ibid., 419.

The Half City

Gina Ciancone (MArch I, MUP), Rodrigo Solé (MUP)
Beyond Reconstruction: Mexico and the 2017 Earthquakes
Instructors: Diane E. Davis, Jose Castillo

In September 2017, Mexico experienced a series of devastating earthquakes. Their effects became both symptoms and evidence of asymmetrical urban, territorial, and social development. For this reason, any ethically defensible response should go beyond "mere" reconstruction and imagine new, more resilient, and equitable forms of urbanization.

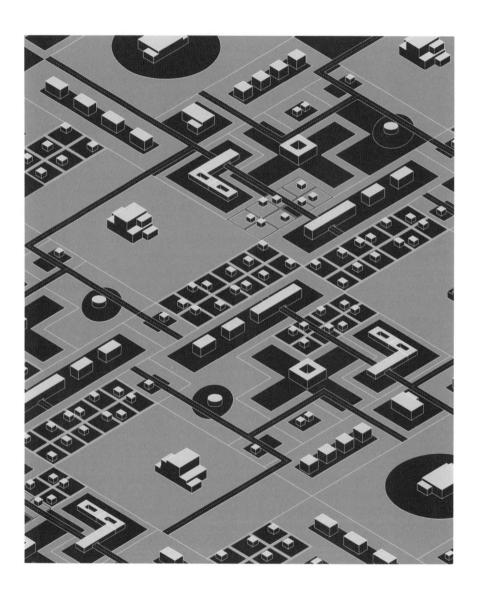

The "Half City" is a method to design community empowerment mechanisms, incentivize annual employment opportunities, and decrease dependency on central authorities. By designing a framework of basic requirements for each plot of collectively owned land, the "Half City" can be transformed based on the needs of individual owners. It is a radical new model of gradual urbanization from the ground up.

Critical Intervention: Alternatives to Preservation in Mexico

Enrique Aureng Silva (MDes CC)
Design Studies Open Project
Awarded the Project Prize in Design Studies
Advisors: Diane E. Davis, Susan Snyder, George Thomas

Historic buildings are the physical signs of the past. They are the material evidence of other times, other peoples, and other ways of understanding life and architecture. Interpreted as such, they are frequently associated with particular historical narratives; they become the objects and recipients of cultural memories, and more often than not, they get connected to notions of national value and particular heritage discourses that tend to emphasize certain historical narratives while neglecting others.

In this way, traditional preservation practices tend to fix historic buildings in a certain particular period of the past. In order to preserve the material qualities and cultural relevance of architectural objects or urban landscapes, the methods and theoretical frameworks of preservation set historic structures, and even their immediate contexts, as landmarks worthy of protection.

But what happens when natural disasters damage historic fabric? What should be done when an earthquake hits and partially destroys a 16th-century monastery listed as a World Heritage Site? Should the same techniques and theories be applied to the natural weathering of a masonry wall as to a collapsed bell tower? What is the role that local communities should play in deciding what to preserve and what to forget?

This thesis proposes, through a reinterpretation of the concept of liminality, that the repetitive nature of earthquakes in Mexico should be seen as an opportunity for change: change in the interpretation of certain historical accounts, change in the relation between historic preservation and historic buildings, and change in the structures of power that dictate the narratives associated with them. All of these should be questioned in order to create new architectures, new urbanisms, and new social interactions that, while still reflecting on the past—on the physical and non-physical fragments left by the catastrophes—use the historic fabric not as a nostalgic element to lament loss, but as a starting point for where to imagine new alternatives.

Conservation
Memory
Reconstruction

L'Enfant's Latency: Camping the Anacostia

Greta Ruedisueli (MLA I AP)
Landscape Architecture Thesis
Advisor: Jill Desimini

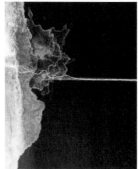
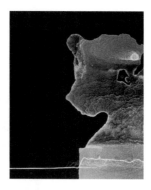
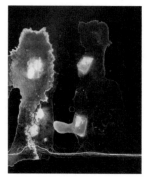

On the one hand, there are the highly regulated, pristine, national landscapes of Washington, and on the other, there are disenfranchised landscapes left out of the planning process. This thesis considers the latter as spaces to reclaim the rights to a collective public realm. It proposes an alternative to systematized maintenance by embracing spontaneous occupation, highlighting the symbiotic potential of plants and humans.

"L'Enfant's Latency" creates an environment for temporary and voluntary camping along the Anacostia River. In opposition to the Washington Mall, this reading of a collective right to the public defines a dynamic and messy democracy.

American City
Democracy
Public Space
Water

Monastery & Brewery in Säynätsalo

Benjamin Hayes (MArch I)
Northern Light
Instructor: Toshiko Mori

In a dynamic society, values change and life shifts, and with that artifacts and buildings disappear while others endure. The potential for buildings to be preserved, be rehabilitated, or simply survive depends on the values of the current times and the building's social contract with its surrounding community.

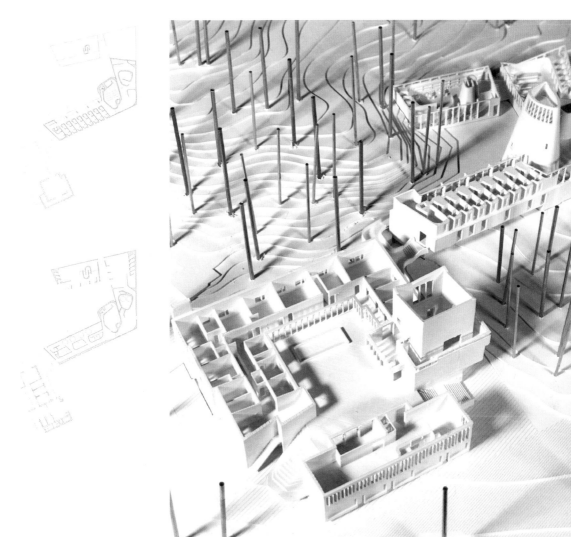

The monastery and brewery reinvigorate Säynätsalo, Finland, by providing a dynamic and self-sustaining social, economic, and spiritual hub for the local community and monks, while also attracting visitors to the island in search of spiritual retreat. Nested among the spruce trees, the monastery makes its presence known with its muted brown brick facade that contrasts with the rich red water-struck brick of Alvar Aalto's Town Hall.

Tabula Plena

Front

1 Elizabeth Savrann
2 Andreea Vasile Hoxha
3 Benjamin Hayes
4 Francisco Ramos

Back

5 Stacy Passmore
6 Jungchan Yee

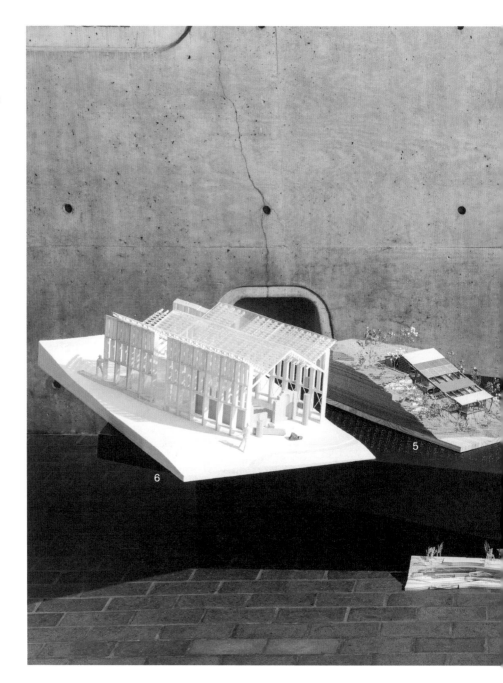

Uninvited Guest

This poem is cut up from the following sources:
HIS 4447 Forest, Grove, Tree: Planting Urban Landscapes
VIS 2344 Constructing Visual Narratives of Place
SCI 6358 Analytic Geometries, Descriptive Geometries:
        Thinking and Making
STU 1101 Architecture Core Studio I: Project
STU 1102 Architecture Core Studio II: Situate
STU 1111 Landscape Architecture Core Studio I
STU 1202 Architecture Core Studio IV: Relate
STU 1212 Landscape Architecture Core Studio IV
STU 1319 Museum Island
SES 5373 Energetics of Urbanization
ADV 9302 Urban Planning and Design Thesis
ADV 9307 Design Studies Open Projects
Lecture   Mayor Rahm Emanuel

Please join us—
    gated communities,
    industrial urbanization,
    monocultures,
    and invited critics—
to pass the scrutiny of
the field of survey.

Addressing the inertia of
war and peace,
a fundamentally optimistic society
tackles
contradictory forces at play,
precluding conventional forms
across diverse territories.

To stake out
possible future scenarios.

Uninvited Guest: *outside agents disrupt this table*

Today's world is inhabited by a number of dominant—yet unsought after—global forces, vying for an ever-greater share of power. When these players enter into existing cultural and social contexts, they act as foreign bodies invading their hosts.

    These actors arrive uninvited. Sometimes through colonization, sometimes through obscene scale, sometimes through capitalistic instruments—the uninvited guest alters the order of things. At this table, the possibility and urgency of resistance is at stake.

At the Still Point in the Turning World

Carson Booth (MLA I), Nai Tzu Cheng (MLA I AP), Helena Cohen (MLA I), Wan Fung Lee (MLA I AP), Danica Liongson (MLA I, MDes ULE), Ann Lynch (MLA I), Melissa Naranjo (MLA I AP), Kai Chi Ng (MLA I AP), Joshua Stevens (MLA I AP), Parawee Wachirabuntoon (MLA I), Tongtong Zhang (MLA I AP), Xiaowei Zhang (MLA I AP)
Landscape Architecture Core Studio IV
Instructor: Pierre Bélanger

If the predominant challenges of the next generation operate on a range of scales and across boundaries of political states, then territorial ecologies offer new synthetic and systemic strategies of spatial intervention. The nation-state is itself a site of design, deterritorialization, and decolonization.

By imagining a future contingent on infrastructural, monumental, and social palimpsests, a new story about sovereignty is told: one that incorporates the voices of territories, citizens, and natural processes.

Democracy
Ecology
Monument
Territory

Bosque Autónomo: Forests as Catalysts of Puerto Rican Autonomy

Anna Curtis-Heald (MLA I), Isabella Frontado (MLA I, MDes ADPD), Mark Heller (MLA I, MUP), Caroline Hickey (MLA I), Juhyuk Lee (MLA I AP), Mengfei Li (MLA I AP), Yanni Ma (MLA I AP), Davi Parente Schoen (MUP, MLA I), Hye Rim Shin (MLA I AP), Stefano Romagnoli (MLA I AP), Chengzhang Zhang (MLA I AP), Xiaoyuan Zhang (MLA I AP)
Landscape Architecture Core Studio IV
Instructor: Sergio Lopez-Pineiro

With ambiguous sovereignty and rapidly changing economic, political, and environmental realities, Puerto Rico lives a dual reality subject to both local and US policies, regulations, impulses, and sway. Our project mobilizes reforestation to open up spaces of sovereignty for Puerto Rico in ways that can prove flexible to multiple futures without being contingent upon a single one.

Ecology
Labor
Policy
Territory

Unitary and Sovereign

Emily Hicks (MLA I), Jiyun Jeong (MLA I), Nam Jung Kim (MLA I AP), Jiacheng Liu (MLA I), Chenxiang Meng (MLA I AP), Isabel Preciado (MLA I), Nadyeli Quiroz (MLA I AP, MDes ULE), Estello-Cisdre Raganit (MLA I), Evangeline Sheridan (MLA I), Melody Stein (MLA I), Ting Fung Wong (MLA I AP), Chuanying Zheng (MLA I AP)
Landscape Architecture Core Studio IV
Instructor: Robert Gerard Pietrusko

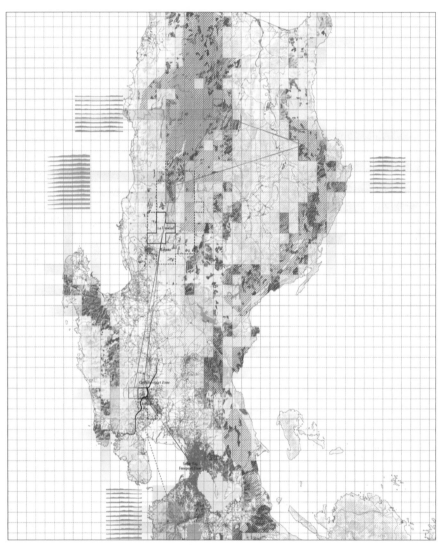

The Subic-Clark-Tarlac Expressway connects the economic freeport zones surrounding vacated American military bases. Officially, the Philippines has been free from foreign occupation since the Military Base Closure Agreement of 1991 following the eruption of Mount Pinatubo. But in reality, the age of foreign occupation is far from over. We prepared a selection of four counterstrategies for managing land and resources that directly address Filipino autonomy and self-governance. Each of these landscape interventions appropriates and redirects channels of governance once used as implements of dispossession in order to manipulate the very institutional structures that put them in place.

Ecology
Mapping
Policy
Social Equity

Hidden by a Legacy of Control

Madeleine Aronson (MLA I)
Forest, Grove, Tree: Planting Urban Landscapes
Instructor: Sonja Dümpelmann

In the Pacific Northwest, a unique mix of local and migrant harvesters follows a yearly trail of fruiting mushrooms from British Columbia to California, depending on which mushrooms are in season and where buyers are stationed.[1] They are picking edible mushrooms that will be sold to local buyers and then distributed to restaurants and global marketplaces, where they demand a high price. Mushroom picking provides a viable income and degree of freedom otherwise unattainable for a diverse group of people. This has included a large percentage of Southeast Asian pickers, initially arriving in the Pacific Northwest in the late 1970s and early 1980s as refugees fleeing war, as well as blue collar workers out of work due to recessions, the decline of the timber industry, and other resource-based economies.[2] As explained by David Arora, "thousands of people in the Pacific Northwest now gather and sell wild mushrooms. Most of them pick locally or opportunistically for a little extra cash or as one of several seasonally based strategies for survival."[3]

Despite the diversity of mushroom pickers, a quick search for articles relating to the mushroom trail reveals a host of sensational stories describing pickers as territorial scoundrels who use shotguns to guard mushroom patches, in a backwoods world of illegal activity.

Articles that misrepresent the mushroom trade as dangerous and rowdy relate to historical tropes of forest as other and forager as social outsider. These perceptions have contributed to the control of mushroom harvesting by national forests today, bringing into question another historically rich concept of forest as commons.

By unpacking and evaluating the Forestry Service's policies and practices impacting mushroom growth and picker livelihoods in Deschutes National Forest in Oregon, I intend to question how forestry practices suppress and devalue human–plant interactions like foraging. What are the historical factors that have led us to this point and to what extent does the contemporary mushroom economy represent the forest as a commons?

1
David Arora, "Migrant Mushroomers," *Whole Earth* (Spring 2000). http://www.wholeearth.com/issue/2100/article/145/migrant.mushroomers.

2
Rebecca McLain, "Controlling the Forest Understory: Wild Mushroom Politics in Central Oregon" (PhD diss., University of Washington, 2000), 15.

3
Arora, "Migrant Mushroomers."

Plants
Policy
Social Equity

From Pipeline to Platform: Imagining Innovation in the Rust Belt

Alexander Yuen (MAUD)
Urban Design Thesis
Awarded the Thesis Prize in Urban Design
Advisors: Felipe Correa, Peter Rowe

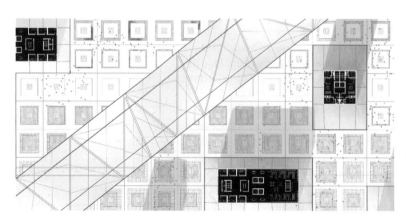

How do we build on economic successes while ensuring that no community is left behind? The project brings together two major contemporary urban phenomena that are not exclusive to the United States but are nevertheless extremely influential in modern American society. The project imagines a new habitat for this ecosystem while simultaneously proposing a refreshed model for the North American innovation campus that rethinks pressing issues of openness, flexibility, sustainability, and relationship to context.

American City
Economy
Urbanism

The Operationalization of the Spanish Territory

Pol Fité Matamoros (MDes ULE)
Design Studies Open Project
Advisor: Neil Brenner

Several scholars have observed a shift during the past decades in the form and dynamics of the contemporary post-1970s landscape and the (g)local manner in which it operates. This phenomenon of "explosion" has fostered the emergence of a number of interpretative frameworks that attempt to address this new reality and update the tools that we dispose to describe—and therefore design—it. This project discusses those interpretative frameworks that appear to be dominant in the current Mediterranean urbanistic discourse to then challenge their applicability to the Spanish context.

Thus, in order to better address the urban transformations of contemporary Spain and its cycles of miraculous growth and crisis, I propose to further examine the "'70s shift" and focus on the role of the state in the provision of infrastructures, acquisition of land, and enactment of policies from the mid-1950s to the early 1980s: that is, the late dictatorial regime and transitioning state. An understanding of the ways in which the state projects itself on the territory to reorganize land and labor when faced with a looming crisis may not only help us to better address the periodization and particularities of Spanish urbanization, but also provide a more consistent narrative that can help interrogate the subsequent periods of the European Union, state decentralization, or the government's failed attempts to implement regional plans.

How Bottled Water Intensifies the Metabolic Shift

Pamela Cabrera (MDes EE), Aurora Jensen (MDes EE)
Energetics of Urbanization
Instructors: Neil Brenner, Kiel Moe

Two significant discourses on energy and urbanization are converging with increasingly parallel questions and concerns. First, a discourse on extended urbanization and global capitalism has begun to stage energy as a central parameter through which to understand historical and contemporary relations regarding territory, accumulation, and urbanization. Second, questions concerning energy in architecture are rapidly cycling up to the scale of urbanization and *longue durée* historical periodizations.

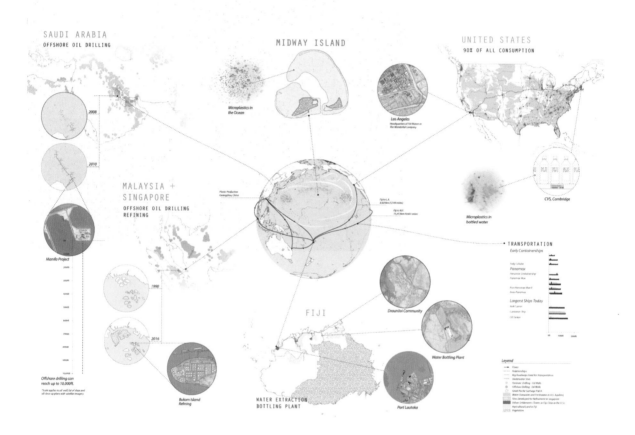

In the last 30 years, the staggering metabolic shift between people and their drinking water has been intensified with the rise of plastic bottles. Companies have actively augmented this shift by disseminating advertisements that undermine local municipal water supplies and convince the public that bottled water is the safest water available. These tactics have successfully normalized the purchasing of bottled water to the point where Americans are willing to pay 2,000 times more for bottled water than they pay for potable municipal water. Through the study of water, a basic resource for human survival, this paper reveals the extent of the metabolic shift between humans and their water resources.

Climate Change
Economy
Energy
Water

Mayor Rahm Emanuel

Public lecture cosponsored by the Harvard Joint Center for Housing Studies
February 20, 2018

Rahm Emanuel is the 55th Mayor of the City of Chicago and has served since 2011. During that time, he has made the tough choices necessary to secure Chicago's future as a global capital.

Mohsen Mostafavi: We have time for one last question.

Aaron Ramirez (MUP): Hi, thanks for coming. My name is Aaron Ramirez. I grew up on the Southwest Side, 50th and Cicero. Happy to be here and to ask you a question. Understanding Chicago and its historical legacy with Chicago-style politics and the embedded corruption there—Edward Burke was my alderman in Archer Heights—my question is related to the idea of corruption. How have you dealt with the corruption that's been embedded in the city that, in my opinion, has prevented you from implementing a lot of the progressive approaches or desired outcomes that you want as mayor of Chicago?

Three Blurred Thresholds: A Sleeping Club

Xianming Sang (MArch I)
Architecture Core Studio II: Situate
Instructor: Elizabeth Christoforetti

The facade is difficult. It is sometimes called upon to pronounce the identity of the activity it conceals even while obliging itself to urban conformance. It is typically a register of scale—of the city, the building, the interior, the program, and construction.

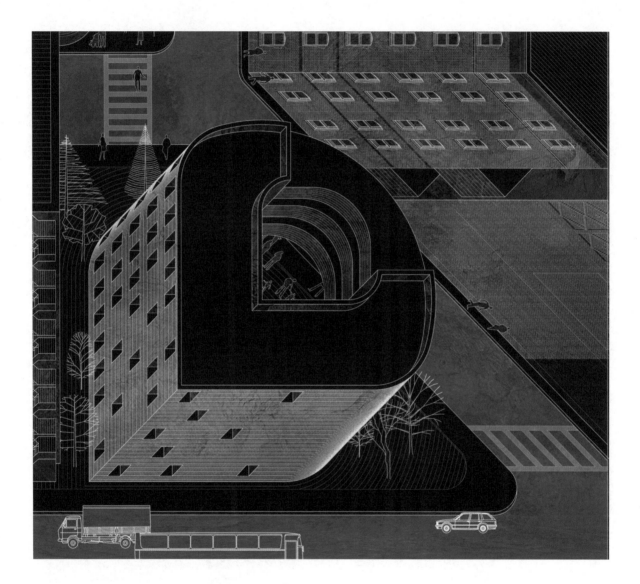

To promote interaction between members while maintaining individual privacy, rooms adjacent to each other are overlapped to create thick thresholds. In this way, the boundary defining each space is blurred, allowing a simultaneous sense of territory and interconnection.

Facade
Program

Talking Stones

Bradley Silling (MArch I AP)
Constructing Visual Narratives of Place
Instructor: Francesca Benedetto

> The themes of the journey and displacement will become a way to describe the metropolitan territory transversally. Its borders, real or imaginary, can render a picture of the new identities that it continues to take on and of how they can be observed.

Tête-à-Tête

Willem Bogardus (MArch I), Golnoush Jalali (MArch I)
Analytic Geometries, Descriptive Geometries: Thinking and Making
Instructors: George L. Legendre, Cameron Wu

Our understanding of the parametric surface depends on the absolute reciprocity between form and texture, between surface and threads: you can't have the one without the other. It may be time to break this covenant. We will explore how the constitutive texture of a "heretical" surface is significantly—and independently—modulated.

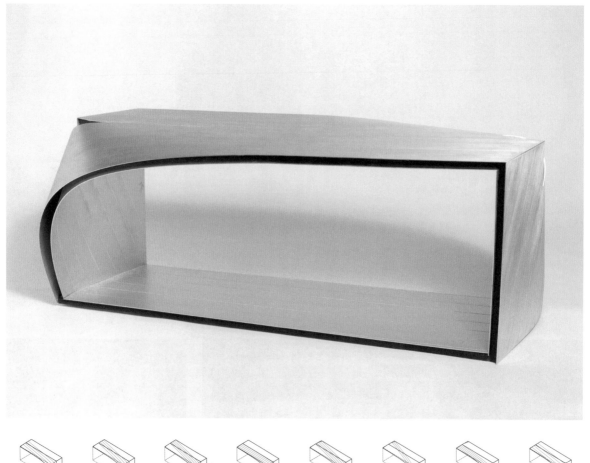

Two planar sitting areas, situated obliquely to each other due to the interstitial placement of conic bends, create a tête-à-tête that facilitates collaboration, collusion, and conspiracy between the bench's users.

Computation
Fabrication
Geometry

Hidden Room

Sum In Sarah Cheung (MArch I)
Architecture Core Studio I: Project
Instructor: Andrew Plumb

Design a group of five rooms, one of which seems to be hidden from the other four. The hidden may involve the art of camouflage and surreptitious passage.

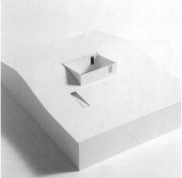

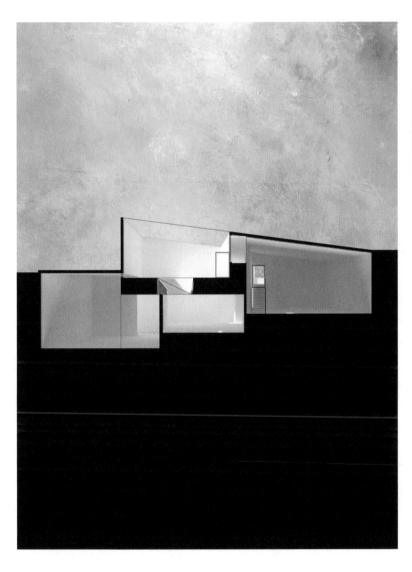

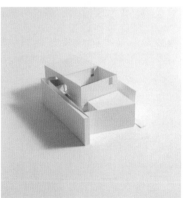

You are fully aware of your subterranean position, yet you wander through each space pondering and chasing the origins of the light. Constantly delivered toward glows, glimpses, and scintillations, you are denied it and made to follow a set path that leads you from room to room.

Revival Revival!

Evan Orf (MArch I), Veronica Smith (MArch I)
Architecture Core Studio IV: Relate
Instructor: Jennifer Bonner

If Denise Scott Brown and Robert Venturi grappled with "nonstraightforward architecture," arguing for messiness over unity, the distorted over the straightforward, the ambiguous over the articulated, and the hybrid over the pure, while Aldo Rossi tackled "nameless architecture," then this studio works toward "ordinary architecture."

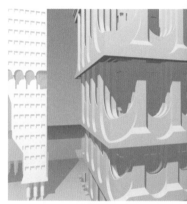

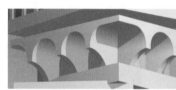

In our three high-density housing proposals in downtown Los Angeles, we suggest an expansion of Revival Style Urbanism, re-spatializing the de-spatialized elements of L.A. Revival architecture without sacrificing the whimsy of mid-century mashups. Reviving the Revival story, we misinterpret the flattened elements of our mashed-up forebears as deep spatial organization that doesn't veil interior monotony, but wholly reconstitutes the internal program and circulation of the standard housing types into which the Revival elements are integrated.

Housing
Precedent
Urbanism
Typology

Illuminating Wild

Zoe Holland (MLA I), Haoyu Zhao (MLA I)
Landscape Architecture Core Studio I
Instructor: Silvia Benedito

Translating the nocturnal landscape through the medium of
photography posed a challenge and forced a confrontation with
the various modes of seeing and navigating a space without
daylight. What results is a new type of wildness, where open
space becomes much more mysterious.

Photography
Plants
Public Space
Representation

Art Depot in Houston

Stefan Sauter (MArch II)
Museum Island
Instructors: Sharon Johnston, Mark Lee
Rather than view island-like monocultures as fissures within the inclusiveness of globalization, this studio will embrace these models as opportunities to promote connectivity through precise demarcation of borders.

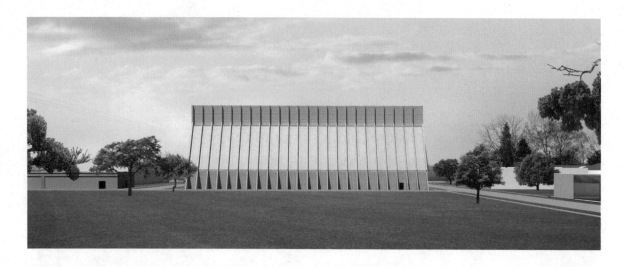

The result of this investigation is an architecture that expresses itself through the limits of material affordance, finding common ground with the architecture of silos such as the ones photographed by Bernd and Hilla Becher. Here, spatial qualities are defined by strict functional determinations. Rather than concealing a large container for art that supports a one-of-a-kind collection, it becomes part of an iconology of intervals where meaning arises in between buildings and oak trees.

Facade
Museum
Timber

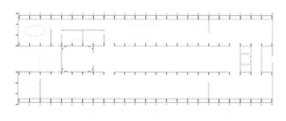

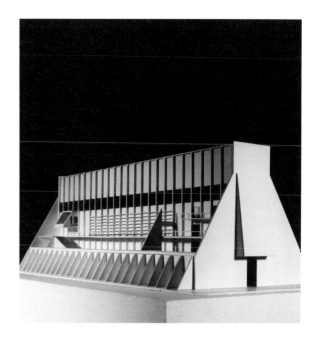

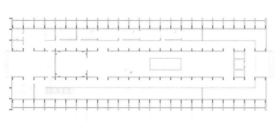

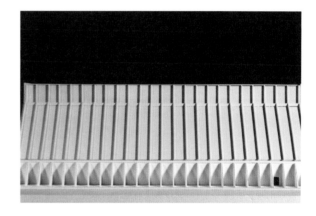

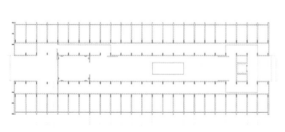

possible future scenarios.

Uninvited Guest

Front

A   Xianming Sang
B   Evan Orf
    Veronica Smith
C   Esther Mira Bang
D   Claire Malone Matson
    Zishen Wen
    Xiaowei Zhang
E   Bradley Silling
F   Alexander Yuen

Back

G   Aiysha Alsane
    Isabel Brostella
    Oi Wai Charity Cheung
    Qiaoqi Dai
    Luis Flores
    Jenjira Holmes
    Varat Limwibul
    Claire Malone Matson
    Sophia Sennett
    Hannah Van der Eb
    Qiao Xu
    Shing Hin
    Bryan Woo
H   Evan Orf
    Veronica Smith
I   Sum In Sarah Cheung
J   Stefan Sauter
K   Willem Bogardus
    Golnoush Jalali

Boys, Bridges, and Blackness

Calvin Boyd (MArch I)
Inspired by and featuring "summer, somewhere" by Danez Smith (2017)[1]
Buildings, Texts, and Contexts II
Instructors: Erika Naginski, Antoine Picon

In a paradise of our own making, black boys worship the god of their choosing, a gargantuan bridge fashioned out of the scraps of brass bullets, and every street in existence radiates out from the life-giving sea in which its mighty foundations rest. On occasion, the bridge will drop boys down from right out of the sky already wet, and after submerging, they balloon to the surface gasping for air.

In paradise, there is a boy named Eugene who falls from the sky with a rock tied to his ankle. Once his body strikes the water, boys watch him plummet ever downward while struggling aback an aquamarine seascape, his body interrogating the crevices of his lungs for any hint of air. Eugene takes on the grace of a meteor while beelining toward the seafloor, burdens showering behind him. His movements are fluid, yet erratic, powerful, but silent; inside him resides a deep struggle, but beneath, the sea is shallow. Surely, he reaches the bottom before expiring. . . . Eugene does not mean to die upon impact like those who jump to finish things. On the contrary, he plans to be born on arrival.

somewhere, a sun. below, boys brown
as rye play the dozens & ball, jump

in the air & stay there. boys become new
moons, gum-dark on all sides, beg bruise

-blue water to fly, at least tide, at least
spit back a father or two. I won't get started.

history is what it is. it knows what it did.
bad dog. bad blood. bad day to be a boy

color of a July well spent. but here, not earth
not heaven, boys can't recall their white shirt

turned a ruby gown. here, there is no language
for *officer* or *law*, no color to call *white*.

if snow fell, it'd fall black. please, don't call
us dead, call us alive someplace better.

we say our own names when we pray.
we go out for sweets & come back.

The night was terribly young, and I was trudging home after a long day of school. It only took 10 minutes to exit the protective gates of the University of Southern California's campus, clear the nearest crosswalk, and make my way down 37th Place to where my apartment poked out to the right. I still recall it as if it happened yesterday, the chorus of bright lights and the cacophony of commanding voices materializing behind me. The doors of stealthy SUVs flinging open and my body shining under the intensity of their headlights. Nothing can truly prepare you for how difficult it is to remain calm in utter chaos, how impossible it is to make out a police officer's gun while blinded by light.

Gender
Justice
Poetry
Race

No matter how hard you practice, performing the role history has assigned you is always tricky. In that moment, hands raised and still, I readied my body to hit the ground and pop up somewhere else under a sun, with my blood-stained hoodie wrung dry. I longed to be somewhere other than America, where "to be a negro and to be relatively conscious is to be in a rage almost all the time."[2] Though in that moment I was not mad; rather, I was oddly patient as my hands were bound and my back was pressed up against my own apartment's chain-link fence.

Surrounded by several men in blue, I was talked over for 30 minutes. Apparently, earlier that night a fellow student reported her purse stolen at gunpoint a couple streets over and I matched the description. My bag was taken and passed around without explanation, and pairs of eyes stared down its throat expecting it to cough up a gun. When it did not, I was asked to hand over my ID, which was on my person, but in one of six possible pockets at the time.

this is how we are born: come morning
after we cypher/feast/hoop, we dig

a new boy from the ground, take
him out his treebox, shake worms

from his braids. sometimes they'll sing
a trapgod hymn (what a first breath!)

sometimes it's they eyes who lead
scanning for bonefleshed men in blue.

we say *congrats, you're a boy again!*
we give him a durag, a bowl, a second chance.

we send him off to wander for a day
or ever, let him pick his new name.

that boy was Trayvon, now called *RainKing.*
that man Sean named himself *I do, I do.*

O, the imagination of a new reborn boy
but most of us settle on *alive.*

Some days, in paradise, the bridge only delivers one or two boys; other days, storms of boys pour down from the sky. After they are fished out of the water and dried by the sun's summer rays, they all skip off. Their internal compasses guide them away from the bridge every which way and boys fill the street marching toward home. Paradise is where protests are simply parades of sun-kissed boys returning home and no one gets lost.

Here in paradise, nothing is off-limits, even the lone bridge and its sacredness. Boys touch, climb on, and jump off its skeletal members, and the bridge still stands though it is beaten and bruised in appearance. Not even the bridge's two abutments—where the gates of both heaven and earth are rumored to be—are restricted, but no boy has ever journeyed there; there is no reason to. Why would someone leave the only place that has ever loved them back? In paradise, black boys see themselves in everything and the very ground they walk on kisses their feet.

sometimes a boy is born
right out the sky, dropped from

a bridge between starshine & clay.
one boy showed up pulled behind

a truck, a parade for himself
& his wet red gown. years ago

we plucked brothers from branches
unpeeled their naps from bark.

sometimes a boy walks into his room
then walks out into his new world

still clutching wicked metals. some boys
waded here through their own blood.

does it matter how he got here if we're all here
to dance? grab a boy, spin him around.

if he asks for a kiss, kiss him.
if he asks where he is, say *gone*.

My student ID was in the last pocket I suggested. A heavy hand removed
it from my hoodie and wasted no time dialing the number of USC
Administration to verify that I was in fact student #7306-8002-90. The
officers were obviously used to neighborhood boys conjuring up fakes when
asked for credentials. What my academic standing had to do with the rob-
bery, I could not tell you.

Moments later, I was released and followed by a lone black officer
back onto my property. I vaguely recall his apology consisting of "you know
the deal" and "these kinds of things happen" as I stared at the ground, twirl-
ing my phone through my fingers. I was not sincerely listening; the damage
had already been done. The now quiet sirens had drawn out quite a few of
my neighbors, all of whom caught a glimpse of my embarrassed counte-
nance. In their eyes I was unquestionably guilty.

Once alone, I checked the time on my phone and saw my mother's
name flash across the screen. I had missed two of her calls.

no need for geography
now that we're safe everywhere.

point to whatever you please
& call it church, home, or sweet love.

paradise is a world where everything
is a sanctuary & nothing is a gun.

here, if it grows it knows its place
in history. yesterday, a poplar

told me of old forest
heavy with fruits I'd call uncle
bursting red pulp & set afire,
harvest of dark wind chimes.

after I fell from its limb
it kissed sap into my wound.

do you know what it's like to live
someplace that loves you back?

In paradise, only black boys exist and no one else is missed. Black boys
never needed anyone anyway; it was always the other way around. Here,

black bodies are no longer used to erect foreign empires they are not welcome in, nor do they fill the walls of prisons, shoulder to shoulder, while lining the pockets of those who put them there. We erect our own monuments devoid of metal detectors crowning the entrances of our architecture; our own names lie carved into the entablatures of our buildings. Here, one cannot tell the difference between a choir and a jury or a church and a courtroom since they are both places to be victorious.

In paradise, black boys are the affluent rulers of a bountiful land and they go wherever they please. Even gates have no sidedness and black bodies pass through them freely. The streets are lined with dazzling steel shovels and water flows abundantly. If you punctured the ground, an impressive geyser would erupt, and possibly spit out a boy or two.

here, everybody wanna be black & is.
look—the forest is a flock of boys

who never got to grow up, blooming
into forever, afros like maple crowns

reaching sap-slow toward sky. watch
Forest run in the rain, branches

melting into paper-soft curls, duck
under the mountain for shelter. watch

the mountain reveal itself a boy.
watch Mountain & Forest playing

in the rain, watch the rain melt everything
into a boy with brown eyes & wet naps—

the lake turns into a boy in the rain
the swamp—a boy in the rain

the fields of lavender—brothers
dancing between the storm.

My mother had always been the more outspoken one between the two of us, so after calling her back, I expected her to speak first. But this time, I could hear my little brother prancing around in the background as she waited for my voice, which was slow to come. I began with an apology of sorts because I so desperately did not want to alarm her. It had only been a couple weeks since the loss of Michael Brown and the onslaught of protests in Ferguson that followed.

I could physically hear the air leave my mother's throat as I hesitantly delivered the news. But by the time I had finished, she had already vigorously beckoned my father over and raised the volume of my voice so he could hear too. Even over the phone it was clear that both my parents were in a state of shock; they could not scold me, seeing that I did everything right, and they did not know whether to be joyful or furious. My mother kept emphasizing how she had merely called to check in, or in her words, "see how I was enjoying the paradise of LA."

if you press your ear to the dirt
you can hear it hum, not like it's filled

with beetles & other low gods
but like a mouth rot with gospel

& other glories. listen to the dirt
crescendo a boy back.
come. celebrate. this
is everyday. every day

holy. everyday high
holiday. everyday new

year. every year, days get longer.
time clogged with boys. the boys

O the boys. they still come
in droves. the old world

keeps choking them. our new one
can't stop spitting them out.

Two years prior to my detainment, a gang rivalry motivated now 25-year-old Brandon Spencer to open fire on USC's campus the night of Halloween. The incident left the entire student body on edge, and the administration was quick to close itself off to the neighboring community. In the months that followed, a campus-wide curfew was instated, fingerprint scanners and a legion of private security guards were stationed at the front of every dorm, and an iron gate metered by brick pillars sprung up from the ground, fully lining the school's perimeter. The impoverished neighborhood of South Central where USC had decided to situate itself was encroaching, and that was unacceptable. Lines had to be drawn, and which side I belonged on soon proved to be a constant issue.

All of this in effect led up to that horrific night, which paradoxically was the closest I have ever been to paradise: a field of rye underneath an ever-present summer sun, somewhere not exactly heaven and not quite earth either. A place somewhere south of somewhere worse, designed for black boys to be boys unencumbered. I have never been there, but on the surface I imagine paradise not to be all that unfamiliar. Paradise looks a bit like home, except there is no such thing as stop-and-frisk, no opportunities for misinterpreted exchanges with the police or whiteness.

ask the mountain-boy to put you on
his shoulders if you want to see

the old world, ask him for some lean
-in & you'll be home. step off him

& walk around your block.
grow wings & fly above your city.

all the guns fire toward heaven.
warning shots mince your feathers.

fall back to the metal-less side
of the mountain, cry if you need to.

that world of laws rendered us into dark
matter. we asked for nothing but our names

in a mouth we've known
for decades. some were blessed

to know the mouth.
our decades betrayed us.

—

there, I drowned, back before, once.
there, I knew how to swim but couldn't.

there, men stood by shore & watched me blue.
there, I was a dead fish, the river's prince.

there, I had a face & then I didn't.
there, my mother cried over me

but I wasn't there. I was here, by my own
water, singing a song I learned somewhere

south of somewhere worse. that was when
direction mattered. now, everywhere

I am is the center of everything.
I must be the lord of something.

what was I before? a boy? a son?
a warning? a myth? I whistled

now I'm the God of whistling.
I built my Olympia downstream.

When black boys dream of paradise, I am sure we all think of the same place: a world where black boys get more time to be children. A world a little less overwhelming; where our bodies are not the subject of difficult conversations we rarely get to take part in. We think how nice it would be if we were simply taken at our word, if our bodies did not rest underneath the tongues of our oppressors and just beyond the barrels of loaded guns. A world where we do not have to be both the mighty bridge and the life-giving sea. In paradise, Brandon Spencer is bestowed a second chance, not a 40-year sentence. In paradise, Eugene walks unburdened by the rock that brought him there.

you are not welcome here. trust
the trip will kill you. go home.

we earned this paradise
by a death we didn't deserve.

I am sure there are other heres.
a somewhere for every kind

of somebody, a heaven of brown
girls braiding on golden stoops

but here—
                    how could I ever explain to you—

          someone prayed we'd rest in peace
          & here we are

     in peace   whole   all summer

1
Danez Smith, "summer, somewhere," in *Don't Call us Dead* (Minneapolis: Graywolf Press, 2017), 3–24. First appeared in *Poetry Magazine* (January 2016): 353–59.

2
James Baldwin, "The Negro in American Culture," *Cross Currents* XI (1961): 205.

The Secret Life of Modern Architecture: We Don't Need Another Hero

Beatriz Colomina
Public lecture organized by Women in Design
March 28, 2018

Beatriz Colomina: The question of collaboration has become increasingly important and urgent. On the one hand, you can say that it's central to contemporary discussions of architecture in general. Consider shared software platforms that allow a large number of people in different locations and disciplines to work together on the same project. On the other hand, I think it's also crucial for historians trying to understand the way in which architecture has traditionally been produced. Architecture has always been collaborative. We all know that, yet it has been very difficult for architects to acknowledge this simple fact—much more difficult than in film. Film has always recognized this. At the end of a film, even the makeup people, the hair people, the catering people are credited. But we credit nobody.

We couldn't be bothered to credit just one person even in situations like the famous and urgent petition to acknowledge Denise Scott Brown as part of the Pritzker Prize—and this is pertinent to Women in Design at Harvard because they started the petition. But it was still denied! How is it possible—even though an architecture firm recognizes and acknowledges Denise Scott Brown in their name—that institutions such as the Pritzker Prize decide it's irrelevant?

I was going to start precisely with this question of how women are credited in architecture and in general—this is an alternative title: "With or Without You: the Ghosts of Modern Architecture"—because in fact, "with" and not "and" is precisely the way women architects are most frequently credited alongside men in official records. And that is if they are credited at all.

The gap between the words "with" and "and," which, as you will see, institutions so vigilantly guard, needs to be rethought. "With" implies a helper, a secondary source of energy; "and" implies partnerships and equality. What is positive about "and" is that it feeds on difference and complexity and may encourage more nuanced forms of production and discourse.

Women have been in architecture for a very, very long time. It's just that we don't see them. In that sense, I can say that women are the ghosts of modern architecture. Here is a ghost, for example: this is a photograph of the Barcelona Pavilion. Has anybody bothered to ask themselves: "Who is this woman standing at the edge of the carpet looking into the Pavilion?" It's Lilly Reich of course, who not only collaborated with Mies van der Rohe on the Pavilion, but was also the one who stayed there while Mies kept going back to Berlin. And she did more than that: she designed 25 industrial exhibits representing Germany in the same international exhibition in 1929. She was crucial to the Barcelona Pavilion, but we continue to refer to it as Mies van der Rohe's.

I will tell you a story of how I got into this whole question of collaboration. Almost 20 years ago I was invited to give a lecture in Madrid. Madrid is incidentally the city where I was born. It was kind of an interesting occasion, because by then I was already a professor at Princeton and I had lectured everywhere. But you know, you're never anybody in your own country. So finally they decided that maybe I was worth their while, and the

Gender
History
Social Equity

Colegio de Arquitectos, which is very much a male kind of institution, invited me to give a lecture.

I was working on Charles and Ray Eames at the time, so I gave a lecture on their work, particularly on the Eames House. And to my surprise, most of the discussion at the dinner after the lecture centered on the role of Ray: her background as a painter, how she had studied with Hans Hofmann—they knew everything about her. I was surprised that they raised this question and that they were so interested in the significance of Ray in the partnership, because I was surrounded by very, very well-known Spanish architects, all of them men, some of whom even teach around here.

The conversation drifted, as it usually does in these occasions, and before we knew it we were talking about Lilly Reich and what an enormous, massive role she might have played in the development of Mies van der Rohe's architecture. They talked about the importance of such projects as the Silk and Velvet Cafe in Berlin—the collaborative project of Mies with Lilly Reich for the Exposition de la Mode in Berlin in 1927—when draperies in velvet and silk were hung from metal rods to form the space.

And everyone, to my surprise, agreed that there was nothing, *nothing* in Mies's work prior to that collaboration with Lilly Reich that would suggest this radical definition of a space by suspended sensuous surfaces, which you could say actually became a trademark of his, as exemplified in the Tugendhat House and the Barcelona Pavilion of 1929.

I was astonished, because I had always thought it was obvious—I had said things like that in seminars—but I never brought myself to write anything about it. And then one of these famous architects said something that has stayed with me ever since. He said it is like a dirty little secret that we—that is, "we" meaning all architects—keep. So these guys who were controlling the entire situation in Spain—the schools of architecture, the institutions—they knew it, they saw it; they were in a kind of spontaneous situation after dinner where they were able to talk about it. But as that architect himself admitted, this was like a dirty little secret that we all know, that we all see, but we don't bring ourselves to talk about. So in fact, this made me think that the secrets of modern architecture are really like the secrets of a family—everybody knows that something happened, but nobody wants to talk about it.

And my prediction is that many more secrets are bound to come out.

Mies van der Rohe and Lilly Reich, *Café Samt und Seide* (*Silk and Velvet Cafe*), Moder der Dame exhibition, Berlin, 1927. Mies van der Rohe Archive, Museum of Modern Art, New York.

Interrogation

This poem is cut up from the following sources:
STU 1202 Architecture Core Studio IV: Relate
STU 1232 Collaborative Design Engineering Studio II
STU 1309 $2,000 Home
SES 5374 Community Development: Past, Present, and Future
ADV 9148 Miami Resilience: Affordability and Health
ADV 9201 Independent Study
ADV 9342 Landscape Architecture Thesis
Exhibition Design and the Just City

Interrogation: *a table for tough questions*

We come to the interrogation table looking for answers. The interrogator enters the room, switches on the spotlight, and looks into the eyes of the subject. With all her evidence in hand, the interrogator prepares her investigation. The subject, heart racing, tries to remain calm, knowing that whatever answers she furnishes will only raise new questions.

    This is the act of interrogation: identifying urgent issues, looking for answers, turning up more queries, and pursuing further solutions. In all disciplines we come to the table to question and test the validity of our inquiries.

Dwelling in Clay: A House for Potters

Aimilios Davlantis Lo (MArch II)
$2,000 Home
Instructor: Marina Tabassum

Three clients, three real project sites, three different stories. Located in the deltas of Bangladesh, these are villagers coexisting with nature through a process of negotiation. They live on minimal means and their livelihood is predominantly sourced from nature. The studio will study and analyze dwelling in a landscape dominated by constant shift and change and will propose living units with a budget of $2,000.

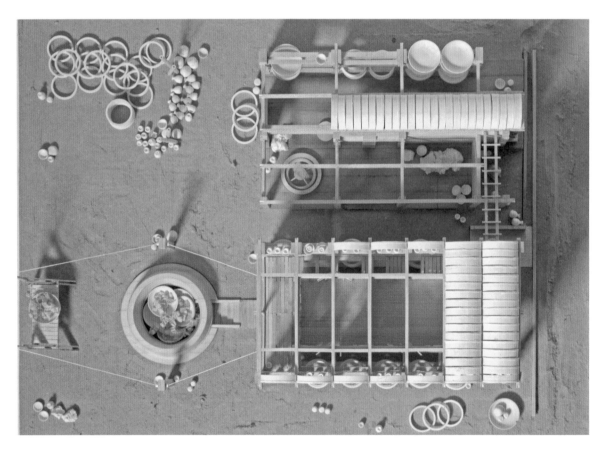

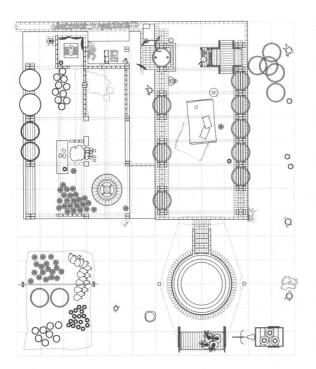
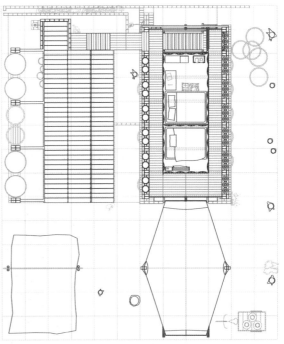

The house has a simple masonry framework that serves as storage for finished and drying pottery. It is a soft exterior boundary that cools the home as the moisture from wet pots evaporates. Inside, stretched *sarees* make up the interior walls, allowing air, ambient light, and color to enter even their most private spaces. The roof is made from a series of arched rings—a commonly produced clay product—but in this case they are divided in half and laid as terracotta roof tiles. The work makes the home and the home feeds the work. It is the act of making that gives breath to their never-finished dwelling.

Turnpike Metabolism

Ernest Haines (MLA I)
Landscape Architecture Thesis
Awarded the Thesis Prize in Landscape Architecture
Advisor: Robert Gerard Pietrusko

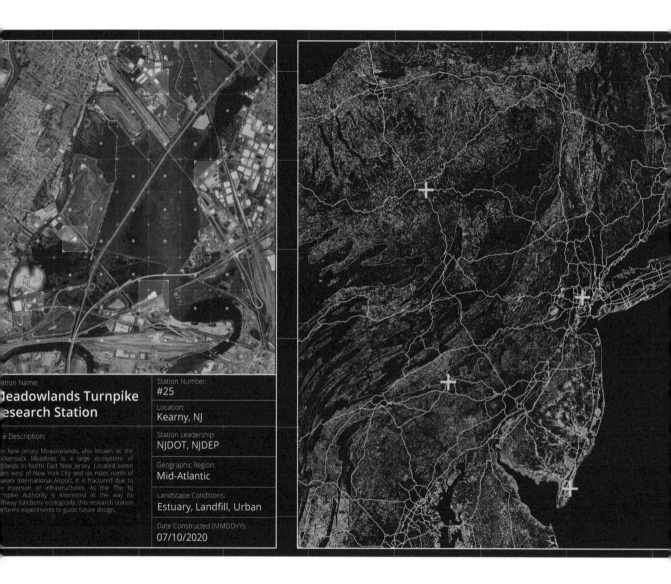

Station Name:	**Station Number:**
Meadowlands Turnpike Research Station	#25
	Location:
	Kearny, NJ
Description:	**Station Leadership:**
The New Jersey Meadowlands, also known as the Hackensack Meadows is a large ecosystem of wetlands in North East New Jersey. Located seven miles west of New York City and six miles north of Newark International Airport, it is fractured due to the insertion of infrastructures. As the The NJ Turnpike Authority is interested in the way its highway functions ecologically, this research station performs experiments to guide future design.	NJDOT, NJDEP
	Geographic Region:
	Mid-Atlantic
	Landscape Conditions:
	Estuary, Landfill, Urban
	Date Constructed (MMDDYY):
	07/10/2020

When one thinks of national infrastructure, the Interstate Highway System immediately comes to mind. Nearly 50,000 miles in length, planned and constructed for over half a century, it is the largest contiguous landscape in the United States of America.

However, in its current state, the highway disproportionately produces the landscape rather than vice versa. This thesis proposes a set of systems and methods that allow the landscape to actively push back upon and define the way that infrastructures are developed in the United States by making landscape formation, composition, and metabolism primary drivers.

As the issue of crumbling infrastructure continues to become more relevant in the face of global instability, there is

American City
Infrastructure
Mapping
Representation

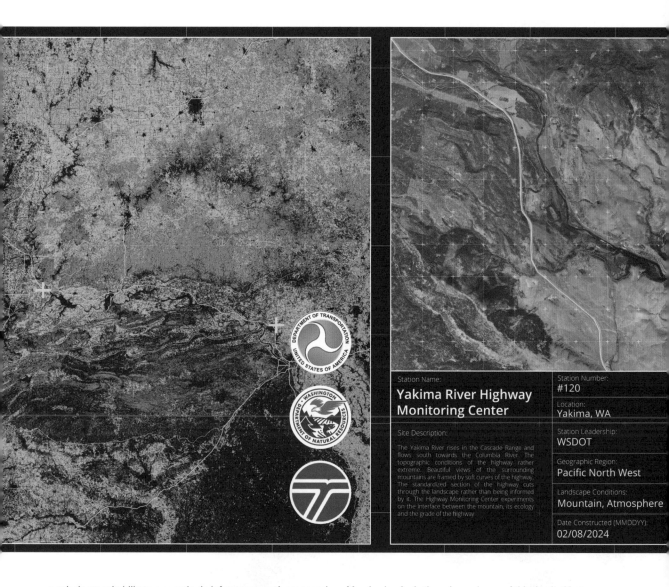

Station Name:

Yakima River Highway Monitoring Center

Station Number:
#120

Location:
Yakima, WA

Site Description:

The Yakima River rises in the Cascade Range and flows south towards the Columbia River. The topographic conditions of the highway rather extreme. Beautiful views of the surrounding mountains are framed by soft curves of the highway. The standardized section of the highway cuts through the landscape rather than being informed by it. The Highway Monitoring Center experiments on the interface between the mountain, its ecology and the grade of the highway

Station Leadership:
WSDOT

Geographic Region:
Pacific North West

Landscape Conditions:
Mountain, Atmosphere

Date Constructed (MMDDYY):
02/08/2024

a priority to rehabilitate our nation's infrastructure. A proposed consortium leverages the responsibilities and interests of existing government agencies by locating their operations in research stations across the country.

These stations collect data, experiment on the ground, and develop standards and guidelines to be used nationally. Research Station #25, located in the New Jersey

Meadowlands, is the primary locus of this thesis. Here, "Turnpike Metabolism" explores the ways in which an active feedback loop between sensing, design, construction, use, degradation, and replacement redefines infrastructural metabolism in the United States.

Community Mealtime

Jessica Liss (MUP)
Community Development: Past, Present, and Future
Instructor: Lily Song

This seminar intends to examine evolving patterns and drivers of urban inequality and poverty, critically analyze community development concepts and strategies, and produce community development agendas and skills, including strategic action, continuous learning, and creative innovation.

The subway car is like a diverse room that people occupy but in which they seldom interact with others. This condition is a missed opportunity requiring further interrogation. To shift the narrative from inhabiting to interacting requires a rethinking of what public transportation, and in this case the subway, means as community-building space. In his January 2018 *New York Times Magazine* piece, "The Case for the Subway," Jonathan Mahler argues for New York City to rebuild its aging system. His ode to the subway highlights this untapped potential, remarking that: "In New York, movement—anywhere, anytime—is a right."[1]

Imagine a subway car filled with a single long table, chairs, and strangers sitting down to a group meal. Rather than jostling for room, subway riders are invited to take a seat at the table, literally and figuratively. People interact over food and moderated discussions. The food served relates to the neighborhoods that a given train route is passing through. Facilitators prompt discussions and then allow people to talk among themselves. Given the scale of the system's ridership, such an intervention would be limited and temporary. It and other such interventions, however, would help people envision a different future for transportation. The next time someone rides the subway and there is no longer Community Mealtime, they may be more willing to take that leap and have a meaningful interaction with a stranger. If interventions on the subway can start to break down barriers between fellow riders, the hope is that this will also translate to life outside the train car.

"Community Mealtime" is based on the belief that gathering around a table and sharing a meal brings people together.

1
Jonathan Mahler, "The Case for the Subway," *New York Times Magazine* (January 3, 2018). www.nytimes.com/2018/01/03/magazine/subway-new-york-city-public-transportation-wealth-inequality.html

How can we encourage interaction on the subway?

Community
Public Space
Transportation

Tropical Dense[city]

Kenner Carmody (MDes EE)
Miami Resilience: Affordability and Health
Instructor: Jesse M. Keenan

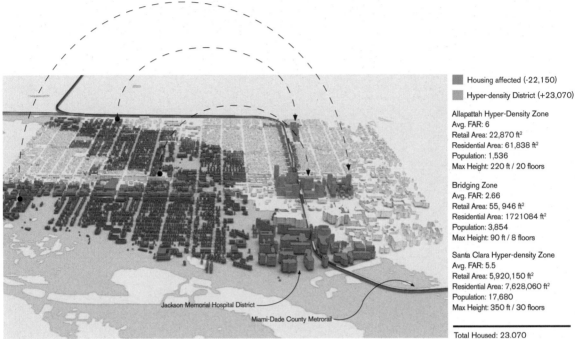

■ Housing affected (-22,150)
■ Hyper-density District (+23,070)

Allapattah Hyper-Density Zone
Avg. FAR: 6
Retail Area: 22,870 ft²
Residential Area: 61,838 ft²
Population: 1,536
Max Height: 220 ft / 20 floors

Bridging Zone
Avg. FAR: 2.66
Retail Area: 55,946 ft²
Residential Area: 1721084 ft²
Population: 3,854
Max Height: 90 ft / 8 floors

Santa Clara Hyper-density Zone
Avg. FAR: 5.5
Retail Area: 5,920,150 ft²
Residential Area: 7,628,060 ft²
Population: 17,680
Max Height: 350 ft / 30 floors

Total Housed: 23.070

Jackson Memorial Hospital District
Miami-Dade County Metrorail

This research aims to visualize and better understand the housing stock necessary to accommodate displaced populations in Miami's Allapattah neighborhood affected by sea level rise and resultant tidal inundation by the year 2100.

Miami must develop a Transfer of Development Rights (TDR) model to diffuse low-lying zones in Allapattah while densifying on higher elevations near mass transit. This model must allow non-contiguous developments to trade densities between vulnerable and more stable areas.

Metrorail in Miami is underutilized compared to Metrobus ridership. With current bridge elevations at only 1 to1.5 feet above sea level (e.g., from Miami to Miami Beach), moving a greater share of ridership to Metrorail and densifying housing, jobs, and amenities along Metrorail transit corridors would be an adaptive solution for the City of Miami. Relocation through TDR that allows for down-zoning of high-risk geographies and up-zoning of low-risk geographies, and that incentivizes management of stormwater, is a key principle in realizing an equitable, mobility-oriented, and hyper-dense future for Allapattah and Miami. Through TDR and hyper-dense development, 23,070 people may be rehoused in various developments within Allapattah.

Sited along Miami's legacy metro system, a densification proposition in East Allapattah tests a hypothesis that a densified urban zone along underutilized existing transit infrastructure can accommodate new (and equitable) densities in Allapattah where housing, employment, and amenities can cluster. Strategic high-density development is critical for Miami's ecological and economic viability in the 21st century.

American City
Climate Change
Policy
Urbanizaiton

Design and the Just City

Exhibition in Frances Loeb Library
Curator: Toni L. Griffin and The Just City Lab
March 26–May 11, 2018

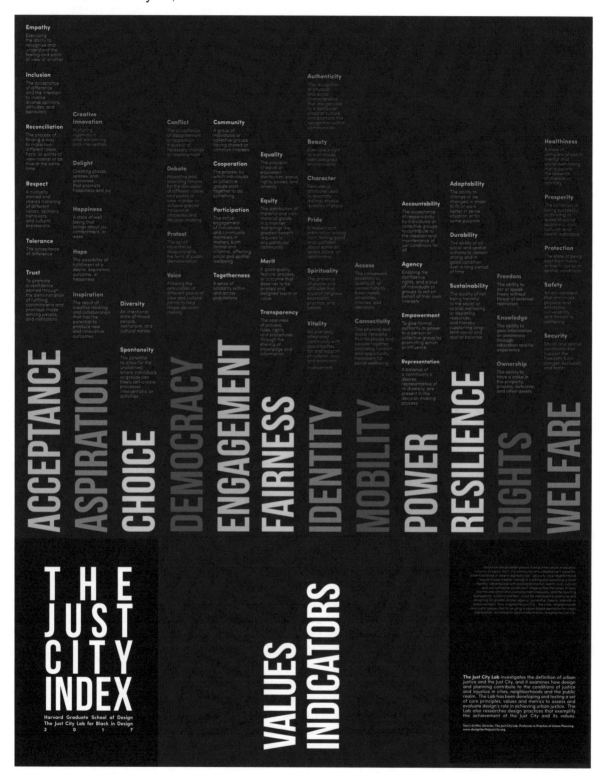

Would we design better places if we

American City
Justice
Policy
Urbanism

Imagine that the issues of race, income, education, and unemployment inequality—and the resulting segregation, isolation, and fear—could be addressed by designing for greater access, agency, ownership, beauty, or empowerment. Now imagine the Just City—the cities, neighborhoods, and public spaces where all people, but especially the "least not," are included, have equitable and inclusive access to opportunities, and have tools that allow them to be productive, thrive, and advance through the ranks of social and economic mobility.

191   put the values of equality, inclusion, or equity first?

The New Futurist Manifesto

Inés Benitez (MDes ADPD), Eric Moed (MDes ADPD),
Penelope Phylactopoulos (MDes ADPD)
Independent Study
Advisor: John Peterson

A collective manifesto unfolded over the course of our independent study.[1] It is composed of the ideas contained in weekly personal statements from each one of us, challenging the current state of architecture and charting a new course into a shared terminology. The shared manifesto was handwritten into a single folded sheet of paper as a representation of the shared stream of consciousness that developed, revealing the process and progress that took place.

1   Architecture does not stop when space is created.
2   Environment-making is the balance of building intentions that trust the impermanence of reality's expression.
3   Making is the present moment of the past. The conception of architecture is a provocation to future-architecture to embellish and improve upon it.
4   Form is never complete: it is waiting to be designated by the architect and defined by the user. Architecture is not an empty semiotic exercise.
5   At best, architecture can set the stage for the theater of life.
6   Architecture must collaborate with communities by embodying the unfrequented lands of hybridization in order to strengthen their publics.
7   Space-making triggers an environment that demands a pastiche of synthesis. Architecture must organize infinite flows of information into a coherent design language.
8   Architects must not be blindly led by technology, which is not in time and tune with what needs to be designed and built.
9   Technology has magnified pensive immobility, abstraction, detachment, and dependence. Architecture should create real movement through environments that promote interaction across space.
10   It is time to formally acknowledge a terminological distinction between different types of architectural practice. Architecture is suffering from an identity crisis. It is time for the practice of architecture to be categorized with distinctions for its varied focuses.
11   We are living in a hybridized virtual and digital reality, since we have already created eternal, omnipresent speed. Architecture will be swallowed up by the sea change of automation and information if it does not morph to embrace the societal shifts that unite us all.

It is here, as architects at their wit's end, that we are issuing this manifesto of hubris and incendiary thought, by which we today are founding the New Futurism, because we want to deliver architecture from its cancerous professors, antiquated tropes, and siloed thought-towers. We the young, strong, and living designers hustling and hybridizing in this multilateral world!

The New Futurists! The New Originals!

1
We conducted a study of existent art and design manifestos, searching for language devices and content which we felt strongly about— either in agreement with or deeply against. Out of all the manifestos that we read, we felt that the *Futurist Manifesto* (1909) by Filippo Tommaso Marinetti was both the most intriguing and the most problematic precedent. We felt it appropriate and necessary to update it.

"FeedBack" is a meal.

"FeedBack" is centered around the unfolding of the "New Futurist Manifesto," an ode to the format of the *Futurist Manifesto*, parts of which are printed on the *sous plat*. Its primary focus is to encourage feedback of our 11-point manifesto. It can be performed anywhere, any number of times.

AFIA: Affordable, Fast, Intuitive, Accurate STI Viral Testing

Julian Siegelmann (MDE), Kenneth So (MDE), Janet Sung (MDE), Kiran Wattamwar (MDE)
Collaborative Design Engineering Studio II
Instructors: Heather Boesch, Jock Herron, Chuck Hoberman, Fawwaz Habbal (John A. Paulson School of Engineering and Applied Sciences), Peter Stark (John A. Paulson School of Engineering and Applied Sciences)

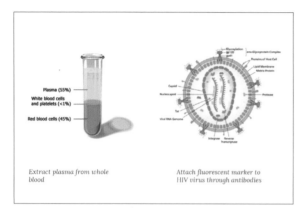

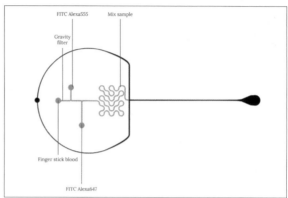

Prepare sample: Extract plasma from blood samples to reduce noise (prevent nonspecific binding) and attach markers to HIV.

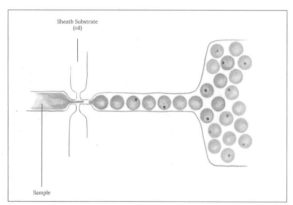

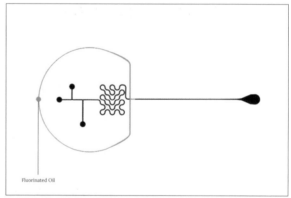

Isolate virus: Advancements in droplet-based microfluidics enable us to isolate viral samples into vesicles labeled based on their fluorescence.

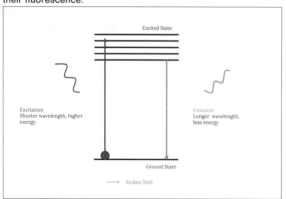

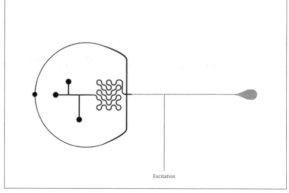

Detect signal: By exciting the fluorescent particles at the right wavelength, we can visualize which vesicles contain the HIV virus.

Engineering
Fabrication
Health
Materials

Why hasn't a point-of-care HIV test

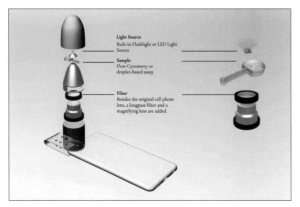

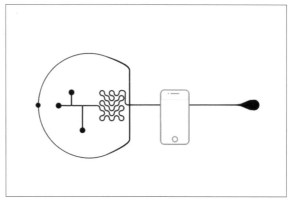

Optical system: An assembly tailored to our fluorescing biomarkers is attached to a cell phone to capture video of the droplets for processing.

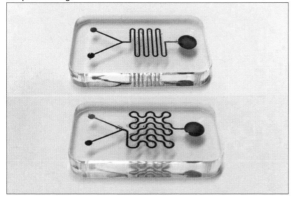

Prototype the device.

Quantify load: Using automated and simple techniques to calculate viral load from radiofluorescently labelled viruses in droplets.

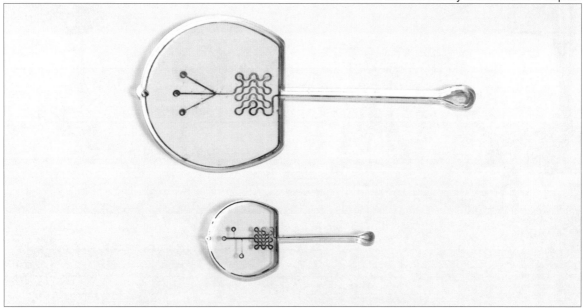

We have created a flow cytometry-based assay that implements microfluidic processes to safely, accurately, and quickly count viral load measurements in one milliliter of blood. The chip will be implemented in concert with a phone accessory and app that will fit all mobile phones, allowing usage in both clinics and homes. To circumvent the need for lab testing, we designed our device to be simple and disposable. The research and solution will cover four different scales: the viral scale (technical interactions), the device scale (components), the human scale (clinical and user experience), and the system scale (national rollout).

Coolth Capitalism

Peteris Lazovskis (MArch I), Thomas Schaperkotter (MArch I)
Architecture Core Studio IV: Relate
Instructor: Matthew Soules

This project explores a convergence between finance capitalist investment power, emerging carbon economies, and the ecological stewardship of dense urbanization. The possibility of that confluence is pursued through a speculative project of 13 towers located on a single site in downtown Los Angeles. The towers are made almost entirely of engineered wood and each contains an earthen cooling chimney. The massive timber construction acts as a carbon sink and the chimneys drop cool downdraft air into pavilions providing public amenities. The cooled air is distributed within a semi-porous canopy that transforms the ground plane into a shaded, ventilated, and accessible hardscape park in downtown Los Angeles.

Economy
Housing
Timber
Urbanization

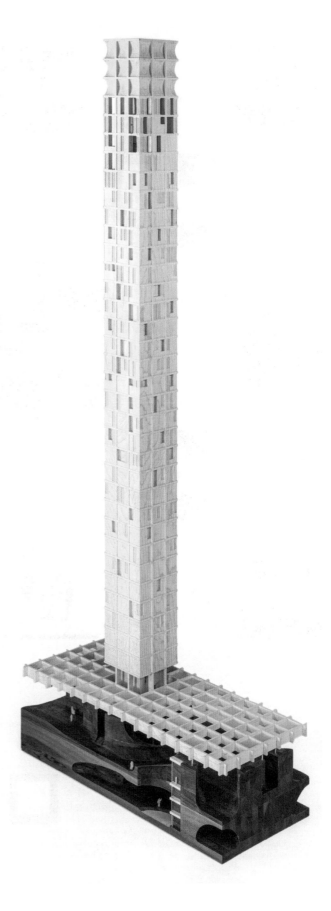

in the context of financialization?

What is the minimum degree of "real" for housing

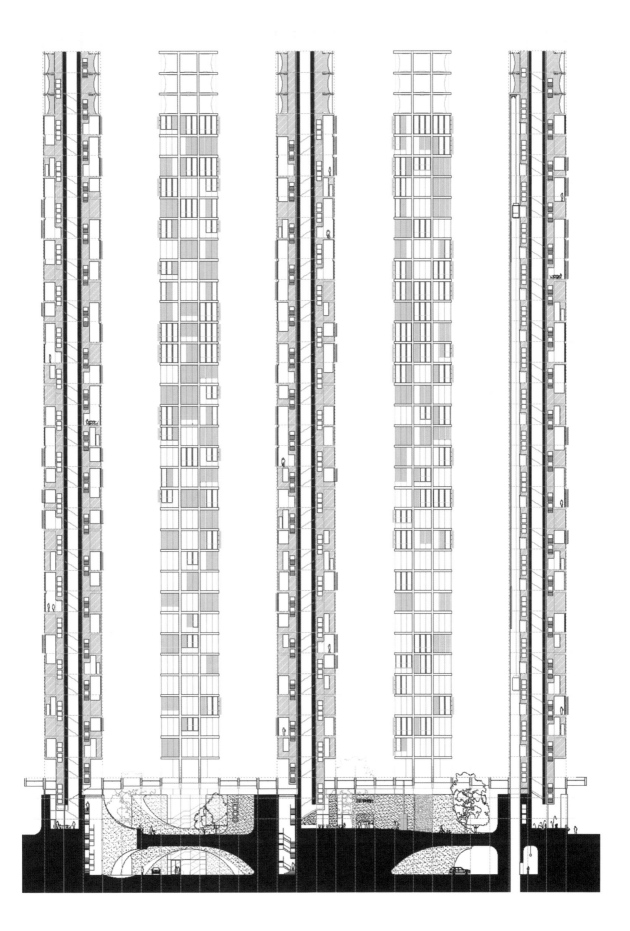

to operate as an accelerating asset?

Interrogation

Front

1 Peteris Lazovskis
  Thomas Schaperkotter
2 Julian Siegelmann
  Kenneth So
  Janet Sung
  Kiran Wattamwar

Back

3, 6 Peteris Lazovskis
  Thomas Schaperkotter
4 Inés Benitez
  Eric Moed
  Penelope Phylactopoulos
5 Aimilios Davlantis Lo

Peace Talks

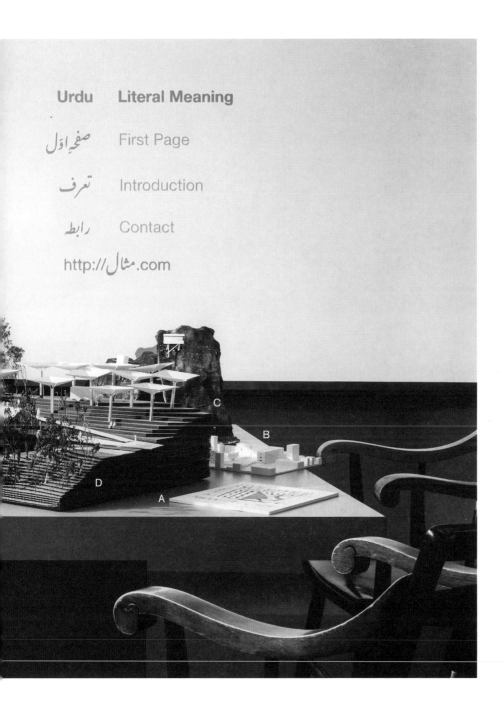

Urdu	Literal Meaning
صفحہِ اوّل	First Page
تعرف	Introduction
رابطہ	Contact
http://مثال.com	

This poem is cut up from the following sources:
STU 1101 Architecture Core Studio I: Project
STU 1122 Urban Planning Core Studio II
STU 1221 Elements of Urban Design
STU 1315 After the Storm: Restructuring an Island Ecosystem
STU 1407 Korea Remade: Alternate Nature, DMZ, and
         Hinterlands
STU 1501 The Unfinished City. Envisioning 21st-Century
         Urban Ideals in Tallinn's Largest Soviet-Era
         Housing District
STU 1502 Refugees in the Rust Belt
ADV 9146 Emergent Urbanism: Planning and Design Visions
         for the City of Hermosillo, Mexico
ADV 9302 Urban Planning and Design Thesis
ADV 9382 Independent Design Engineering Project
Lecture   Border Ecologies, Malkit Shoshan
Lecture   Borderwall as Architecture, Ronald Rael

At the center of conflict,
an expanded notion
of simultaneous existence.

Fragile willingness
to redraw boundaries.

How do we go forward
      walled off,
      reunified,
rebuilding
a seamless verdant territory?

The sharing of progress
serves as the backbone
to create an atlas
of thoughtful responses.

Shaping the future
of new urbanities.

Peace Talks: *a negotiating table*

As factions form and conflict seems imminent, we come to the table to
mediate a peace—to prevent the building of walls or divisions between
us. At this table we seek to find common ground, shared values, and new
pathways forward.

Forging ahead toward a shared future, these projects propose new
tools of communication, enact more democratic processes, and plan more
welcoming and inclusive communities.

Therefore, we declare that the War Room (Gund Hall, Room 111)
shall be known from now on as the Peace Room.

The Urdu Keyboard

Zeerak Ahmed (MDE)
Independent Design Engineering Project
Advisors: Neil Brenner, Susan Crawford (Harvard Law School),
Krzysztof Z. Gajos (John A. Paulson School of Engineering and Applied Sciences)

This project, the design of the "Urdu Keyboard," is situated in a complex political and social environment where the lingua franca of one of the most populous countries in the world—and a language native to tens of millions of people—struggles to be represented in technology. The result is a debate about how to formulate technical vocabulary in the education system of Pakistan as it moves increasingly toward English as the language of science and progress.

The project proposes a renewed life for Urdu stemming from technological representation and utilizes the development of production-grade consumer software to start this process. The "Urdu Keyboard" is rethought from the ground up, with specific concentration on mobile devices, which will be how most of the world—especially those yet to come online—will interact with Urdu text. Using features of the Arabic script and educational techniques for teaching the script, this project develops new interactions that enable more effective Urdu text entry.

In addition, the keyboard is launched with a public initiative that collectivizes the ownership of the software, the language models, the standards of language representation, and the discourse around all these issues. This includes questions like: How do we standardize the alphabet? Which language is it appropriate for the keyboard to represent? How do we include regional languages that use slightly different alphabets in this design discussion? How do we prevent the encoding of geographical, cultural, and religious bias in the artificial intelligence of auto-correct and auto-complete technologies?

The keyboard and the public initiative are both live. The keyboard has gone through Apple's beta review process and is in people's hands. Public access has been restricted as we design a research study so we can publish a scientific analysis of our findings and contribute to a human-computer interaction domain that has few if any empirical discussions about typing methods in the Arabic script. The public initiative had a successful launch: the announcement was seen over 25,000 times (organically, with no financial support) and about 150 individuals have already signed up for early access to the keyboard.

Ultimately the project included presentations, important URLs, and addenda with additional information, posters, interim design explorations, writing, code, and research study materials presented to the Institutional Review Board.

This project presents a rethinking of how we conduct our digital practice and the impacts that it can have not only on how we communicate but on how we think. The ideas of an entire nation are curtailed by the

absence of effective technology to represent the language of those ideas. As a result, the keyboard uses digital media to affect class divides, educational barriers, and the very fabric of language in a world where a billion people who have been disenfranchised from technology are expected to come online in the immediate future.

The keyboard is just the beginning. The website, and the project as a whole, concentrates on Urdu software and on using the smartphone to generate new design paradigms centered on the non-Latin world. By giving software developers and designers the digital tools needed to effectively and efficiently design in other scripts, the keyboard and parallel interface enable a greater set of possibilities.

Redefining the State-Society Interface

Colleen Brady (MUP)
Urban Planning Thesis
Awarded the Thesis Prize in Urban Planning
Advisors: Michael Hooper, Janina Matuszeski (Harvard Kennedy School)

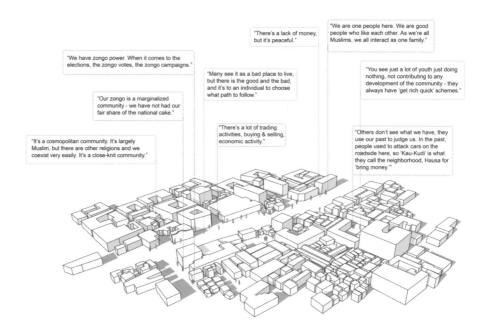

"There's a lack of money, but it's peaceful."

"We are one people here. We are good people who like each other. As we're all Muslims, we all interact as one family."

"We have zongo power. When it comes to the elections, the zongo votes, the zongo campaigns."

"Many see it as a bad place to live, but there is the good and the bad, and it's to an individual to choose what path to follow."

"You see just a lot of youth just doing nothing, not contributing to any development of the community - they always have 'get rich quick' schemes."

"Our zongo is a marginalized community - we have not had our fair share of the national cake."

"There's a lot of trading activities, buying & selling, economic activity."

"Others don't see what we have, they use our past to judge us. In the past, people used to attack cars on the roadside here, so 'Kau-Kudi' is what they call the neighborhood, Hausa for 'bring money.'"

"It's a cosmopolitan community. It's largely Muslim, but there are other religions and we coexist very easily. It's a close-knit community."

Global trends focusing on accountability and community participation have led many governments to address marginalized populations previously left behind by urban development. This thesis examines how governments engage with socio-spatially marginalized populations through the policies and programs they adopt, focusing on the state-society interface in which government priorities and marginalized communities interact. It focuses on a case study of Ghana's newly created Ministry of Inner City and Zongo Development (MICZD), an emerging government initiative that is engaging with a marginalized community. The MICZD's stated objective is to improve the social and infrastructural development of Zongos, or "stranger's quarters," which have historically housed northern Hausa migrants and over time have become associated with slum-like conditions.

Building upon the literature of state-society engagement, community participation, and urban citizenship, the study draws on 38 interviews with government stakeholders, community-based organizations, and local leaders as well as four focus groups of Zongo residents. The results reveal several key findings related to this effort of state-society engagement.

Considering some of these challenges, this thesis identifies two potential paths toward more productive and empowering state-society engagement—creating continuous engagement platforms and counterbalancing powers—and proposes how lessons from the case of the MICZD can serve as a learning opportunity for governments engaging with marginalized populations worldwide.

Reintegrate/Restructure

Yue Shao (MArch I AP), Chenglong Zhao (MAUD)
The Unfinished City. Envisioning 21st-Century Urban Ideals
in Tallinn's Largest Soviet-Era Housing District
Instructor: Andres Sevtsuk

Eliel Saarinen's 1913 Masterplan for Grand Tallinn proposed a four-mile-long sunken channel to connect the city with its eastern expansion district of Lasnamäe. The studio will investigate new programmatic, typological, and institutional designs to better integrate and regenerate Lasnamäe as a vital part of 21st-century Tallinn.

Grid
Precedent
Urbanism

A Vision for the International Village

Mariana Paisana (MAUD)
Refugees in the Rust Belt
Instructor: Daniel D'Oca

Working with national and local refugee resettlement organizations in the Rust Belt cities of St. Louis, Detroit, and Cleveland, students will make proposals at a range of scales aimed at helping refugees thrive.

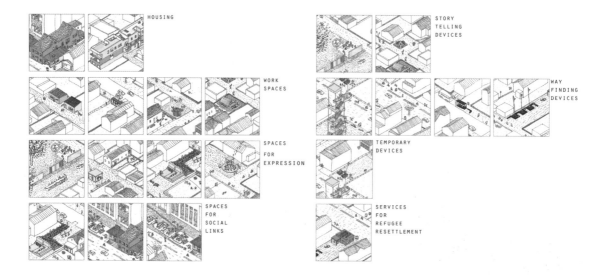

The International Village is a neighborhood in Cleveland that supports the arrival of refugees and thinks about ways to facilitate their integration. The center of the neighborhood is the Thomas Jefferson School, an institution that prepares non-English speakers with the necessary knowledge to transition to the American school system. As this school offers a transition space and time for the integration of newcomers, the International Village aims to do the same at the neighborhood level—to create a strong neighborhood community that helps the integration of refugees.

My proposal is a spatial strategy for the principles and objectives of the International Village. The project proposes a series of unusual programs that provide spaces for newcomers to express their culture and individuality, relate to their community, and create bonds with the residents of the neighborhood—besides providing affordable and diversified spaces to work and live. These new spaces are designed with three main principles: first, to provide different scales of public spaces; second, to focus not just on housing but on other programs that are essential for a thriving community: spaces for work as well as cultural and religious expression; third, to provide multiple landmarks as wayfinding strategies.

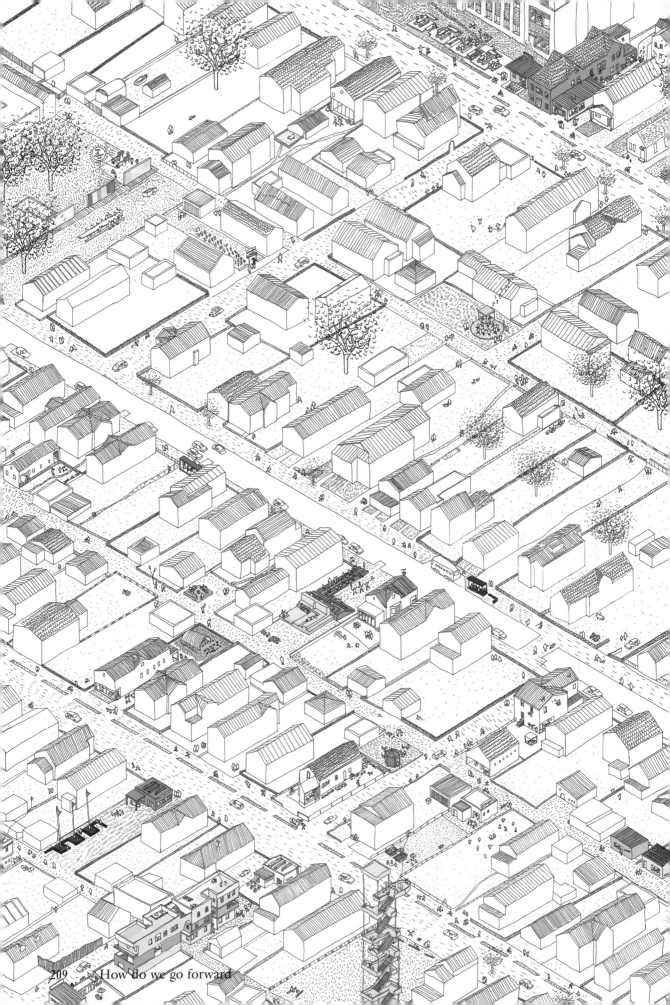

Topographic Centrality

Evan Shieh (MAUD), Luke Tan (MAUD)
Elements of Urban Design
Instructor: Felipe Correa

The moment is ripe to question and redefine the role of the urban project within current landscapes of urbanization. What should guide the designer conceiving new relationships among existing urban parts? How can design act as a critical agent in these contexts?

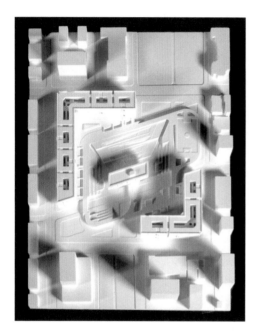

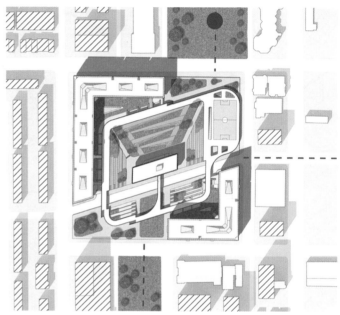

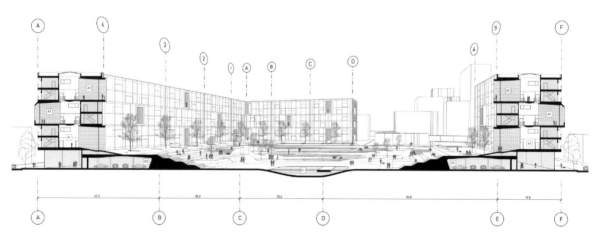

Situated in the former Cabrini-Green area of Chicago, this project introduces a civic park that catalyzes new development in the neighborhood and refocuses the city's development inland. The project proposes a thickened ground plane that organizes private mixed-income housing at its corners, embeds parking and retail in its section, and frames a public community center in the middle. The intervention is a public amenity that defines diverse types of publicness over a topographic gradient from center to edge, blurring boundaries between public/private and interiority/exteriority.

American City
Housing
Landform
Urbanization

The Layered Refugee Experience

Kimberly Bernardin (MUP), McKayla Dunfey (MUP)
Urban Planning Core Studio II
Instructor: Stephen Gray

What makes a great gateway city? What are the social and physical qualities that help immigrants and refugees thrive? And to what extent can things like housing, transportation, open space, urban design, and economic development better serve the needs of immigrants and refugees?

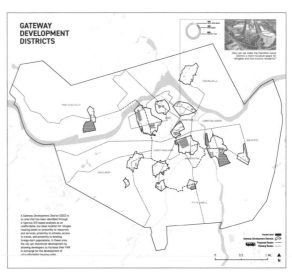

This project addresses the affordable housing shortage in Lowell, Massachusetts, through a policy-based inclusionary development recommendation. The central goal of the policy is to spur development of ultra-affordable housing in well-positioned areas of the city of Lowell: new homes that will foster immigrant success not just through affordability, but through access to public transportation, services, and existing immigrant community connections.

Though the project is targeted toward improving the immigrant housing experience, inclusionary zoning in Lowell would serve the entire low-income population, as well as wealthier Lowellians, by ensuring that the city retains its accessible, diverse, and welcoming character.

Infrastructure
Mobility
Policy
Transportation

El Hit: The Family's Right to the City

Patricia Alvarez (MDes REBE), Aaron Ramirez (MUP), Samuel Matthew (MDes RR), Theodore Kofman (MAUD)
Emergent Urbanism: Planning and Design Visions for the City of Hermosillo, Mexico
Instructors: Diane E. Davis, Felipe Vera

Students' final objective will be to propose a project, or a set of projects, that will lay the groundwork for creating a more livable, economically vibrant, socially inclusive, and sustainable future for the city of Hermosillo. Students will use research findings, advocacy strategies, and participatory exercises, as well as other forms of social and spatial practice, to produce alternative, speculative, and creative solutions for the city.

6:00 a.m.–9:00 a.m.
Families wake up in their homes and go about their day. Children play in the courtyards and grandparents greet each other. Parents take their children to school or exercise under tree-lined pathways.

8:00 a.m.–10:00 a.m.
People go to work or arrive on site via the Mass Rapid Transit.

10:00 a.m.–3:00 p.m.
Students and workers make their way to the business education center and incubation hub.

4:00 p.m.–8:00 p.m.
After work, parents play tennis on adjacent facilities.

5:00 p.m.–10:00 p.m.
After work, people shop, eat, and drink.

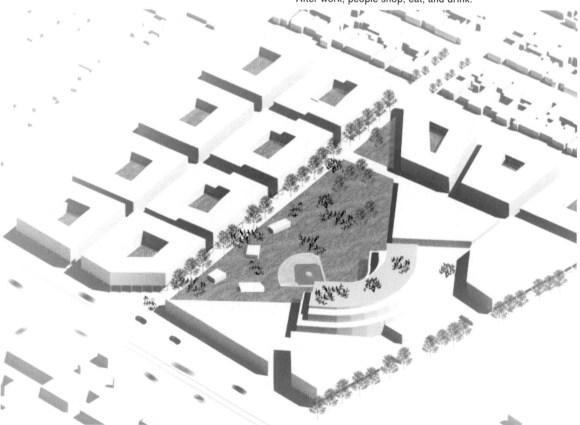

"El Hit" is a mixed-use, transit-oriented development. The project models a family-friendly way of living that provides an alternative to sprawl and segregation while promoting the site's unique culture and identity.

Community
Mobility
Public Space
Transportation

In and Out and Roundabout

Suthata Jiranuntarat (MArch I)
After the Storm: Restructuring an Island Ecosystem
Instructors: Jeanne Gang with Claire Cahan

As we zoom in to the architectural scale, we will explore ways in which patterns observed at the ecological scale can be applied to impact real projects and communities.

How can we create more sustainable and resilient island ecologies in light of climate change, ecological degradation, water scarcity, and resource depletion? At the center of St. John, U.S. Virgin Islands, the Susannaberg Transfer Station is now overwhelmed with waste and debris produced in the aftermath of Hurricanes Irma and Maria. The project seeks to transform the site into a sustainable living center: a laboratory for innovative ways of thinking about waste and resources and a public space for collaboration and engagement.

Climate Change
Community
Ecology

Ground Switching: Building as Filter

Sheng Zhao (MArch I)
Architecture Core Studio I: Project
Instructor: Jenny French

The most intelligent ordering systems that define rich architectural space must negotiate the complexities of material and programmatic demands, as well as the logics of metric dimension. The process of bringing order and hierarchy to a set of heterogeneous parts that form a whole—whether coherent, diffuse, or idiosyncratic—is a primary directive of architectural design. In this project, you are asked to integrate architectural elements from different proportional scales ranging from building/envelope scale to more intimate human/furniture scale while navigating a specifically shaped residual space. It has been said that we as architects are either adders or dividers. In lieu of using the repetitive modulation of similar parts to produce accretive shape and hierarchy, this project will begin with figuration and spatial variety in search of logics of organization and repetition.

Border Ecologies

Malkit Shoshan
GSD Talks Public Lecture
November 6, 2017

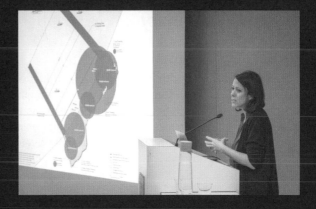

Borders shape and consolidate relations between states, people, jurisdictions, political entities, and territories, and they often lie at the center of conflict between them. They are tools entangled in complex sociopolitical and economic ecologies. While some borders are relatively stable, others are in a constant flow. They regulate economic relations and people's access to places, resources, and rights.

Borders determine the way our surroundings are organized, inhabited, and controlled, and the ways communities relate to one another—while some break through borders to survive, others fence themselves off. In this lecture, Malkit Shoshan presents case studies from the Foundation for Achieving Seamless Territory's ongoing investigations and engagements with conflict and post-conflict areas.

Borderwall as Architecture

Ronald Rael
GSD Talks Public Lecture
November 14, 2017

Despite recent attention to wall-building as a security measure, the building of barriers along the United States—Mexico border is not a new phenomenon. The Secure Fence Act of 2006 funded the single-largest domestic building project in the 21st century and financed approximately 700 miles of fortification, dividing the United States from Mexico at a cost of up to $16 million per mile. Today, approximately one-third of the 1,954-mile-long border between the United States and Mexico has been walled off.

Ronald Rael discusses his book, *Borderwall as Architecture: A Manifesto for the U.S.—Mexico Boundary* (2017), a timely reexamination of the physical barrier that divides the United States of America and both a protest against the wall and a projection about its future.

Rewilding the Imaginary

Matthew Wong (MLA I)
Korea Remade: Alternate Nature, DMZ, and Hinterlands
Instructors: Jungyoon Kim, Niall Kirkwood, Yoonjin Park

Reunification of the two Koreas will address, among other topics, the erasure or redrawing of national boundaries, population displacement, the provision of new industrial development and the enhancement of existing infrastructure, the technological issues of live landmine removal and soil contamination remediation, and a reimagined role for the landscape and the future inhabitation of the Korean Peninsula.

The reunification of the Korean Peninsula may come in the form of an agreement between the land and its constituents. As a product of the Korean War, the ground on which the Demilitarized Zone (DMZ) was established remains deeply scarred by ad hoc infrastructural security measures and decades of cultural separation. The implications of such disparity have resulted in a static divide perpetually frozen in time, giving rise to a new form of wild. This proposal seeks to explore reunification as a state of transition, mediated through the Baekdu-daegan Mountain Range on the eastern side of the peninsula. In this scenario, the DMZ is reconceptualized as a porous territory of cultural, material, and ecological exchange, acting as the ground on which future negotiations take place.

Borders
Ecology
Mapping
Representation

217   of thoughtful responses.

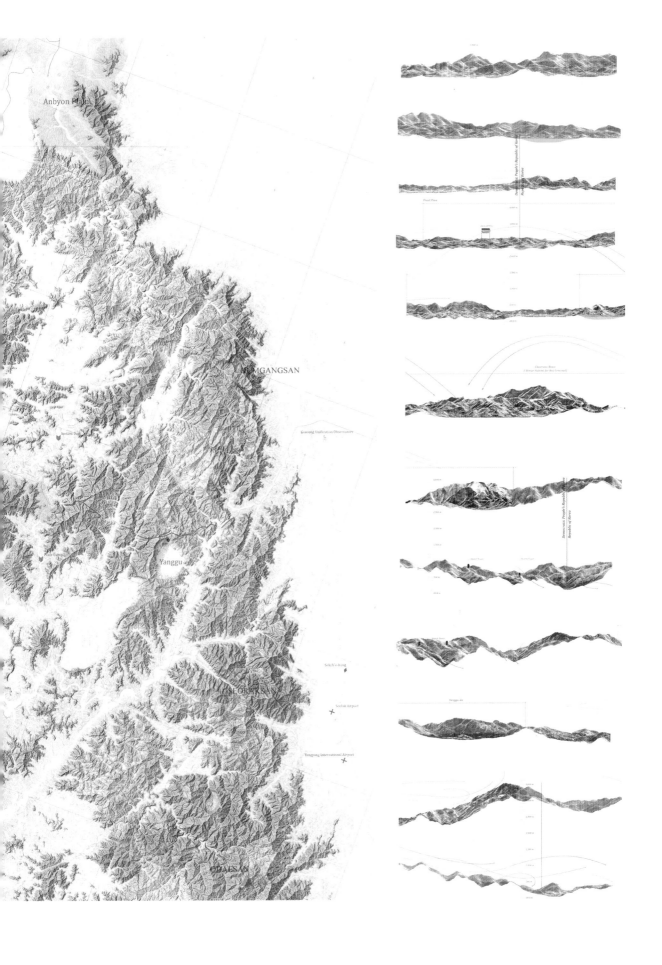

of new urbanities.

Peace Talks

With/in

Interdisciplinary Art and Design Practices
Instructors: Silvia Benedito with Jill Johnson (Harvard Dance Center) and Silvia Kolbowski
This seminar investigates the exploratory character of art and design practices across modalities found within contemporary culture.

This practice-oriented seminar follows a series of exploratory workshops with/in new forms, expressions, time scales, and media as transformative contributions to life in the space and place of the city and its public domain. They investigate and exercise the histories and methods associated with various media used interchangeably in art and design, such as installation, sound, performance, nomadic design, and projection with the associated artists/designers of the program. While an emphasis is placed on the making and development of projects, lectures on the history of the medium and discussions of key readings will be equally relevant. Issues of techniques and methods, presentation and re-presentation, author's agency, and the overall polemic/position will be tested and analyzed.

Fundamental goals of the seminar are:
1   To exercise the "why/for whom," "what," and "how";
2   To expose the students to methods, techniques, and positions of various interdisciplinary art and design practices;
3   To creatively explore the potentials of various media in the realization and expression of ideas;
4   To raise relevant questions and to test them through the development of projects;
5   To raise more questions rather than solve "problems."

Throughout the term, students will be exposed to a series of media, methods, and the histories of the various modes of practice. Each assignment promotes the interdisciplinary art/design approach and asks students to exercise skills and develop knowledge and references within a wide variety of media. Also, and importantly, it will immerse students within the trajectory of the corresponding medium of each project.

Art Practices
Community
Film
Representation

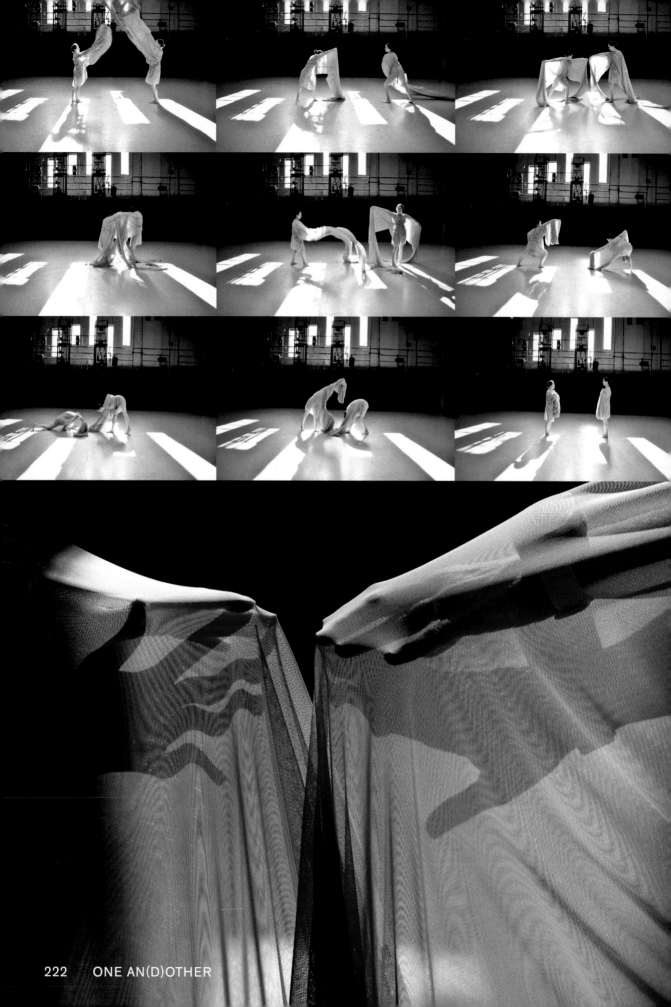

ONE AN(D)OTHER

ANXIETY SANDWICH

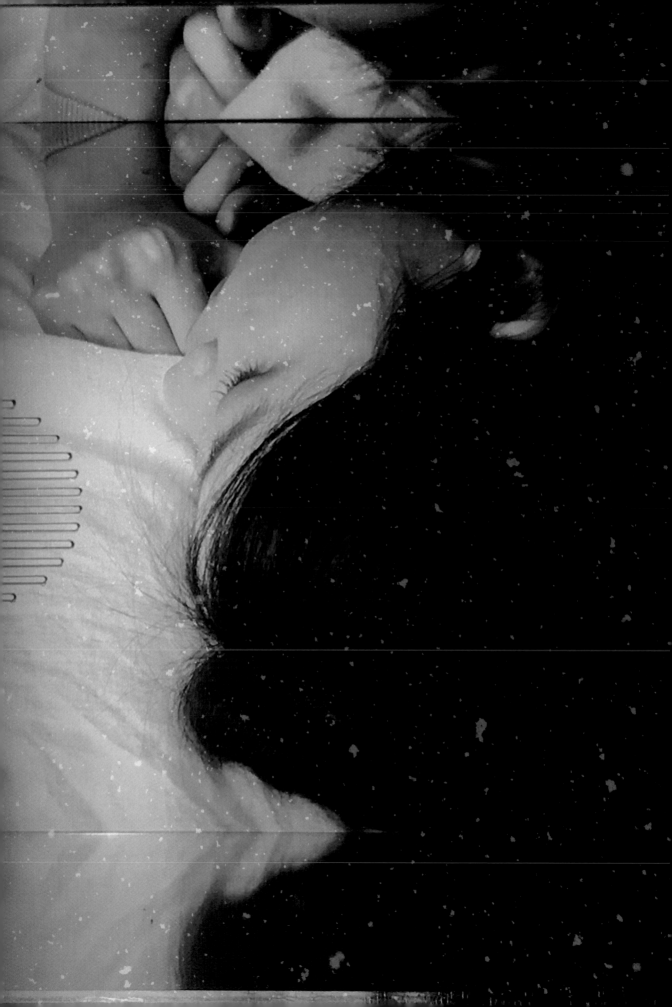

One An(d)other

Inés Benitez (MDes ADPD)
Hanna Kim (MDes ADPD)

Clothing represents an omnipresent second skin to which
we have grown familiar. Without it, we feel vulnerable and
discomposed. We share our space inside clothing as a symbol
of physical and emotional closeness.

"One an(d)other" explores a narrative of proximity and
distance through motion. As two separate bodies come into
contact, a new intimacy is born, for the culmination of proximity is touch.

In the title, "(d)" represents an invisible distance that
separates the performers. By becoming proximate in their
most vulnerable space, the performers overcome "other" and
become "another."

Anxiety Sandwich

Eric Moed (MDes ADPD)
Alicia Valencia (MDes ADPD)

"Anxiety Sandwich" is a body.

"Anxiety Sandwich" is a performance. A performance by
bodies on a host body. The host body is pregnant with meaning; it contains multitudes; a layered surface.

"Anxiety Sandwich" is a table. A table that at first glance
looks over-built. A table with 20 legs. A table with multiple
layers of surfaces. Multiple layers of materials. Multiplicities
that appear to be strong.

Enter our bodies. We are rough. We have appendages
on our appendages. Surfaces on our skin more coarse than
the blood that is coursing through our bodies. Quick and
deliberate movements begin to engage the body. The anxiety
sandwich begins to reveal itself. Showing its naked layers,
shedding its strong appearence, losing its legs. The irony of its
many steel legs becomes as apparent as its red underlayer.

Air to Air

Inés Benitez (MDes ADPD)
Stella Kuma (MDes ADPD)

This project is inspired by our desire to materialize and isolate
the atmosphere. We impose a finite space that keeps the air
from dispersing in physical space, removing the intimate atmo-
spheric engagement of the viewers with the screen.

What does it mean to exchange and share the atmosphere, in the physical sense and the abstract sense? Is it
possible to contain an affective atmosphere? What is the role
of media in this process?

There is something unspeakable and indescribable about
atmospheres. How do you possibly describe that moment,
that feeling, that atmosphere you keep thinking about? We are
exploring air as a medium of mixtures. A mixture of molecules,
movement, affects that cannot be isolated or separated. In that
sense, the box poses a paradoxical existence. What is inside
are perhaps irreconcilable relationships between material and
immaterial, imagined and real.

First
Dates

A landscape of intrinsic beauty and terror
looking each other in the eyes.

      A new facade to the inner core
      sets the rhythm.

Searching for novelty, ugly or weird,
an exceptional moment.

      Deadpan portraits
      send shivers through the spines of many.
      Unlikely juxtapositions
      do not shy away from reality.

Putting the human being at the center
a myriad of ways.

      Something between two-dimensional flatness
      and three-dimensional depth
      allows for a dialogue to occur—
      partners will be required.

This poem is cut up from the following sources:
HIS 4368 Making Sacred Space
HIS 4373 Bavarian Rococo: Heterotopias
VIS 2314 Responsive Environments: The Future of Shopping
VIS 2481 Public Projection: Projection as a Tool for
         Expression and Communication in Public Space
STU 1112 Landscape Architecture Core Studio II
STU 1202 Architecture Core Studio IV: Relate
STU 1301 Entropy, History, Time. Architectural Infrastructure
         for a Gravel Pit in Spain
STU 1302 Tibet Contemporary: Building in the Himalayas
STU 1303 A Bank for Burbank and Other L.A. Stories
STU 1314 Model as Building—Building as Model
STU 1318 In the Details: The Space between God and the Devil
STU 1402 The Anatomy of an Island
STU 1407 Korea Remade: Alternate Nature, DMZ,
         and Hinterlands
STU 1502 Refugees in the Rust Belt
ADV 9301 Architecture Thesis
ADV 9662 Methods of Research in Art and Design:
         A Workshop-Tutorial

The idyllic and the real,
a dilemma of identity,
work and play,
everyday life.

     Re-presenting
     intellectually curious
     one-to-one
     love making.

The meeting of the sky and the earth,
a notion of time,
the will to perpetuate
beauty, and the sublime.

     Fantastical otherness
     in an extreme anachronism.

The ritual starts—
break the ice.

First Dates: *a table for two*

At this table we play Tinder. If graduate school is a time for working in pairs then it's also a time for seeking other partnerships. A good place to start? Why not with your buttmate, cheekmate, or facemate (that is to say, the student at the desk behind, beside, or in front of you)?

    Here we set up a series of matches between projects, as if they were extensions of the students who authored them. On some dates chemistry is based on first impressions (materiality and form), while on others it heats up through witty banter (discourse). Their mutual attraction is based on common backgrounds (site), habits (processes), ideas (concepts), or goals (objectives).

    With more than 900 potential matches in the studio trays, who's going home alone tonight?

Vransducer: A New Way of Communicating

Je Sung Lee (MDes ADPD)
Methods of Research in Art and Design: A Workshop-Tutorial
Instructor: Krzysztof Wodiczko

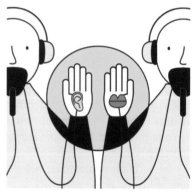

"Vransducer" is a communication device that utilizes the characteristics of the medium of sound. Unlike ordinary conversations that transmit vibrations remotely through the air, the "Vransducer" is a device that communicates physically. In order to communicate using voices, the two devices must be in physical contact.

Art Practices
Borders
Communication

Healing Scape

Mengfan Sha (MLA I)

Korea Remade: Alternate Nature, DMZ, and Hinterlands
Instructors: Jungyoon Kim, Niall Kirkwood, Yoonjin Park

The hypothesis underlying the studio is that the unification of the Korean Peninsula will be initiated by the re-territorializing of the DMZ and the Hinterlands as a spatial mediator between north and south.

233   looking each other in the eyes.

The Urban Edge

Xingyue Huang (MLA I)
Landscape Architecture Core Studio II
Instructor: Silvia Benedito

"The Urban Promenade" elaborates on the urban threshold along Boston's northern boundary on Sever Street.

The Urban Journey

Xinyi Zhou (MLA I)
Landscape Architecture Core Studio II
Instructor: Kristin Frederickson

"The Valley" aims at finding a particular moment of linkage and connection between the journey and the promenade, to expand the depth of the urban promenade, and to bring people to the inner core and lower levels of the park and its varied landscapes.

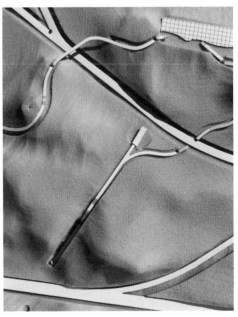

A Eulogy for Mr. McMaster

Nada AlQallaf (MArch II, MLA I AP), Sampath Pediredla (MArch II), Julia Roberts (MArch I),
Şevki Topçu (MArch II), Zachary Weimer (MArch II)
Bavarian Rococo: Heterotopias
Instructor: Andrew Holder

> Nowhere was Rococo taken up with greater intensity than in the southern part of Germany, where it was promulgated as the house style in an ambitious building program initiated by the Catholic Church. Design a mausoleum for the author of the McMaster-Carr catalog.

We who knew him, though, know that even from the very first nuts and bolts his catalog was full of emotion. It flowed from every number, every image of every object. It was the essence of him.

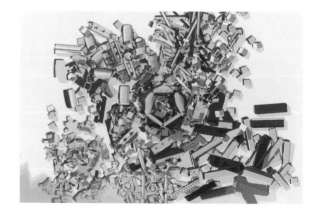

Cathedral Rises Again

Jianing Zhang (MArch II)
Making Sacred Space
Instructor: Christine Smith

Many recently built churches are ugly as sin. Others are great as design but don't work well functionally or symbolically. Most are just boring. How can it be that, having been the avant-garde of design and engineering for almost 2,000 years, church design today has so failed?

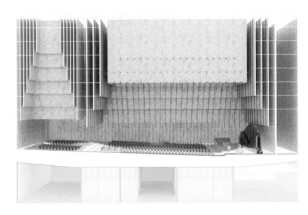

237   an exceptional moment.

OOPS . . . Architecture is a Collection of Happy Accidents

Madelyn Willey (MArch I)
Architecture Thesis
Advisor: Jennifer Bonner

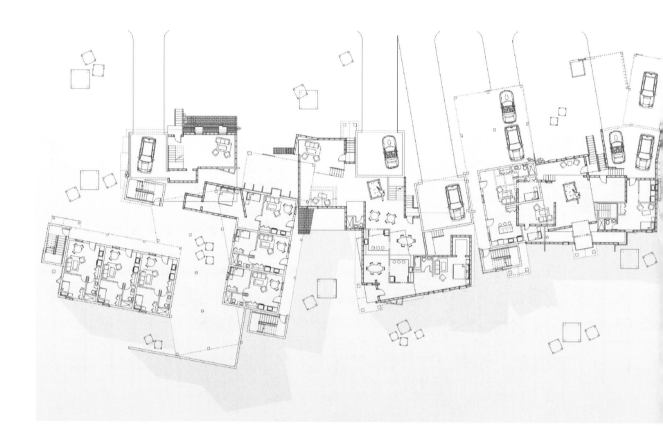

 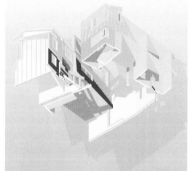 

The typical thinking that objects are solely the results of creative intellect is an important tradition but ultimately insufficient, begging for a new aesthetic that does not shy away from the reality of error and chance. The thesis operationalizes these "happy accidents" found in different suburban landscapes to create an architecture filled with misalignments between surfaces, architectural elements, rooms, and the intended use of those rooms. The result not only challenges the image of the suburban home but attempts to generate new types of living and spatial adjacencies that are produced only through embracing an aesthetic of the accidental.

Commodity
Economy
Housing

A Bank (& Trust) for Burbank

Sophie Juneau (MArch II), Elias Logan (MArch II)
A Bank for Burbank and Other L.A. Stories
Instructors: Andrew Atwood, Anna Neimark

Often, these loose building assemblies are formed by the exigencies of the urban environment and are therefore guided more by accident than by design. The models will be presented as *houses of cards*, leaning on one another for support.

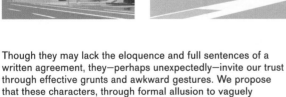

Though they may lack the eloquence and full sentences of a written agreement, they—perhaps unexpectedly—invite our trust through effective grunts and awkward gestures. We propose that these characters, through formal allusion to vaguely familiar pop objects, forge some new kind of architectural agreement.

Façade
Program
Typology

OOPS . . .

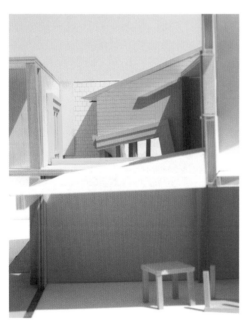

A Bank (& Trust) for Burbank

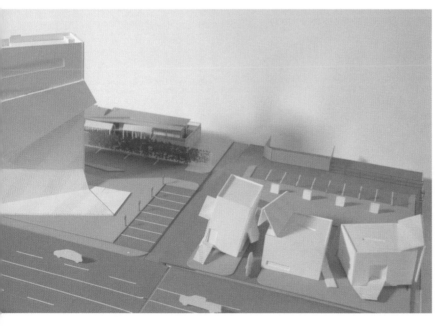

do not shy away from reality.

Upwardly Mobile

Christopher Liao (MLA I), John David Wagner (MArch II)
Refugees in the Rust Belt
Instructor: Daniel D'Oca

Working with our partners in St. Louis, Detroit, and Cleveland to develop initiatives aimed at integrating refugees in the Rust Belt, it will be our goal to generate a collection of projects that deeply resonate with residents, policy makers, community-based organizations, and other change-makers.

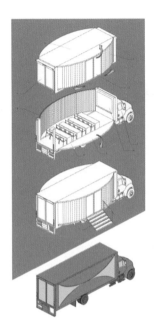
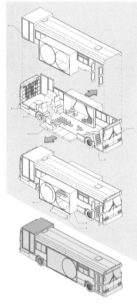
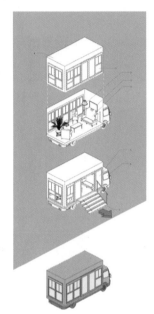
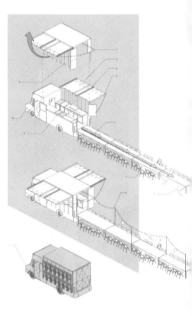

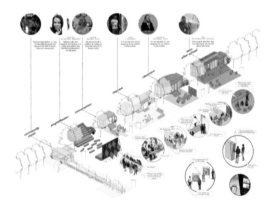
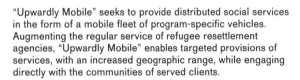
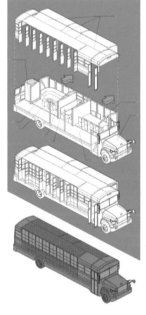
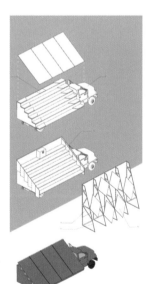

"Upwardly Mobile" seeks to provide distributed social services in the form of a mobile fleet of program-specific vehicles. Augmenting the regular service of refugee resettlement agencies, "Upwardly Mobile" enables targeted provisions of services, with an increased geographic range, while engaging directly with the communities of served clients.

American City
Community
Public Space
Transportation

Ship Shop

Nada AlQallaf (MArch II, MLA I AP), Danielle Aspitz (MArch II), Martin Fernández (MArch I),
Karen Mata (MAUD)
Responsive Environments: The Future of Shopping
Instructors: Allen Sayegh with Stefano Andreani

Design research often deploys simulations and scenario-based projections to reveal latent potentials for future conditions. What is the impact of certain qualities of the built environment in the sensory experience of retail places and in affecting people's shopping experience?

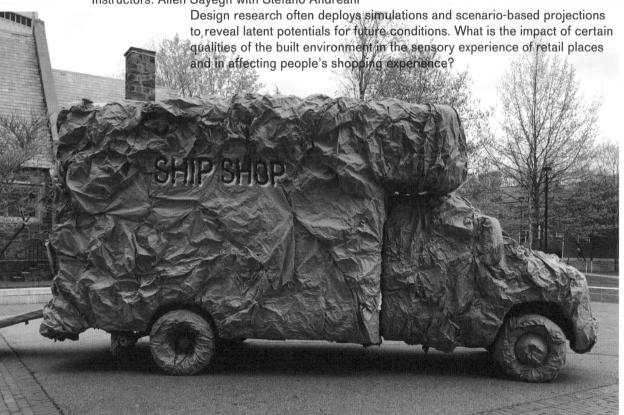

Our invention is to bring the BOPUS (buy online pick up in store) idea to a mobile vehicle—a truck. This idea is meant to reduce endless debates for customers by giving them the ability to see, touch, and try things before committing, reduce costs and losses for retailers by centralizing shipping and returns, and reduce the time that items are in limbo.

16" on Center

Madeline Eggink Lenaburg (MArch I)
Architecture Thesis
Advisor: Andrew Holder

This thesis contemplates the diagrams that we reference, tutorials that we watch, catalogs that we shop, and browsers that we search. Recommended prescriptions are followed, but resources are not only consulted. Instead, instructions are taken literally and used as raw material. Digital landscapes are mined for componentry and computer interface gewgaws inevitably intervene. Through moving images, residual digital artifacts are preserved as construction phases are performed. The project insists on earnestly following advice but always in the wrong medium. The result is something between two-dimensional flatness and three-dimensional depth, virtual space and real place, stage set and suburban home. A construction process is reenacted. A house gets built.

Commodity
Materials
Typology

CD to SD: A Nonstandard Approach to Design

Matthew Gehm (MArch II), Şevki Topçu (MArch II)
In the Details: The Space Between God and the Devil
Instructors: Dwayne Oyler, Jenny Wu

The sequence of development in the studio will move back and forth between this idea of the detail and the inlay. By working on a series of objects related to the idea of inlay, each project will then be asked to develop a smaller, detailed section of the object and to stake out a conceptual position with regard to those details. The details will then be used as a way of guiding the development of the overall building proposal.

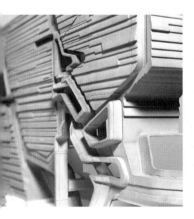

This project began with an antithetical approach to standard practice by first looking at the architectural detail as the basis for its design logic. By moving between scales, the project investigated how conceptual ideas that can be executed at the micro scale can then reappear at the macro scale in new ways. The main ideas that we were interested in expressing are the translation and implications of seams across materials, the expression of a hidden or coy volume, and how tolerances can be used as a design element as opposed to a limitation.

Detail
Fabrication
Materials

allows for a dialogue to occur—

CD to SD

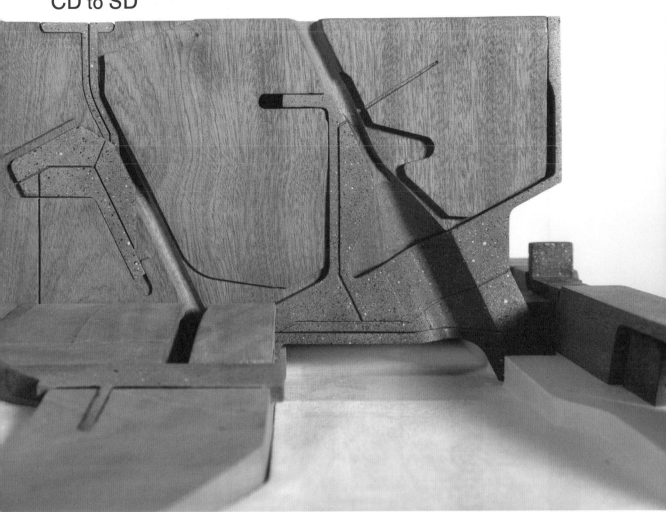

partners will be required.

Plateau: Brewing Spectacle in the Sublime

Andrew Bako (MArch I AP)
Tibet Contemporary: Building in the Himalayas
Instructor: Zhang Ke

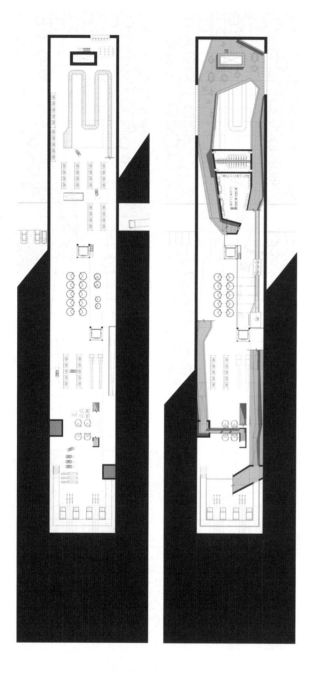

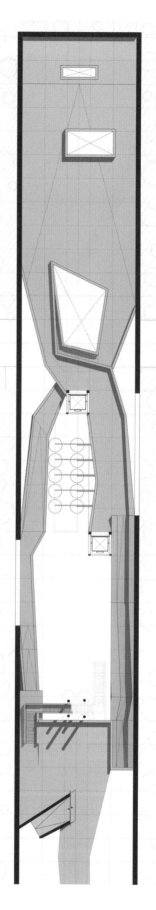

This project is a response to the recent surge in tourism and overbuilding in Tibet by providing a model of how these issues can be integrated with local cultural practice. By rethinking how a factory can negotiate the flow of people with the flow of production, tourists can productively engage with locals through their culture.

Landform
Program

Otium Negotiosum: At Work and Play in the Fields of Rome

Eric Zuckerman (MArch I)
Architecture Thesis
Advisors: Erika Naginski, Cameron Wu

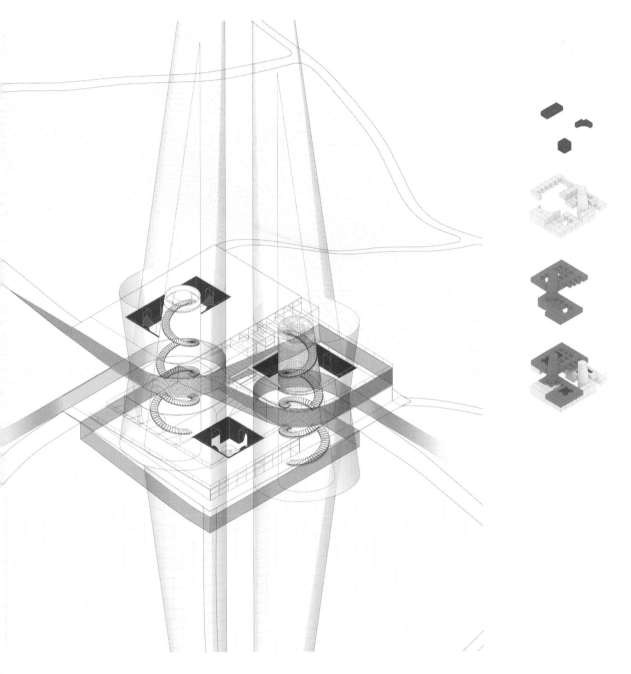

Yet Rome's growth fundamentally fissured the once unified relationship between culture and cultivation, transforming the inhabitation of the countryside into a contradictory mix of *otium* (leisure) and *negotium* (work). The villa became both the rural retreat for the rich and the center of agricultural production for the empire, solidifying the conflict between newfound luxury and traditional values, the idyllic and the real, leisure and work,

in the form of the inextricable *pars urbana* space of cultural production and *pars rustica* space of agricultural production. This productive leisure, "Otium Negotiosum," defined the ambiguous essence of the villa's ancient past.

Geometry
History
Precedent

Plateau

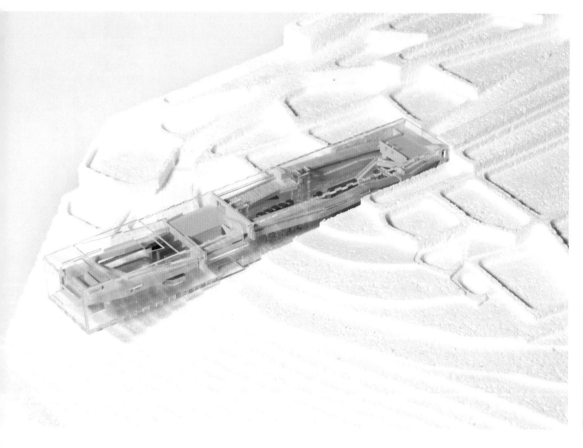

work and play,

Otium Negotiosum

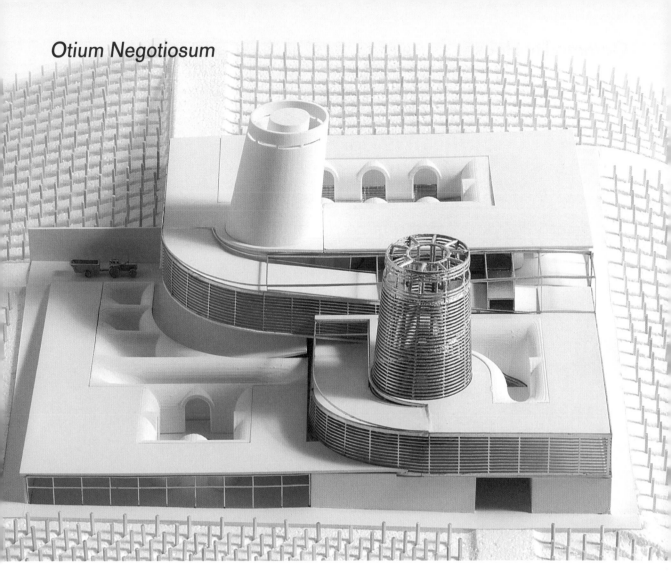

everyday life.

Commodity House

Kai Liao (MArch II)
Architecture Thesis
Advisor: John May

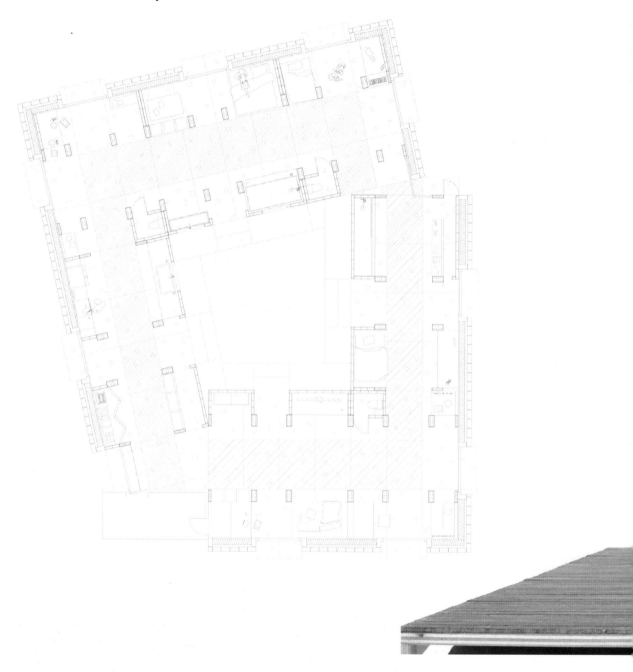

If everyday commodities are considered products of labor
vis-à-vis architectural production and not merely capital,
then this project leverages the systemic circulatory logics of
commodities to materialize—in renewed exchanges and with
renewed value—the invisible labor embedded in the process of
design and homemaking.

The Same House, Twice

Grace McEniry (MArch I)
Model as Building—Building as Model
Instructor: George L. Legendre

This studio explores the reemergent phenomenon of "Model as Building—Building as Model" whereby projects of any size or purpose are designed and built anywhere but on site.

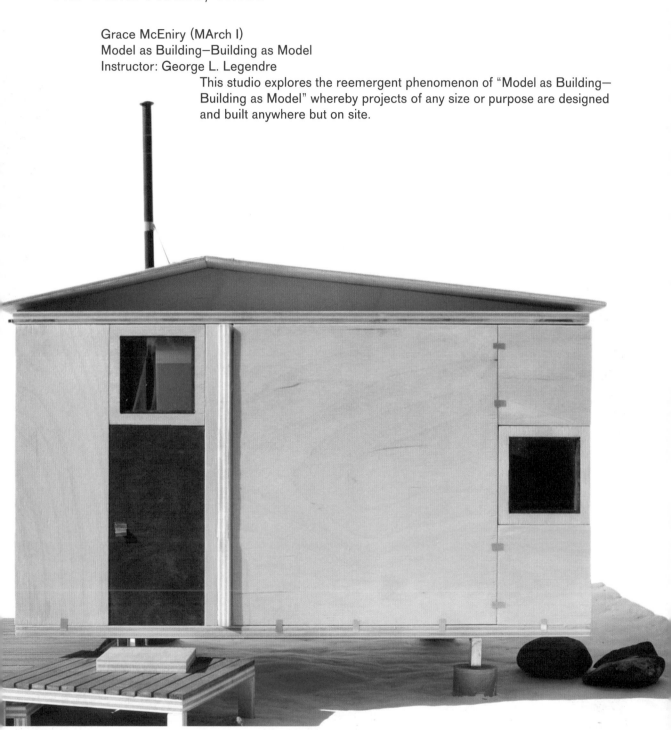

The project references an old riddle: "I know a farmer who says he has had the same ax his whole life—he only changed the handle three times and the head two times. Does he have the same ax?" (Howard Mansfield, *The Same Ax, Twice: Restoration and Renewal in a Throwaway Age* [Hanover, NH: University Press of New England, 2001.]) How would this cabin be the same 100 years from when it was built? This project seeks to demonstrate an understanding of off-site manufacturing (OSM) as a part of a continuum of people and places that allows for adaptation to life in one cabin over time.

Commodity House

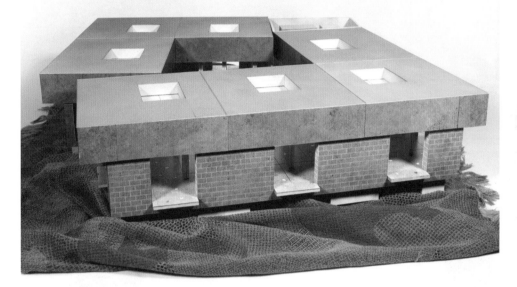

The Same House, Twice

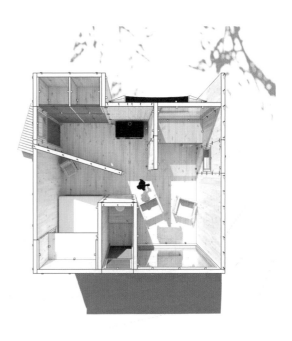

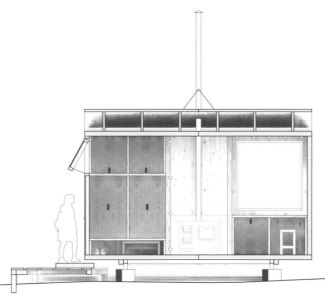

Infrastructural Picturesque

Mariel Collard (MLA I AP, MDes RR)
Entropy, History, Time. Architectural Infrastructure for a Gravel Pit in Spain
Instructor: Iñaki Ábalos

> The Sorigué gravel pit in Lleida, Spain, is undergoing a process of change, thus becoming a territory of experimentation where the building of new infrastructure for its artistic collections is just a first step of a more ambitious project to build a new future and public sense for the whole landscape.

There is a vertical force whereby we understand our place on this site, in one sense grounding us and connecting us to the center of the earth through geological strata, and in the opposite sense transporting our attention to the cosmos. This project is caught in between: a captured walk to inhabit time in a future that will soon become history.

256   The meeting of the sky and the earth,

Cadillac Mountain Skyland

Lane Raffaldini Rubin (MArch I, MLA I AP)
The Anatomy of an Island
Instructors: Bridget Baines, Eelco Hooftman

Landscape may be defined as a state of continuous becoming, never quite started and never quite finished. Not an object but a process. Above all, the studio engages with the notion of how we look at the landscape: the landscape as view and point of view. Our eyes explore the horizon and navigate through it in order to view all the aspects of the landscape and to find out how figures relate to each other.

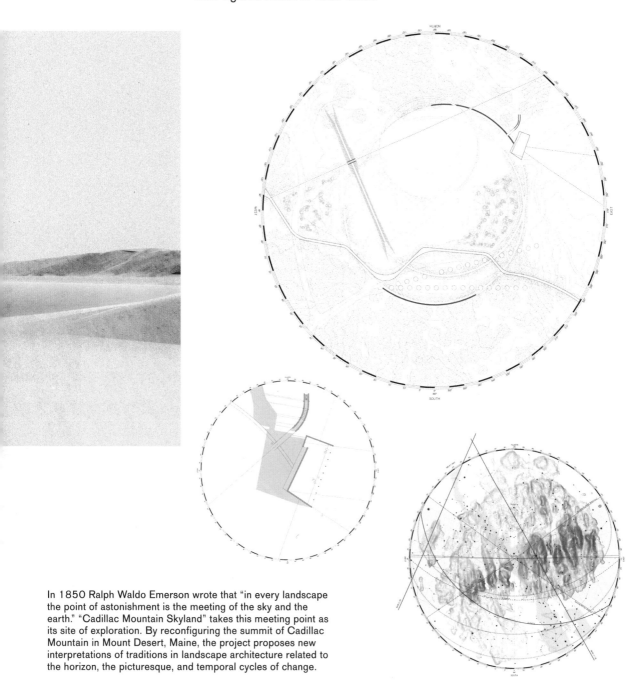

In 1850 Ralph Waldo Emerson wrote that "in every landscape the point of astonishment is the meeting of the sky and the earth." "Cadillac Mountain Skyland" takes this meeting point as its site of exploration. By reconfiguring the summit of Cadillac Mountain in Mount Desert, Maine, the project proposes new interpretations of traditions in landscape architecture related to the horizon, the picturesque, and temporal cycles of change.

Infrastructural Picturesque

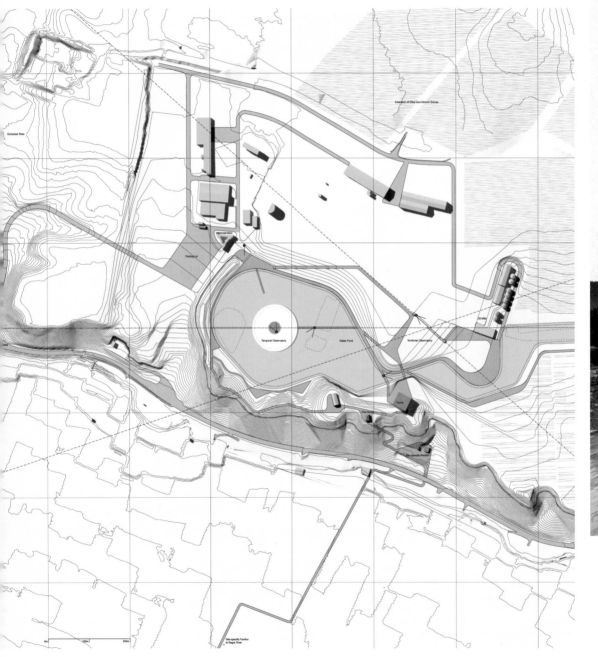

Cadillac Mountain Skyland

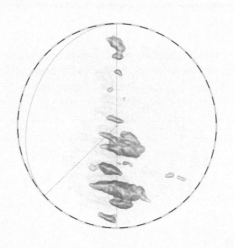

beauty, and the sublime.

Flighterotopia

Panharith Ean (MArch I), Zhixing Wanwan Fei (MArch I)
Architecture Core Studio IV: Relate
Instructor: Andrew Holder

Our studio will claim to discover an extreme anachronism. We will develop an extended analogy with neolithic, stacked-stone constructions. The heterogeneous rocks and found objects of cairns will be taken for the units and enclosures of private property that, when stacked, coproduce an entire world of gaps and misfits bound together in huge, eidetic monuments.

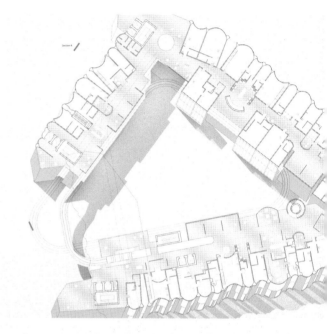

The fundamental need for shelter is not only to store dormant bodies overnight but also to celebrate the gregariousness of human society. Identical shoebox living units are no more than cargo trunks that package humans into lifeless possessions of an industrially constructed environment. The aim of this project is to combat the segregated living experience in high-density housing and the aloof image of megastructures in cities.

Ware/House

Tammy Teng (MArch I), Euipoom Estelle Yoon (MArch I)
Architecture Core Studio IV: Relate
Instructor: Andrew Holder

"Ware/House" integrates a housing complex with an Amazon warehouse distribution center in downtown Los Angeles. By locating a warehouse in the center of the city with housing, the project brings a new proximity between goods and consumers, housing residents and warehouse workers. This project attempts to transform Los Angeles, a city of industry-specific districts, into one that merges all industries inside a single housing complex.

in an extreme anachronism.

Facade
Housing
Urbanism

Feed or Devour

Tianhui Hou (MAUD), Zhengyu Qin (MAUD)
Public Projection: Projection as a Tool for Expression and Communication in Public Space
Instructor: Krzysztof Wodiczko

Our project aims to break the ice. It is a partition panel in the
middle of the dining table, separating visual contact between
two people sitting face-to-face at the same table. When they
start eating, their faces are projected onto each other's food.
People can choose to react to each other's behavior, feeding
the projection or ignoring their tablemate and devouring the
facial projection.

break the ice.

First Dates

Mirror Mirror

This poem is cut up from the following sources:
J-Term   Inside Architecture
VIS 2121 Architectural Representation: Origins + Originality
STU 1101 Architecture Core Studio I: Project
STU 1111 Landscape Architecture Core Studio I
STU 1201 Architecture Core Studio III: Integrate
STU 1202 Architecture Core Studio IV: Relate
STU 1231 Collaborative Design Engineering Studio I
STU 1602 Phantom Coast: Transforming San Francisco's
               Eastern Waterfront
Lecture   Black in Design: Designing Resistance,
               Building Coalitions
News   Statement from Women Faculty of the GSD

Learning to see
a subtle balance
    highly subjective,
      provocative and perhaps unexpected.

The inner psyche,
reflecting the outside world,
confronts but also exposes
different points of view,
      questioning what each offers.

We face
figurative riffs
positioned between
barriers
and moments of awakening.

Demanding transparency
requires articulation of both.

Mirror Mirror: *a table of reflection and representation*

When we look into the mirror, we do not see ourselves. The mirror [re]constructs our face, projecting a new image by means of reflection. When we look upon these two faces, we are confused as to which image is the true likeness—perhaps both images are true, perhaps neither.

    Holding a mirror in front of this table allows us to discover what is not apparent upon first glance. This grants us a view of the work's twinning, thickening, bridging, and hinging, showing us that the mirror is not a surface of duplication but of multiplication, not of representing but of revealing.

The Shadow of Light

Jianing Zhang (MArch II)
Inside Architecture J-Term Course
Instructor: Luisa Lambri

> Translate a subjective and personal approach to image-making based on experimental techniques that reveal the inner psyche of the participants and concentrate on the human condition rather than reflect the outside world.

Art Practices
Detail
Light
Photography

Serial

Euipoom Estelle Yoon (MArch I)
Inside Architecture J-Term Course
Instructor: Luisa Lambri

a subtle balance

Art Practices
Detail
Photography
Representation

twin *twin*

Antonio Casalduc (MArch I), Kenneth Hasegawa (MArch I)
Architecture Core Studio IV: Relate
Instructor: Jennifer Bonner

Los Angeles has several locatable twin conditions, from mirrored and rotated towers to an economy of means found in copy-paste dingbat housing. Imagine an exaggerated city where twinning not only serves as the stand-in typology, but also structures a methodology for working in pairs.

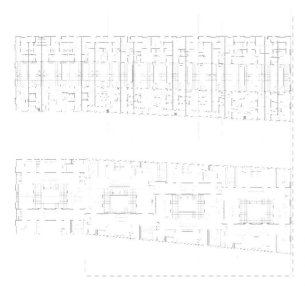

The weird thing about twins is not that they look alike but that they look slightly different. Twins produce uncanniness through the proximity of nearly identical objects. Twins position an architecture that is neither copy nor icon but somewhere in between.

Housing
Representation
Typology

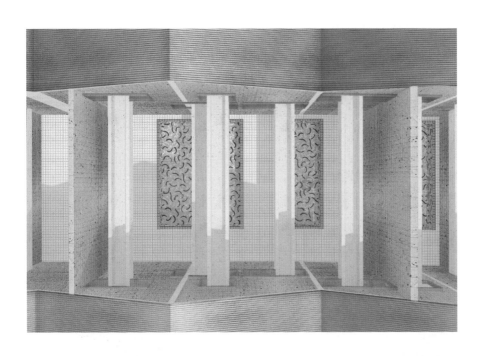

271   provocative and perhaps unexpected.

Apeirogon

Humberto Ceballos (MDE), Saif Haobsh (MDE), Katherine Spies (MDE)
Collaborative Design Engineering Studio I
Instructors: Jock Herron, Andrew Witt, Fawwaz Habbal (John A. Paulson School of Engineering and Applied Sciences), Peter Stark (John A. Paulson School of Engineering and Applied Sciences)

Propose a sensory therapy environment: a tangible spatial experience that will deliver on the project's therapeutic aims.

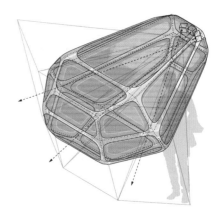

As a neighborhood access point in settings from urban to rural, "Apeirogon" provides an individual therapy enclosure where one can deeply relax to cope with immediate stress and anxiety, or focus on long-term cognitive behavioral therapy (CBT) to improve symptoms over time.

Engineering
Fabrication
Health
Responsive Environments

Rift

Julia Schubach (MArch I)
Architectural Representation: Origins + Originality
Instructor: Megan Panzano

> Architectural representation is an ideology. It is integral to the design process and the production of architecture—it is present and future tense: an active participant in exploring and making.

  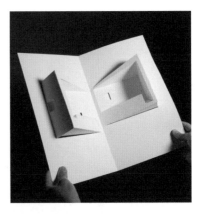

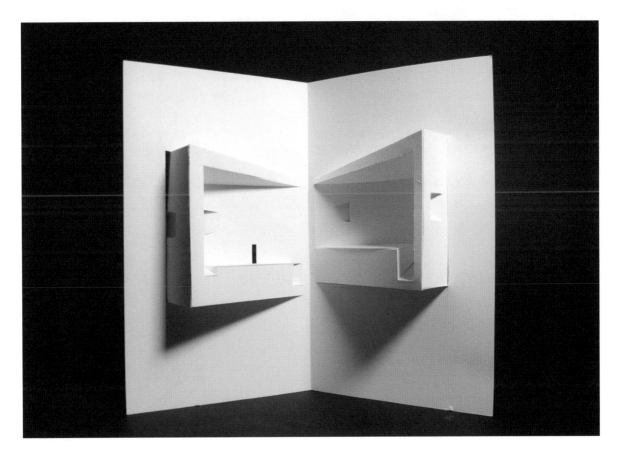

reflecting the outside world,

Detail
Representation

3 Cones, 3 Cylinders

Ashley Hickman (MArch I)
Architecture Core Studio I: Project
Instructor: Sean Canty

"Jump Cut" references a technique in film editing where there is an abrupt transition, typically within a sequential clip, that makes the subject appear to jump from one spot to the other.

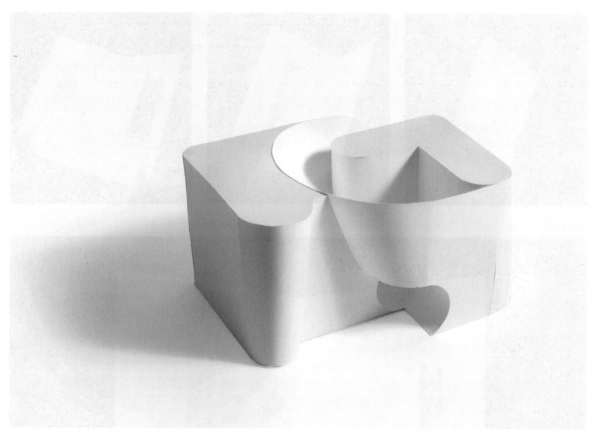

The project takes the two given section cuts and treats them as separate, adjacent buildings. One building is dominated by verticality, the other by horizontality. A sculptural conic element is inserted between the two buildings to unite them. This sculptural move joins the horizontality of the floor with the verticality of the wall. On the interior, this gesture merges the sectional difference between the two adjacent buildings.

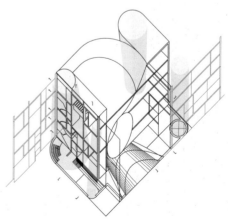

Stilt City: Framework for a Transient Shoreline

Zephaniah Ruggles (MLA I AP)
Phantom Coast: Transforming San Francisco's Eastern Waterfront
Instructors: James Lord, Roderick Wyllie
> Explore the imaginative potential of the San Francisco Seawall as both innovative infrastructure and dynamic and engaging public open space. This infrastructure can become a new forum for civic engagement and activism.

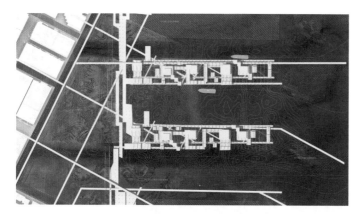

The project proposes a deconstruction of the city. Block by block, these risky lands will be returned to the bay. The displaced housing, businesses, and people will then densify along the Embarcadero in new urban frameworks. This new "Stilt City" will embody the ideal of living with water, suggesting a future where the water is a part of the city and not opposed to it.

Infrastructure
Public Space
Urbanism
Water

Students Respond to the "Shitty Architecture Men" List

Banners hung in the Gund Hall trays on April 6, 2018.

Statement from Women Faculty of the GSD

April 23, 2018

As members of the GSD we, the women faculty, are united in support of the student body in denouncing discrimination, harassment, and aggressions against any member of our community. We will not tolerate it, we will not stand silent. We do so by acknowledging that we too have suffered and still do from this culture in our own daily encounters, both here and in the broader design community.

We support student activism and we respect our students speaking out against injustices in our community and demanding transparency. As faculty we will enter this conversation and work to create a manifesto and other tools to combat pervasive prejudices and disrespectful behaviors which may be systemic in our culture and discipline.

This is a crucial moment of awakening and a pivotal opportunity to promote awareness and actively pursue our goal for a fair and just society, accepting across gender, race, nationality, sexuality, and religion. We will join hands with our students and invite our male colleagues and all staff to join us in seeking and executing a new path forward.

questioning what each offers.

Gender
Justice
Social Equity

Black in Design: Designing Resistance, Building Coalitions

Conference organized by African American Student Union
October 6–8, 2017

We are framing the upcoming conference across the forms of design, to unearth our agency as designers to envision more radical and equitable futures.

ACT UP (Gran Fury), *SILENCE = DEATH*, neon sign, featured in "Let the Record Show. . .," New Museum, New York, 1987.

Toni L. Griffin: I need the black brothers to stand up. I need the women in this room to stand up. If you are a proud member of the LGBTQ community, I need you to stand up. If you are a person who practices a religion that is not Christianity, please stand up. If you are a person in this room who lives in this country but was not born in this country, please stand up. You are the people who live in fear in this country every day. You are who the Just City is for.

Gender
Justice
Race
Social Equity

Collected Towers: Life as a Spectacle

Kaoru Lovett (MArch I)
Architecture Core Studio III: Integrate
Instructor: Belinda Tato

Programmatic organization considers the relationships of program, and the sequencing of their experience, as well as their critical adjacencies. Distinct from function and use, program takes on a new quality as a generative tool. Often understood as a given, program has become a site for organizational invention.

Flr. 00
...
Rehearsal spaces

Flr. 01
...
Gallery . Event

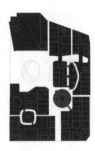

Flr. 02
...
Performance Theater
Classrooms
Admin Offices
—
Library
Garden
Research Chamber

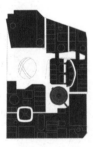

Flr. 03
...
Performance Theater
Classroom
Workshop
Admin Offices
—
Library
Garden
Research Chamber

Flr. 04
...
Opera Lobby and Event Space

Flr. 05
...
Opera Theater

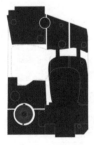

Flr. 06
...
Opera Theater
Residential

Flr. 07
...
Opera Theater
Residential

Flr. 08
...
Opera Theater
Residential

Performance
Program
Theater

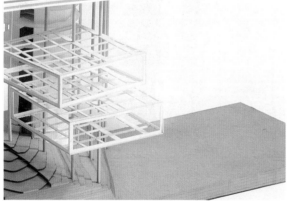

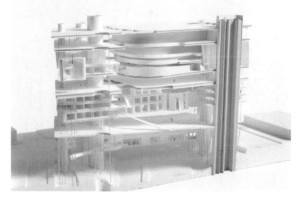

Nested within Boston's urban topography, the opera house serves as a campus for two prominent music conservatories. The project turns toward city life as the performance. The various activities and internal workings of the academy are exposed through sectional and scalar heterogeneity. Just as program between the two academies is divided into shared and independent spaces, the architecture finds reciprocity between the collective and the autonomous through the aggregation of program towers. This relationship generates a scalar spectrum of interlocking spatial components, alternating between room, tower, and urban block. As spectators navigate through the building, the internal performances unfold as exhibition.

Soft [edge] Hard

Andreea Vasile Hoxha (MLA I)
Landscape Architecture Core Studio I
Instructor: Francesca Benedetto

Detail
Public Space
Water

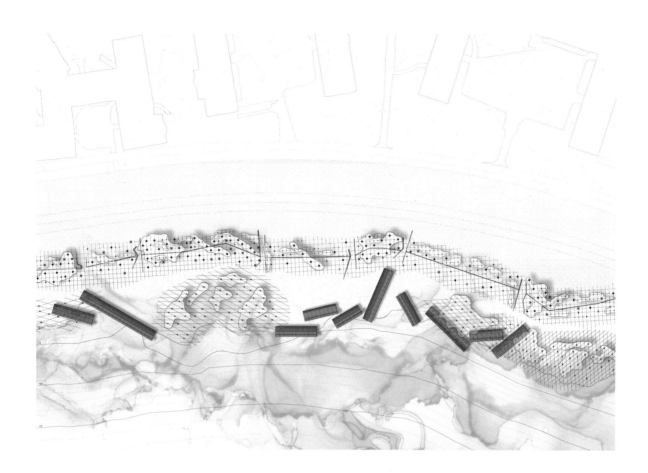

The project seeks to create a sequence of unique experiences along the Charles River by physically isolating particular moments and further articulating the water's edge. The outcome is depicted through a series of landscape objects placed strategically to create views towards the water and the bridges, which also define the soft edge populated by willows and bald cypresses.

281   and moments of awakening.

Charles River Malleable Edge

Xingyue Huang (MLA I)
Landscape Architecture Core Studio I
Instructor: Danielle Choi

The River Park will address the threshold between the river and the city, water and land, solid and aqueous.

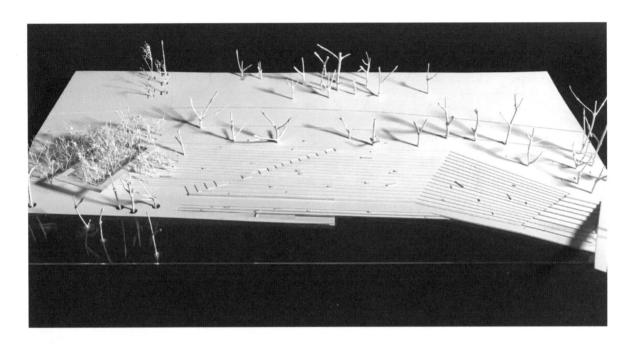

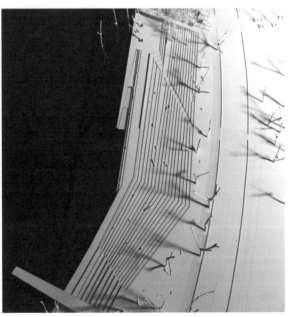

Landform
Public Space
Water

In Between: Mass and Mound

Kenneth Hasegawa (MArch I)
Architecture Core Studio III: Integrate
Instructor: Jon Lott

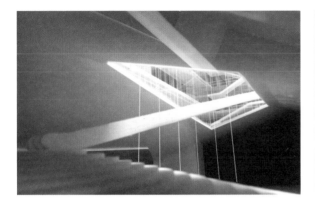

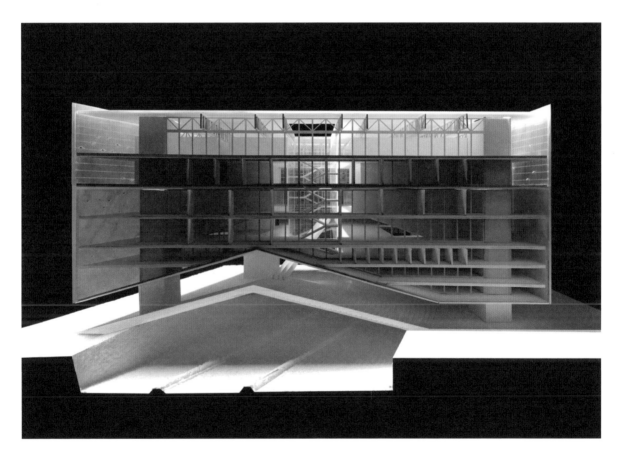

The cut into the bottom of the mass takes the shape of a gable
and forms a roof for the spaces below it. This surface—the
mound—is doubled in function to engage with both urban
contexts. It acts as a ceiling for the cars traveling along the
freeway, forming a gateway to the city, and creating another
type of theater space for the vehicular traffic.

Landform
Program
Theater

Mirror Mirror

Front

A, B Antonio Casalduc
     Kenneth Hasegawa
C   Kaoru Lovett
D   Mojdeh Sadat
     Mahdavi Moghaddam

Back

E, H Boxiang Yu
F   Euipoom Estelle Yoon
G   Kenneth Hasegawa
I   Kaoru Lovett
J   Andreea Vasile Hoxha
K   Ashley Hickman
L   Xingyue Huang
M   Zephaniah Ruggles

Pleasing to the Touch

Material Systems: Digital Design and Fabrication
Instructors: Martin Bechthold with Jose Luis Garcia del Castillo y López (DDes)
Ceramics Studio Consultant: Kathy King (Harvard Ceramics Program)

Over the past decade, advances in material development have been catalyzed by increasingly robust implementations of digital design and fabrication techniques that have empowered designers through digital modeling, simulation, and the increasingly digital augmentation of all physical processes. Creative applications of material-related technologies have produced new forms of expression in architecture, have triggered a debate on digital ornament, and continue to advance the performative aspects of buildings. Yet we are only at the beginning of a new age of digital materiality.

The course positions material systems as combinations of design technologies with material processing and manipulation environments. Material systems are positioned as central to a research-based design inquiry that capitalizes on opportunities that emerge when craft-based knowledge is synthesized with CNC machines, robotic technologies, additive manufacturing, and material science.

This year's course will focus on ceramic systems. Ceramic is the first-ever material created by mankind and it is omnipresent in the craft studio as well as in industrial manufacturing settings. Pleasing to the touch and easily manipulated by hand, it can just as easily be subject to digital technologies and robotic approaches. While ceramic-specific aspects of material design and manipulation will be taught, emphasis is on understanding ceramics as a microcosm of material research that offers insights that transfer to work with almost any material used in architecture.

The technical and systems knowledge imparted in the class will be complemented by the teaching of research methods in the area of technology, through a combination of readings and writing exercises. Students will propose and work on a research-based ceramics project throughout the semester, culminating in a substantial experimental prototype and a conference-level paper that frames the project as an instance of design technology research in ceramic material systems.

Computation
Engineering
Fabrication
Materials

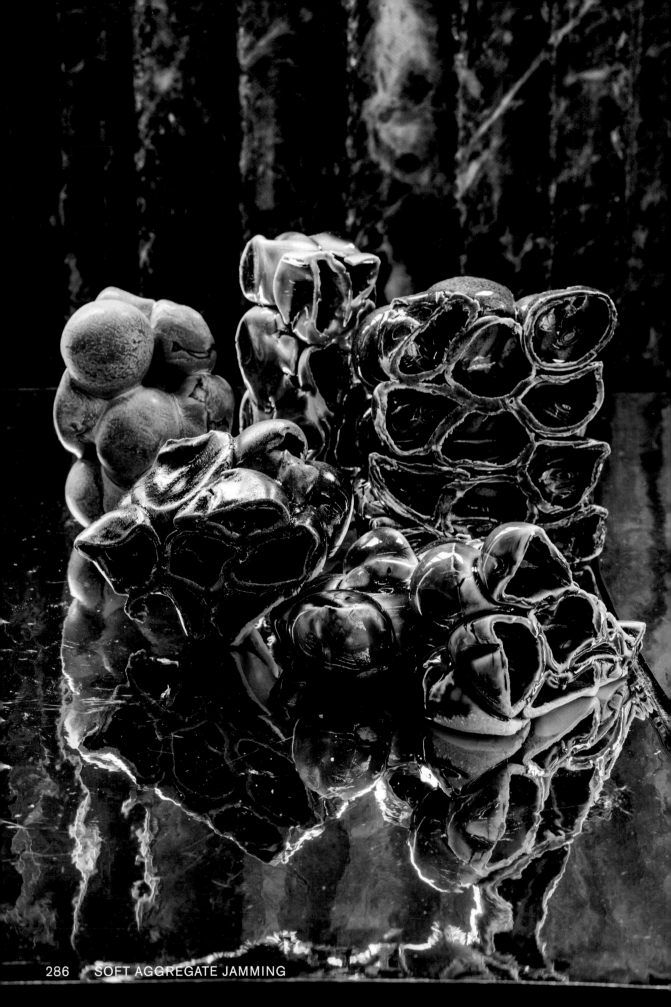

SOFT AGGREGATE JAMMING

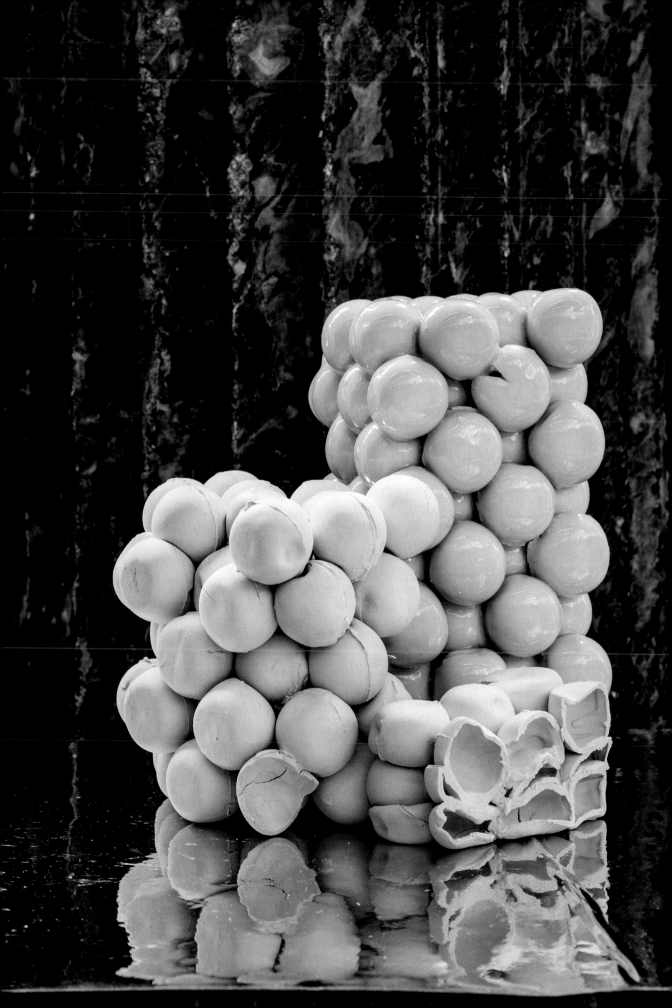

Soft Aggregate Jamming: Customizable Compression of Soft Clay Aggregate for Thermally Tuned Ceramic Units

Iain Gordon (MDes EE)
Aurora Jensen (MDes EE)
Peter Osborne (MDes EE)

This study began by exploring the opportunities offered by aggregating ceramics as a building tectonic in its plastic phase. By documenting the formal and thermal properties of the variable-density bricks, this research reveals the emergent qualities and flexibility of this soft aggregation process.

The starting point involved studying the properties of deformation and aggregation of a variety of soft clay forms. The scope was then refined to focus on the aggregation of simple hollow spherical clay units, due to their pure form and lack of rotation bias. The size of the spherical unit, its wall thickness, and the porcelain clay body were held constant throughout this study of the aggregate system. Therefore, this investigation fundamentally explores the relationship between mass, voids, and exposed surface area that result from the compression process.

Through experimentation and close study of the clay body, the soft aggregation of clay spheres was translated into a novel material system in which modules might be designed with specific thermal characteristics. The project demonstrates the principles of soft aggregate jamming for architectural-scale applications using uniform-density unitized building blocks.

Controlling Material Behavior with Printspeed, Feedrate, and Complex Printpath

Sulaiman Alothman (MDes Tech)
Hyeon Ji Im (MDes Tech)
Francisco Jung (MDes Tech)

Current digital soil fabrication techniques comply with the innate behavior of the material being extruded by printing the soil in two-dimensional layers. This method inevitably uses an excess amount of building material and is a time-consuming process that does not take advantage of the viscous properties of clay.

The extrusion behavior of the material can be controlled by utilizing spatial print trajectories with embedded print parameters (e.g., speed and extrusion rate) that simulate the actions of anchor, drag, and pull of the soil at the nozzle tip. The printpath can be scaled up to exploit the potential of digital fabrication at the construction scale.

Instead of stacking bricks or interlocking prefabricated structures, the clay lump construction primitively piles material on top of itself, resulting in a monolithic structure, very similar to the process of additive 3-D printing.

This is the basis of the research investigation in which the viscosity of clay is utilized to form a self-supporting lattice system out of spatial print trajectories. The exponential ramifications when scaling the printpath and introducing fibers for tensile reinforcement will be studied to validate its use in construction.

The Mixology Table: Controlling Porosity in Ceramic from Nano-Porous to Micro-Porous

Haeyoung Kim (MDes Tech)
Sejung Song (MArch II, MDes Tech)
Hyeji Yang (MDes Tech)

This research explores the porosity of ceramic as a means of a potential architectural filtration system. The emphasis is set on controlling a scale and position of porosity in ceramics from nano-porous (the inherent property of ceramic) to micro-porous (the engineered property of ceramic). The level of nano-porosity is experimented through differentiating the thermal curing temperature of a kiln. The size of micro-porosity is dependent on the size of a swollen hydrogel and its position is specified through rotation and time.

Through research and experiments, robotic integration in controlling the micro-porosity in ceramic translated into a new fabrication framework. The size and the positions of the hydrogels in slip were controlled due to the rotation angle and the time duration in the fabrication process. The catalogue of different porosity designs proved that it is now possible to control and create the desired porosity in ceramics with two-axis rotation.

Conveyor Belt

This poem is cut up from the following sources:
STU 1101 Architecture Core Studio I: Project
STU 1102 Architecture Core Studio II: Situate
STU 1111 Landscape Architecture Core Studio I
STU 1112 Landscape Architecture Core Studio II
STU 1121 Urban Planning Core Studio I
STU 1201 Architecture Core Studio III: Integrate
STU 1211 Landscape Architecture Core Studio III
STU 1301 Entropy, History, Time. Architectural Infrastructure
          for a Gravel Pit in Spain
STU 1306 Idiom, Identity, Id
STU 1404 Civic Spaces in an Age of Hyper-Complexity:
          From Protest to Reverie
STU 1505 The Industrious City: Rethinking Urban Industry
          in the Digital Age
STU 1604 Between Earth and Sky: A Building for the
          HafenCity, Hamburg
ADV 9301 Architecture Thesis
ADV 9307 Design Studies Open Projects
ADV 9342 Landscape Architecture Thesis

UNDERPINNING (296) EVERYDAY (297) MET
HODOLOGICAL (298) CLICHÉS (299) ASERIE
S (300) OFMECHANISMS (301) ASET (302) OFPRO
TOCOLS (303) ASTANDARD (304) OFCOMPLET
ION (305) DIGITAL (306) ANDANALOGUE (307)
MULTIPLE (308) RATHERTHAN (309) SINGUL
AR (310) EXPANDING (311) ANDCONTRACTI
NG (312) ATAPESTRYOF (313) COMPLEX (314) E
XPERIMENTS (315) RADICALLY (316) RECON
SIDERED (317) HUNDREDSOFYEARS (318) OF
MASSPRODUCTION (319) SEQUENTIAL (320)
TRANSFORMATIONS (321) ACROSSVARIO
US (322) MEDIUMS (323) POWERFUL (324) CATA
LYSTS (325) INVENTING (326) NEWTYPES (327)

Conveyor Belt: *an assembly line*

One after the other, we produce, we discard, and we start over again. Our
working process resembles an assembly line: always making and remaking.
We are told "Iterate!" and, like machines, we burn the candle at both ends
in order to keep up.

   At this table—somewhere between a workbench and a roll of trace
paper—students work through and throw away ideas, striving for the best
possible outcome. But this is not simply a process of mass production;
this is a means by which schemes are sharpened, forms refined, tools mas-
tered, and concepts ironed out.

   Scraps pile up, but our projects would be nothing without them.

Infrastructure for a Gravel Pit

Noam Saragosti (MArch II)
Entropy, History, Time. Architectural Infrastructure for a Gravel Pit in Spain
Instructor: Iñaki Ábalos

The territory consists of a large plain of gravels of different origins and periods that serve as a base for the fertile orchards of Lleida, Spain, and for the oldest and most important gravel pit of the Sorigué company. This company has begun a process to recover the landscape and the physical surroundings for the long term.

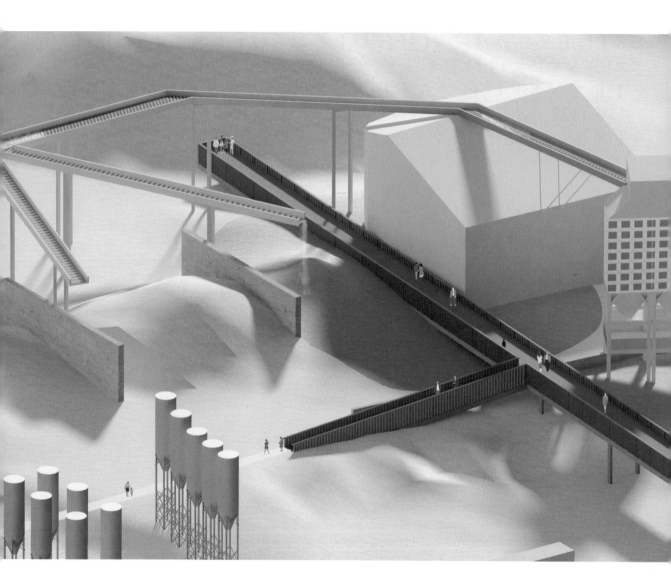

A bridge spans the extraction site to the south and the processing plant in the center of the site. While atop the bridge, one begins to form an understanding of the various elements of the site and their interrelationships. The bridge animates the existing simple industrial sheds and allows visitors a safe perspective inside the plant to understand the processes of extraction, sorting, and asphalt and concrete production.

The bridge may seem like part of the existing industrial infrastructure of steel sheds and gravel conveyors. While the bridge appears initially like a light steel structure, upon encounter the visitor begins to understand its materiality—a refined precast concrete construction produced on site. The relationship of the bridge to the material and form of the surrounding structures becomes apparent.

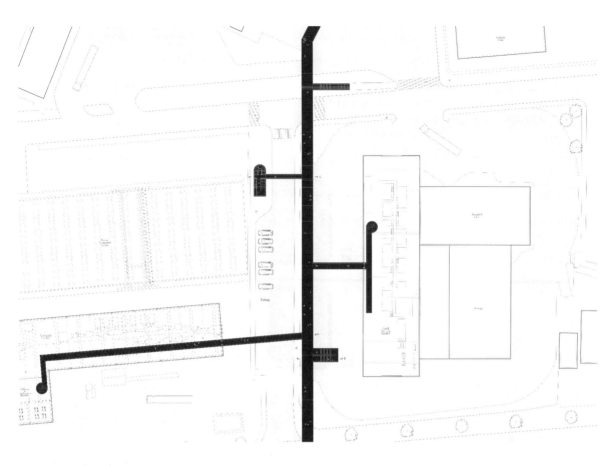

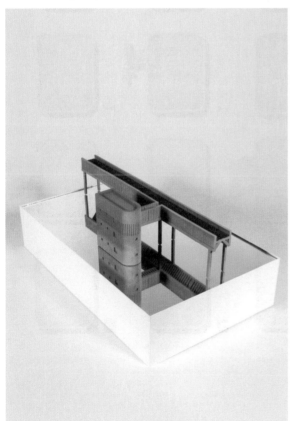

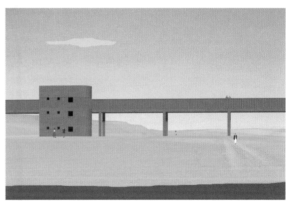

Ballast Urbanism

Claire Malone Matson (MLA I), Zishen Wen (MLA I AP), Xiaowei Zhang (MLA I AP)
Landscape Architecture Core Studio III
Instructor: Sergio Lopez-Pineiro

Work iteratively through topographic studies that consider hydrological processes.

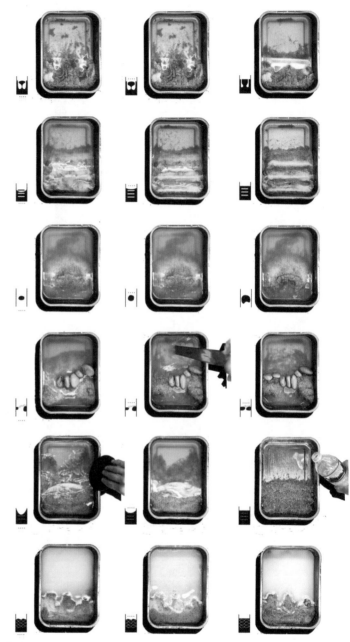

This project proposes the collection of discharged ballast water from international cargo ships at the Conley Container Terminal in South Boston and the redistribution of these waters into individual pools associated with their sources. The infrastructure of capturing and holding these waters becomes the spatial backbone for a new neighborhood on the 100-acre abandoned, post-industrial site adjacent to the terminal.

Infrastructure
Landform
Water

Analytical Assembly Line

Projects that use analytical iterative methods.

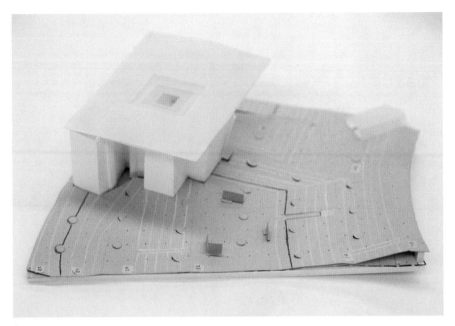

1

2

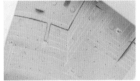

3

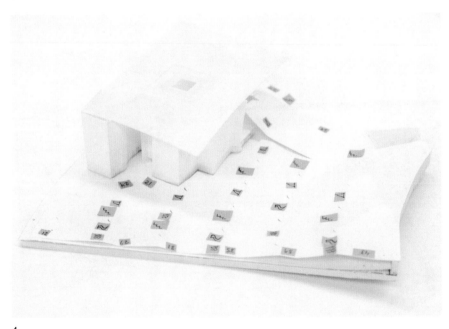

4

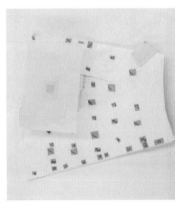

5

6

1–6
Study for City Hall Plaza: Slides, Stairs, and Ramps
Carson Fisk-Vittori (MLA I)
Landscape Architecture Core Studio I
Instructor: Francesca Benedetto

299   CLICHÉS

Circulation
Detail
Landform
Program

7

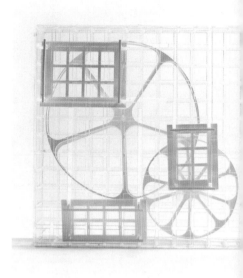

8

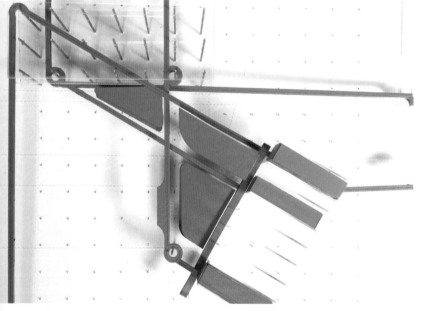

9

10

7
A Future Archaeology
Rana Aksoy (MArch I)
Architecture Core
Studio I: Project
Instructor: Jenny French

8
The Spinning Babylon
De Qian Huang (MArch I)
Architecture Core
Studio II: Situate
Instructor: Jenny French

9
Terminus
Aria Griffin (MArch I)
Architecture Core
Studio I: Project
Instructor: Jenny French

10
Sound Pluralism
Elif Erez (MArch I)
Architecture Core
Studio III: Integrate
Instructor: John May

11

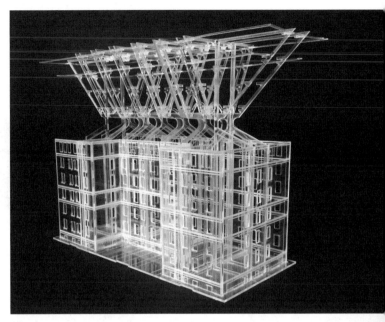

12

13

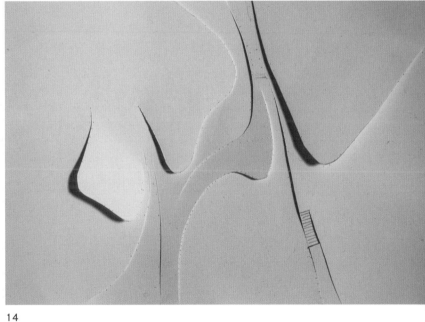

14

11
A Theater Within A Theater
Xiangyu Guo (MArch I)
Architecture Core
Studio III: Integrate
Instructor: Belinda Tato

12
Clouds and the New Columbia
Khoa Vu (MArch I)
Idiom, Identity, Id
Instructor: Preston
Scott Cohen

13
A Cultural Hub
Jonathan Tsun Hong
Yeung (MArch I)
Architecture Core
Studio III: Integrate
Instructor: Belinda Tato

14
A Geography of the Senses
Zeqi Liu (MLA I)
Landscape Architecture
Core Studio II
Instructor: Silvia Benedito

It's Id and Super-Ego, So to Speak

Idiom, Identity, Id
Instructor: Preston Scott Cohen
The synthesis of these investigations and analyses will be applied to two important and complex contemporary challenges: to confront the increasing demand for urban university housing and to spatialize an identity that expresses and distinguishes a particular university's culture from that of others.

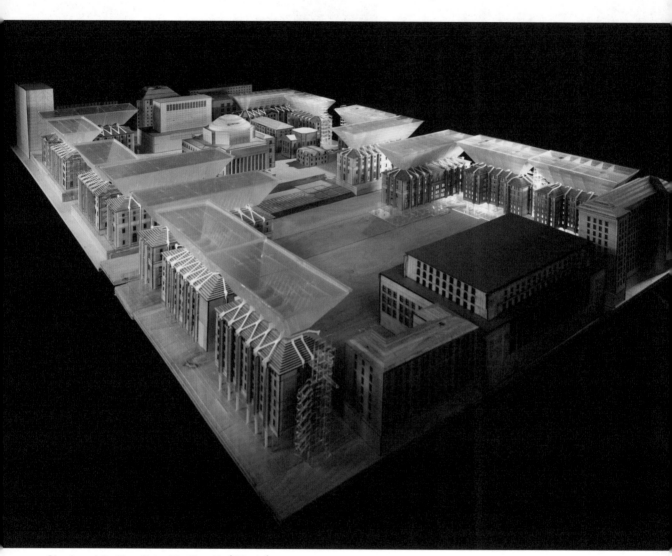

Clouds and the New Columbia, Khoa Vu (MArch I)

Revealing the Boundary, Jun Ho Han (MArch I AP)

Two Worlds, Wilson Harkhono (MArch I AP)

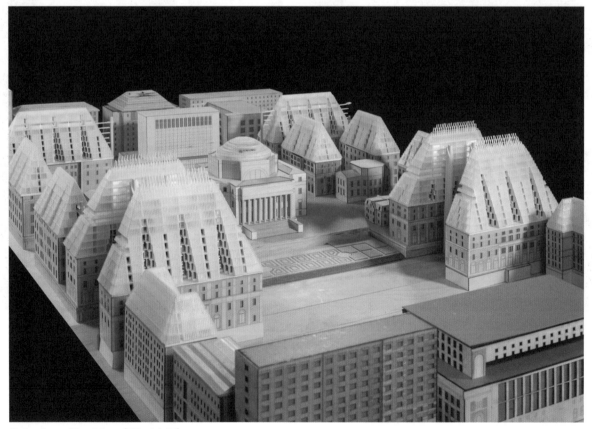

Alpine Dorm, Yungi Jung (MArch I AP)

A Frame of Type, Benjamin Pollak (MArch II)

Even More McKim for Columbia University, Igsung So (MArch I AP)

Wild: Manhattanism Unhinged

Seok Min Yeo (MLA I AP)
Landscape Architecture Thesis
Awarded the Thesis Prize in Landscape Architecture
Advisors: Craig Douglas, Rosalea Monacella

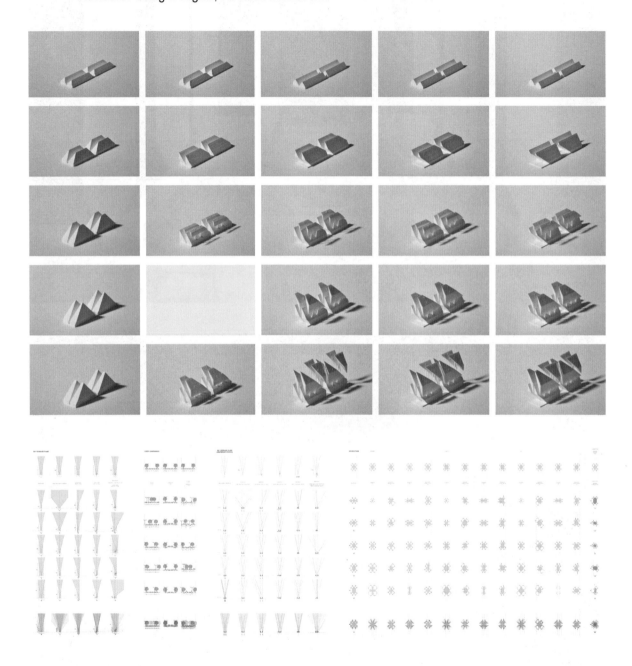

The Manhattan grid, and its ability to absorb manic heterogeneity, emancipates each block as an island of its own identity and ideology, inspiring architectural ecstasy. Manhattanism fearlessly soars to the sky, projected from the grid through a logistical framework that can support even the wildest dreams. The podium—a straight extrusion of the existing formal logic of the grid—is the datum of reliability that acts as a stage for expressions above. Consequently, the space in between the podiums—the streets—where the public experiences the city, has been neglected. Through the exploitation of the variability built into the zoning apparatus that gives rise to the form of the island, "Wild" posits the street and its composition as the catalyst, the public as the agent, and the built form as the byproduct.

Grid
Urbanism

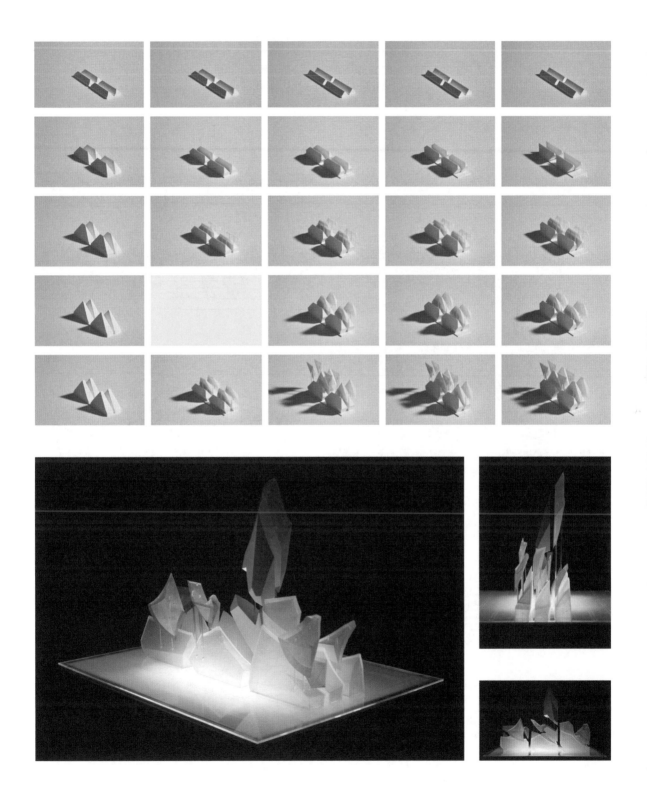

Layered Fab-City

Konstantina Tzemou (MAUD), Xiyao Wang (MAUD)
The Industrious City: Rethinking Urban Industry in the Digital Age
Instructors: Hiromi Hosoya, Markus Schaefer

Cities have always been places where commerce and production, working and living, are physically and functionally integrated. Only with the rise of industry have zoning regulations been introduced to separate these functions in space. But what is the role of such regulations when industry becomes more digitized, small-scale, agile, increasingly emission-free, and based on innovation more than mass production?

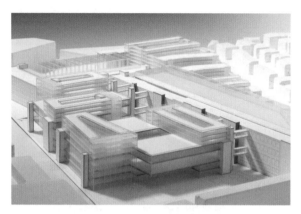
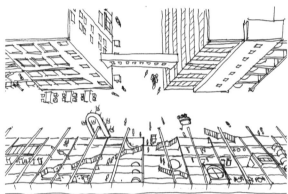

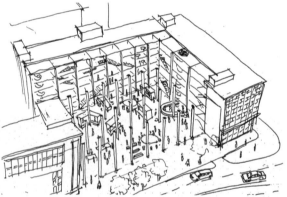

The project proposes the programmatic augmentation of the site in Oerlikon, Zurich, by sliding layers of civic nature into the industrial complex. By combining working, living, making, learning, and recreation facilities, the city is remixed to the maximum and the district enjoys economic diversity as well as urban friction.

Labor
Urbanism

A Civic Center for Billebogen and Baakenhafen

Theodore Kofman (MAUD)
Between Earth and Sky: A Building for the HafenCity, Hamburg
Instructor: Eric Parry

The eastern, undeveloped end of the HafenCity is defined by the rail and road bridges marking the historic approach to Hamburg from the south. Here it is intended to build a 200-meter-high tower that will mark the skyline from all directions, adding to a number of significant 20th-century and historic towers.

Sunrise   Midday   Sunset

Facade
Typology

Forms of the Oblique: A Center for Performing Arts

Zi Meng (MArch I AP)
Architecture Core Studio III: Integrate
Instructor: Belinda Tato

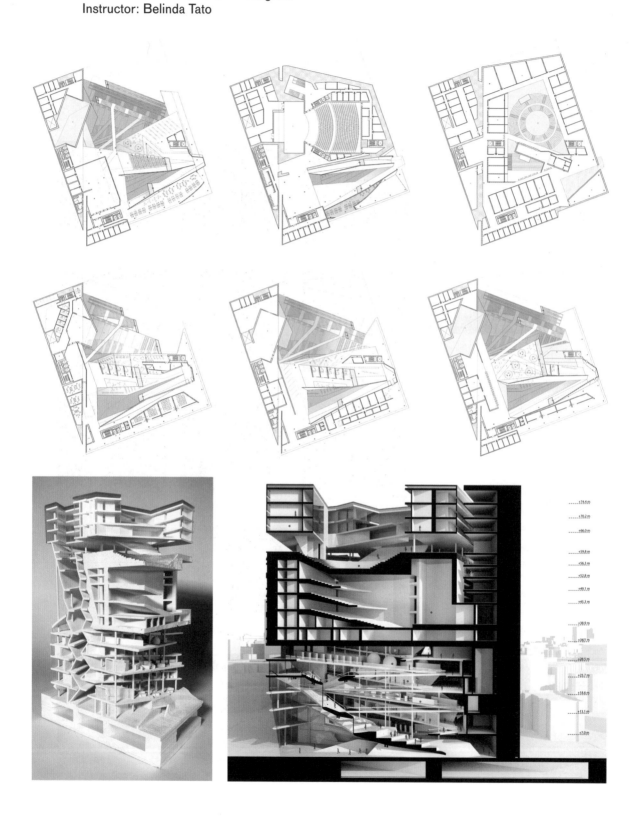

Circulation
Theater

Productive Collision

Milos Mladenovic (MArch I)
Architecture Core Studio III: Integrate
Instructor: John May

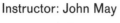
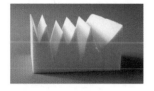
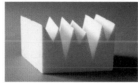
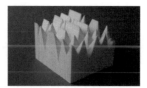
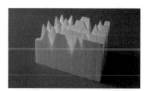

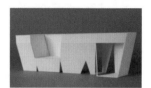

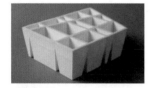

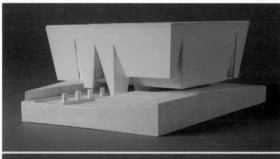
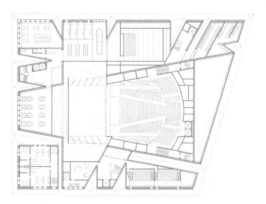

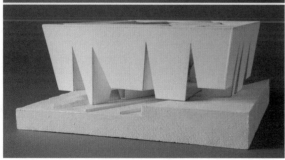
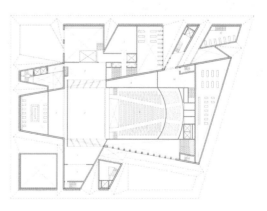

This project approaches the problem of a large-volume building as one of aggregation and subdivision, considering the acts of both mixing and segregation to be equally requisite in managing an excessive number of programs, institutions, and agendas.

Program
Theater

Ornament in the City of Industry

Juhee Park (MArch II), Noam Saragosti (MArch II)
Architecture Thesis
Advisors: Sharon Johnston, Mark Lee

In the big box, architecture is limited to the envelope. Whether it is a stripe of paint or faux brick adorning the facade, these buildings superficially attempt to deal with scale, order, and identity. When only the necessary exists, ornament as appliqué is a contradiction. Rather than surface-level adornment, ornament embedded in its construction and material processes can emerge as the expressive agent that civilizes the big box, from facility to a work of architecture. The thesis is a series of portraits of big boxes in the City of Industry, each reexamining techniques of tilt-up concrete construction to approximate the role of ornamentation.

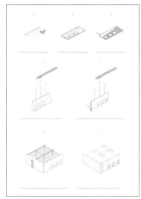

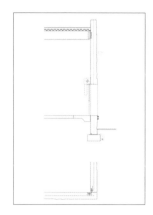

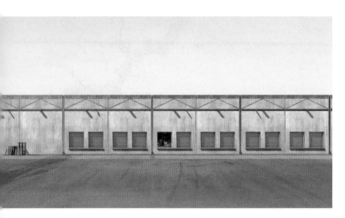

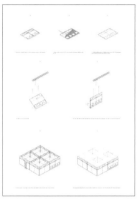

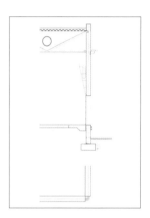

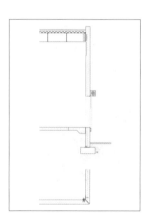

The Sapphire Bracelet: A Tool for Environmental Justice

Daniel Becerra (MUP)
Urban Planning Core Studio I
Instructor: Sai Balakrishnan

The most compelling plans will demonstrate knowledge about the area, its context, relevant planning ideas, and ethical issues involved in planning (e.g., fairness and equity, social justice, concern for the future).

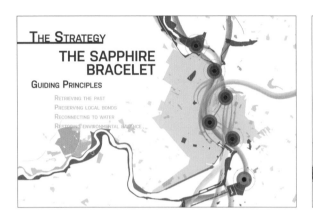

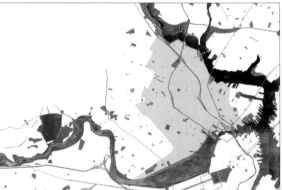

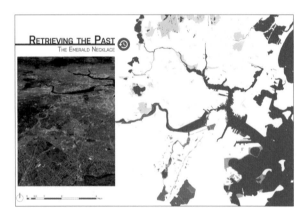

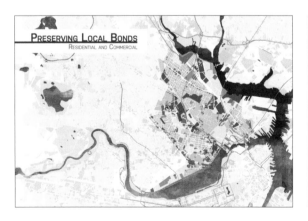

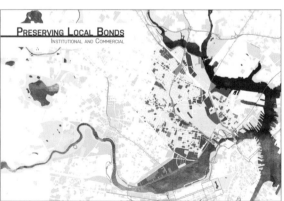

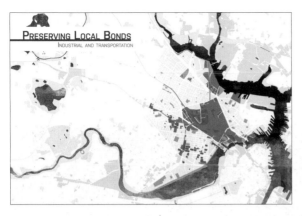

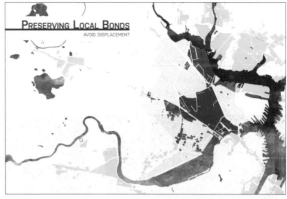

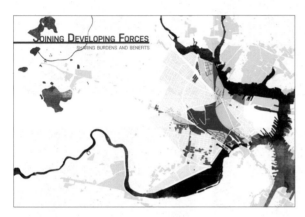

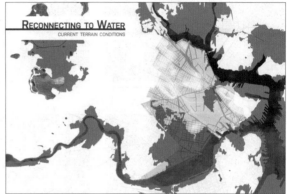

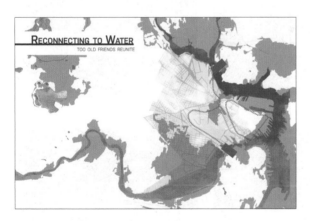

During the 18th and 19th centuries, the shorelines of the Charles and Mystic Rivers experienced environmental degradation caused by the impact of processing centers, manufacturing plants, munitions depots, antiquated sewer lines, and illegal plumbing, among other outcomes of industrialization. Water quality deteriorated as both rivers were used as the city's earliest transportation and waste management infrastructures.

However, as years passed, differentiated development of the built environment shaped each river's ecological narratives.

Combining four principles, the project proposes an urban intervention that will serve as a tool to restore natural equilibrium along the Charles and Mystic Rivers: retrieving the past; preserving local bonds; reconnecting water; and restoring environmental balance.

Pattern Mapping

Elissavet Pertigkiozoglou (MDes Tech)
Design Studies Open Project
Advisor: Andrew Witt

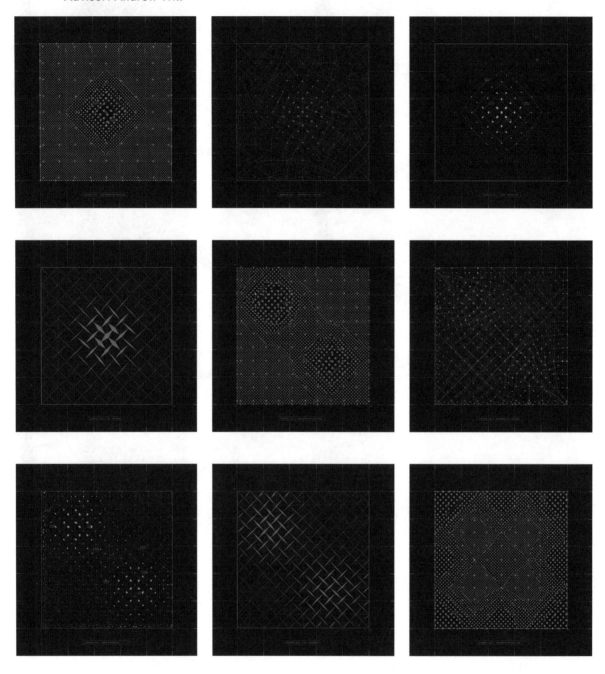

The technical description of objects and processes usually disregards the agency of the designer's perception in the creative process. The thesis shifts the focus to explore the potential of computational media to trigger interpretation through visual perception. "Pattern Mapping" suggests a computational environment for the design, making, and learning of a geometric material system: three-dimensional surfaces that can be created out of planar material through patterned cuts and deformation. Informed by studies that describe creativity as emerging associations between different concepts and situations, the proposed computer interface attempts to facilitate learning through multiple representational modes and scales of operations.

Computation
Fabrication
Materials

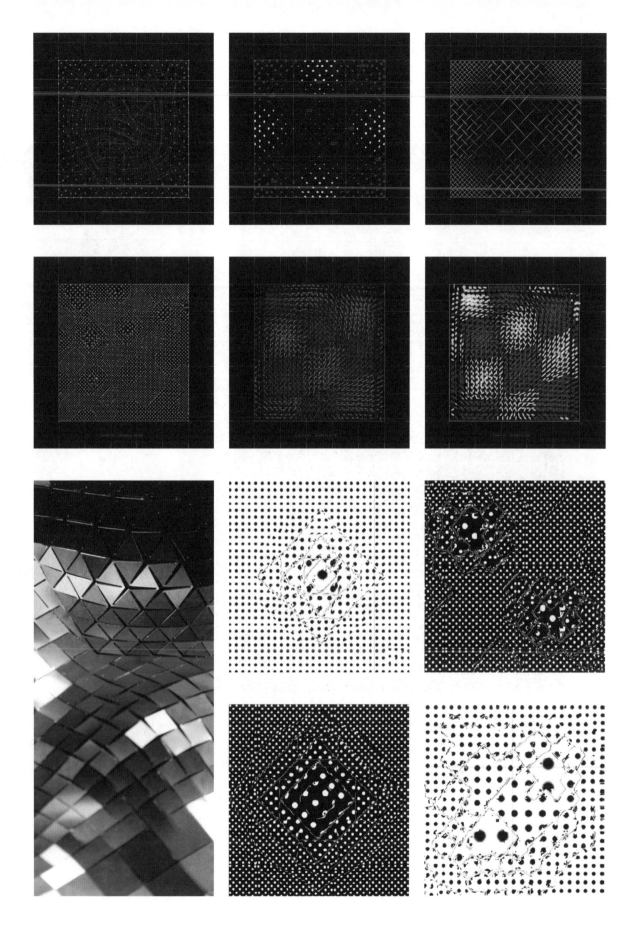

Structural Assembly Line

Projects from Architecture Core Studios exploring structural logics.

15

16

15
The Scenographic Machine
Jihyun Ro (MArch I)
Architecture Core Studio III: Integrate
Instructor: Belinda Tato

16
Aggregating Vaults
Yuna Kim (MArch I)
Architecture Core Studio II: Situate
Instructor: Sean Canty

Detail
Materials
Representation
Structure

17

18

19

17
Mitosis Magna
Aria Griffin (MArch I)
Architecture Core Studio II: Situate
Instructor: Tomás dePaor

18
The Real Table Tennis Club
Aria Griffin (MArch I)
Architecture Core Studio II: Situate
Instructor: Tomás dePaor

19
Shavings
Evan Kettler (MArch I)
Architecture Core Studio II: Situate
Instructor: Tomás dePaor

Tectonics for Parametric Geometry: Forms of Fabric Formwork

Yumiko Matsubara (MArch II)
Architecture Thesis
Advisor: Martin Bechthold

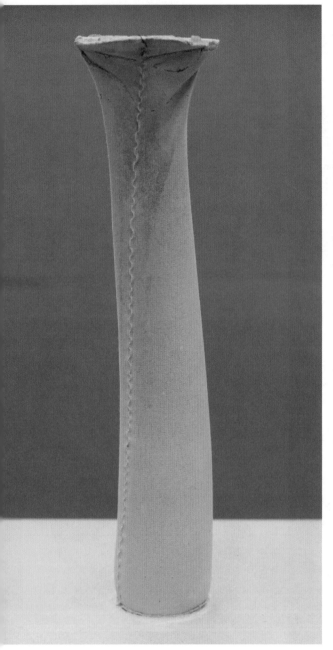

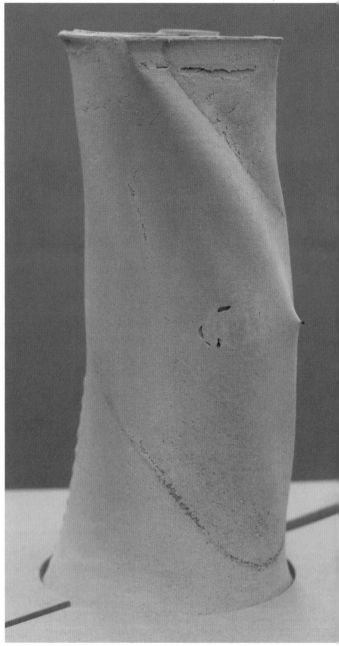

Prototype 1: Solid

Prototype 2: Pinch

While it is possible to draw and fabricate almost any form using today's digital tools, parametrically designed forms are often challenging to build. They are typically approximated by standard parts and assembled manually, consuming extra cost and materials. The goal of this project is to explore more suitable ways to materialize parametrically designed architecture.

Detail
Fabrication
Materials

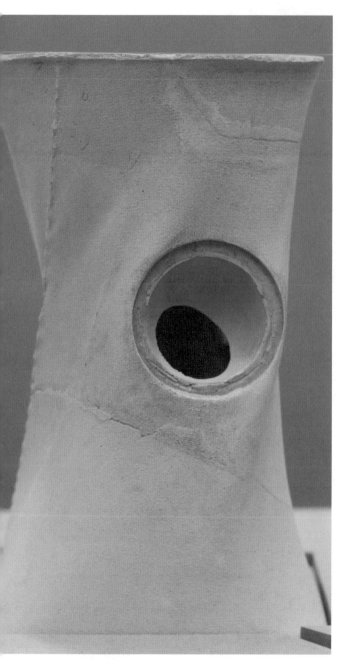

Prototype 3: Window

Prototype 4: Button

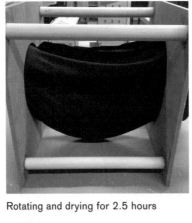

Lycra fabric held by a jig

Rotating and drying for 2.5 hours

Removing fabric after three nights

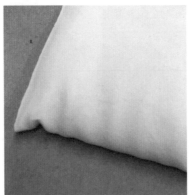

Texture of fabric

Waving

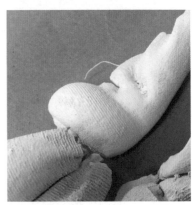

Seams by sewing

Drape

Twist

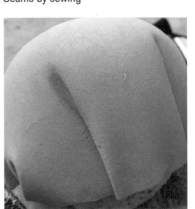

Folded surface by hanging

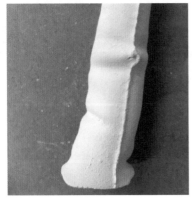

Seam

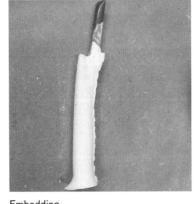

Embedding

Pattern of fabric

Invented Techniques

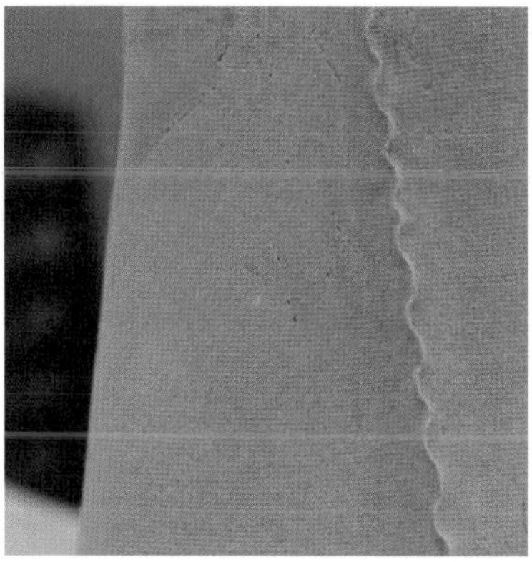

Sewing

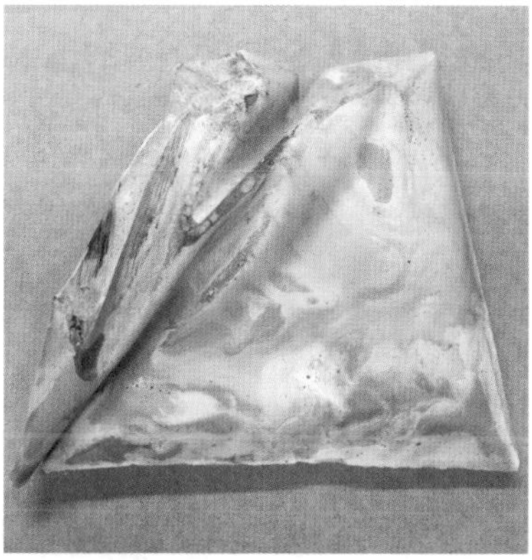

Heat sealing plastic sheets

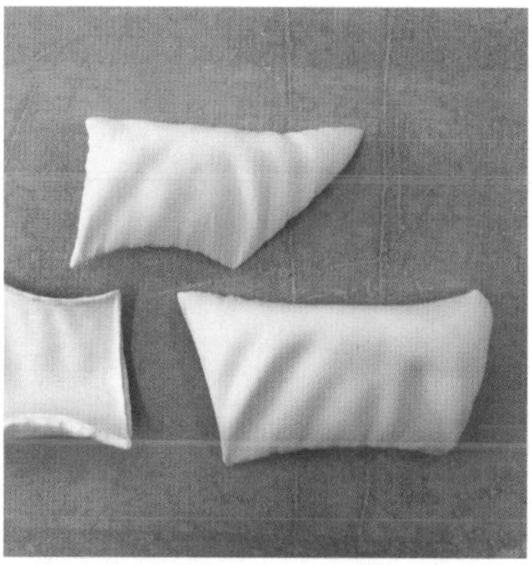

Shell slip casting

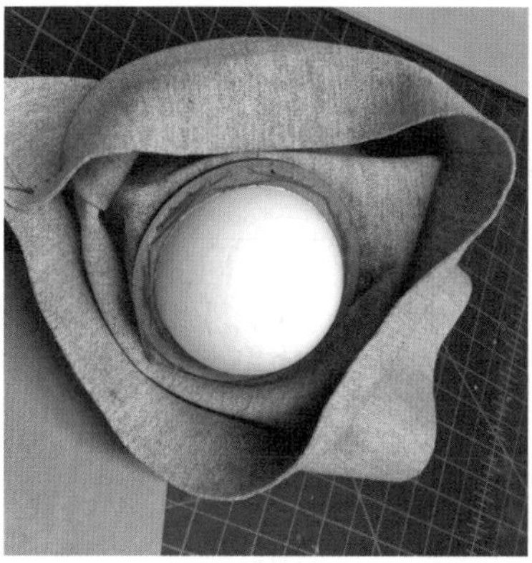

Opening

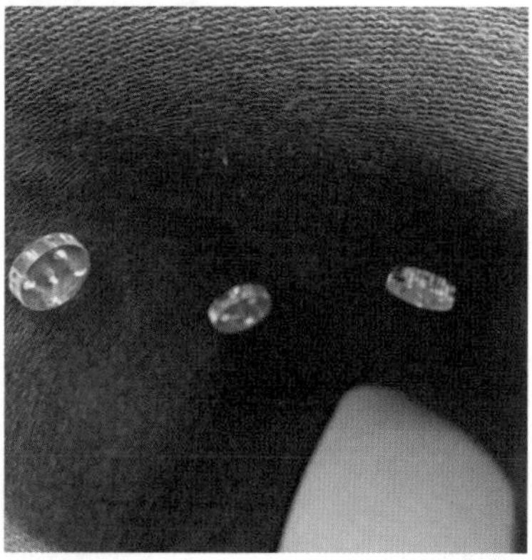

Button

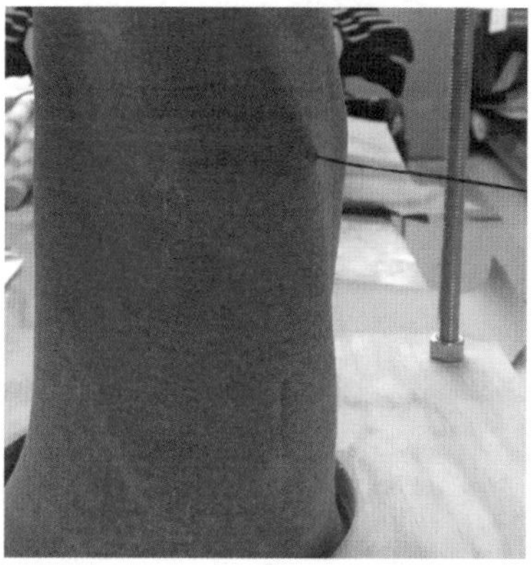

Pinching

Typical Failures

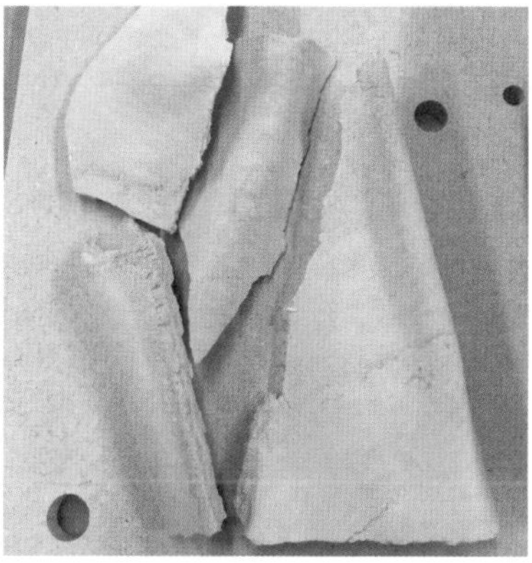

Detaches from mold

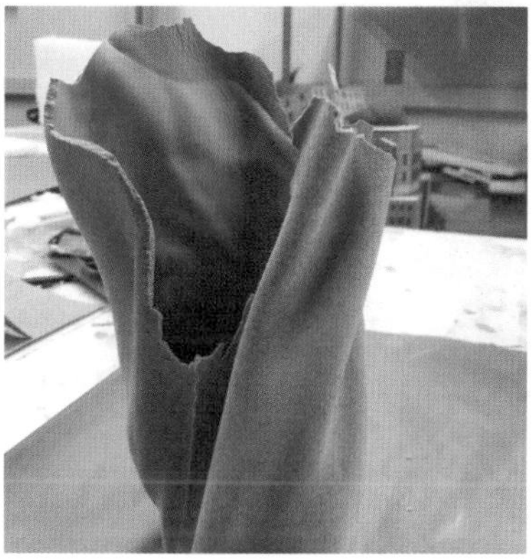

Fractures due to thinness

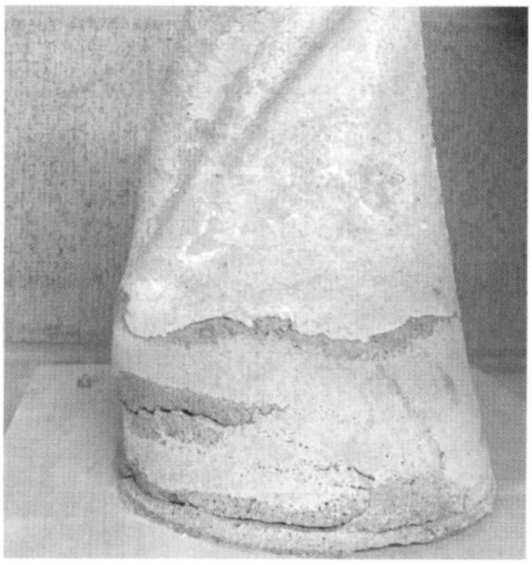

Bottom breaks

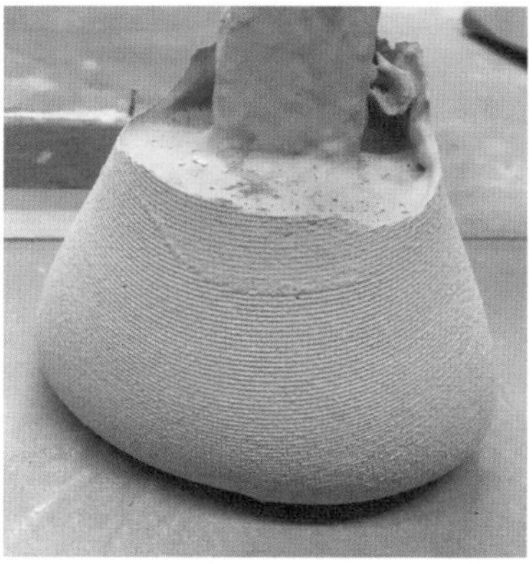

Excessive bulging

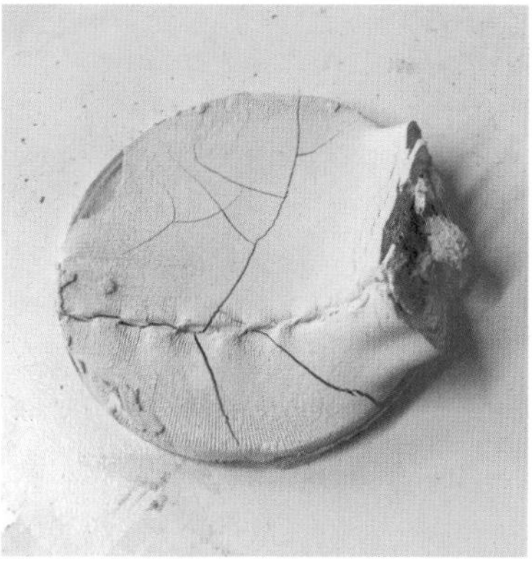

Cracks due to shrinkage

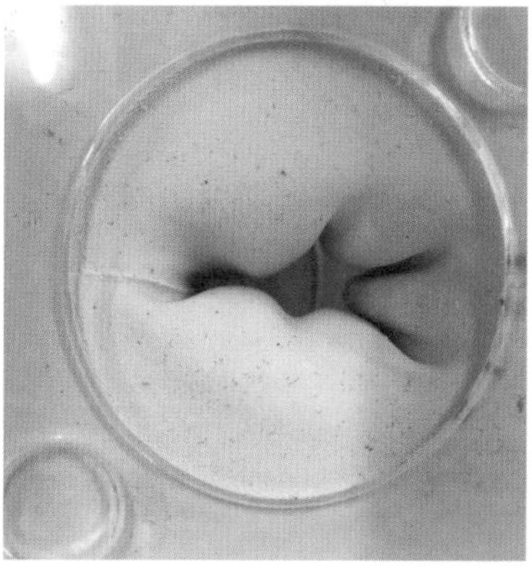

Mold cannot be removed

Treading Lightly: Addressing Urban Soil Compaction

Madeleine Aronson (MLA I)
Civic Spaces in an Age of Hyper-Complexity: From Protest to Reverie
Instructors: Mikyoung Kim with Bryan Chou

As civic spaces must now address manifold demands, more innovative and potent tools are necessary for their design. Invent a unique design language through a series of design exercises to develop landscape and architecture that focus on both large- and small-scale experiences.

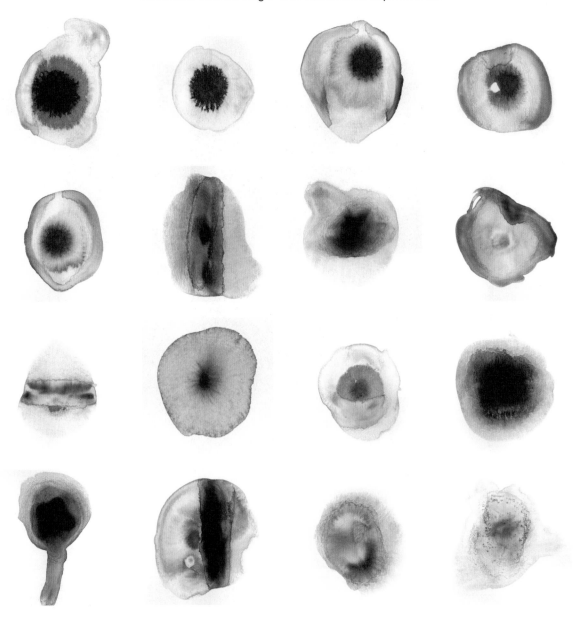

Working from a conceptual framework that explores processes of dissipation, blurring, wicking upward, and the idea of saturation at the center, this project asks how the SoWa (South of Washington) neighborhood in Boston can be a highly saturated center—saturated not only with plants and water, but also with civic activity and community.

Materials
Representation

Landscape Tales

Landscape Architecture Core Studio II
Instructors: Silvia Benedito, Montserrat Bonvehi Rosich, Kristin Frederickson, Belinda Tato
With Italo Calvino's *Invisible Cities* (1972) as an intellectual and discursive basis, the students are asked to imagine a particular landscape/environment in one of the described cities. With the suggestive power of the imagination, embodied knowledge, and projective goals, the student will invent and experiment with ideas of hybrid and multi-layered spaces.

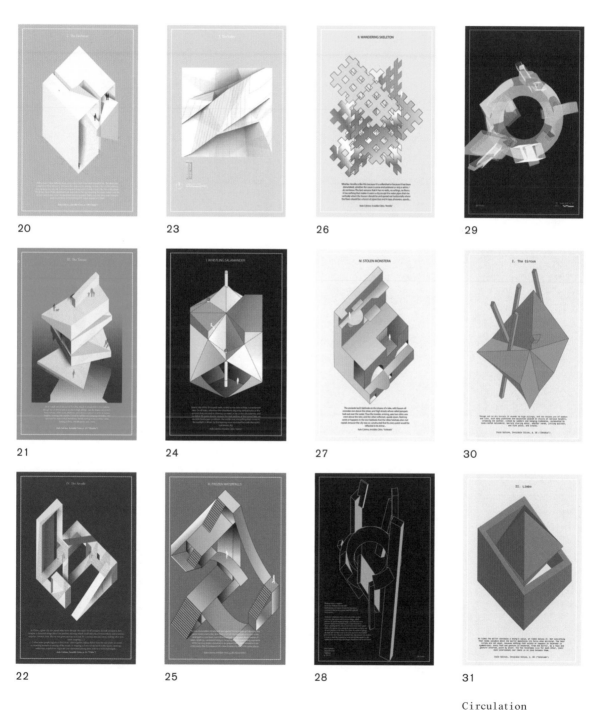

20

23

26

29

21

24

27

30

22

25

28

31

Circulation
Energy
Literature
Representation

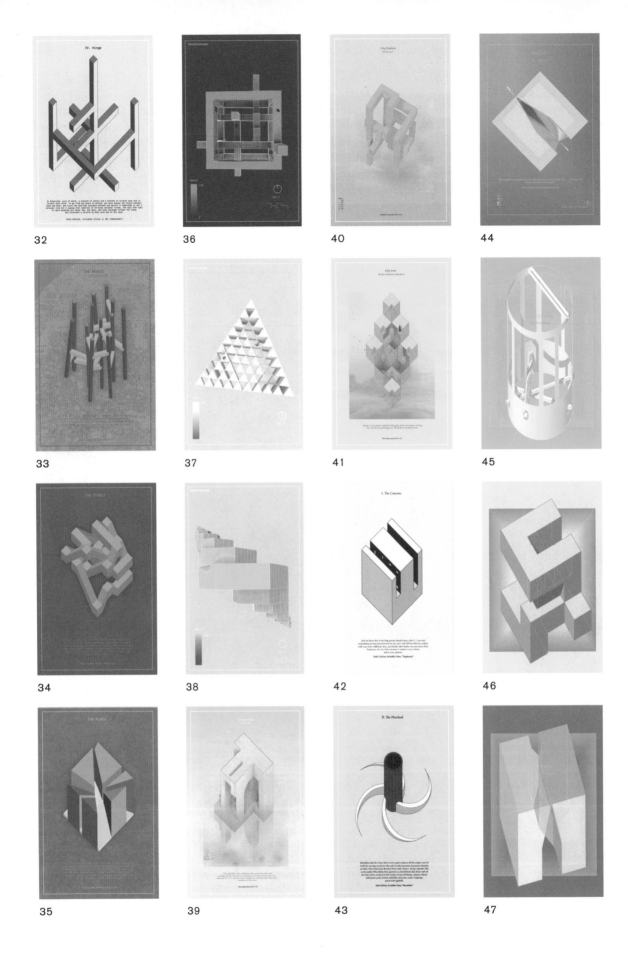

32

36

40

44

33

37

41

45

34

38

42

46

35

39

43

47

48

52

56

49

53

57

50

54

58

51

55

59

Conveyor Belt

Front

1 Khoa Vu
2 Elif Erez
3 Jonathan Tsun
   Hong Yeung
4 Noam Saragosti
5 Zi Meng
6 De Qian Huang
7 Aria Griffin
8 Seok Min Yeo

Back

9,11 Aria Griffin
10 Brayton Gregory
12 Evan Kettler
13 Madeleine Aronson
14 Seok Min Yeo
15 Yumiko Matsubara
16 Juhee Park
   Noam Saragosti
17 Jonathan Kuhr

Also seen in
plan view (p. 18)

Andreea Vasile Hoxha
Xingyue Huang
Milos Mladenovic
Julia Schubach
Xinyi Zhou

Appendix

Harvard GSD Leadership 2017–2018

Drew Gilpin Faust
President of Harvard University

Mohsen Mostafavi
Dean and Alexander and Victoria Wiley Professor of Design

Patricia J. Roberts
Executive Dean

HARVARD GSD EXECUTIVE COMMITTEE

Anita Berrizbeitia
Professor of Landscape Architecture; Chair of the Department of Landscape Architecture

Diane E. Davis
Charles Dyer Norton Professor of Regional Planning and Urbanism; Chair of the Department of Urban Planning and Design

Mark Goble
Chief Financial Officer

K. Michael Hays
Eliot Noyes Professor of Architectural Theory; Associate Dean for Academic Affairs; Interim Chair of the Department of Architecture

Beth Kramer
Associate Dean for Development and Alumni Relations

Erika Naginski
Robert P. Hubbard Professor of Architectural History; Director of Doctoral Programs

Jackie Piracini
Assistant Dean for Academic Services

Antoine Picon
G. Ware Travelstead Professor of the History of Architecture and Technology; Director of Research

ARCHITECTURE

K. Michael Hays
Eliot Noyes Professor of Architectural Theory; Associate Dean for Academic Affairs; Interim Chair of the Department of Architecture

Jon Lott
Assistant Professor of Architecture; Director of the Master in Architecture I Program

Jennifer Bonner
Assistant Professor of Architecture; Director of the Master in Architecture II Program

LANDSCAPE ARCHITECTURE

Anita Berrizbeitia
Professor of Landscape Architecture; Chair of the Department of Landscape Architecture

Gareth Doherty
Assistant Professor of Landscape Architecture; Senior Research Associate; Director of the Master in Landscape Architecture Programs

Chris Reed
Professor in Practice of Landscape Architecture; Codirector of the Master of Landscape Architecture in Urban Design Program

URBAN PLANNING AND DESIGN

Diane E. Davis
Charles Dyer Norton Professor of Regional Planning and Urbanism; Chair of the Department of Urban Planning and Design

Ann Forsyth
Professor of Urban Planning; Director of the Master in Urban Planning Program

Felipe Correa
Associate Professor of Urban Design; Director of the Master of Architecture in Urban Design Program; Codirector of the Master of Landscape Architecture in Urban Design Program

DESIGN STUDIES

John May
Assistant Professor of Architecture; Director of the Master in Design Studies Program

DESIGN ENGINEERING

Martin Bechthold
Kumagai Professor of Architectural Technology; Director of the Doctor of Design Studies Program; Codirector of the Master in Design Engineering Program

Woodward Yang
Gordon McKay Professor of Electrical Engineering and Computer Science at Harvard SEAS; Codirector of the Master in Design Engineering Program

DOCTORAL PROGRAMS

Erika Naginski
Robert P. Hubbard Professor of Architectural History; Director of Doctoral Programs

Martin Bechthold
Kumagai Professor of Architectural Technology; Director of the Doctor of Design Studies Program; Codirector of the Master in Design Engineering Program

RESEARCH

Antoine Picon
G. Ware Travelstead Professor of the History of Architecture and Technology; Director of Research

Academic Programs

ARCHITECTURE

Master in Architecture I (MArch I)

MArch I students come from a mix of backgrounds: some enter the GSD with a bachelor of arts in architecture, while others have majored in the sciences, liberal arts, or fine arts. The core program involves two years of required courses, followed by one year of option studios, elective classes, and a final thesis semester. Each semester, students take one studio course (or thesis) and typically three additional courses (or the equivalent of half-semester modular courses).

Master in Architecture I Advanced Placement (MArch I AP)

MArch I AP candidates typically hold a four-year bachelor of science in architecture from an intensive undergraduate program. AP students place out of the first year of the MArch I program and join the class in its third semester. While enrolled in second-year core studios, some AP students may be able to place out of one or more required courses and take electives instead. Students may be able to waive required courses if they can provide supporting evidence of successful completion of an equivalent course at another institution.

Master in Architecture II (MArch II)

MArch II candidates come to the GSD with a prior professional degree in architecture—at minimum, a five-year bachelor in architecture—and many have gained professional experience before returning to school. The MArch II is a two-year program, with students beginning at the option-studio level. In their first semester, MArch II students take a required proseminar. Afforded a high degree of flexibility, MArch II candidates are in the enviable position of designing a large portion of their own curriculum.

LANDSCAPE ARCHITECTURE

Master in Landscape Architecture I (MLA I)

The MLA I is a first professional degree for students with a four-year bachelor's degree in any field of study. MLA I students follow a core curriculum for their first four semesters, after which they are eligible to pursue option studios, thesis, and/or electives during their final year.

Master in Landscape Architecture I Advanced Placement (MLA I AP)

Those who hold an accredited professional degree in architecture, a preprofessional undergraduate degree in landscape architecture, or a preprofessional undergraduate degree in architecture with an exceptionally strong design portfolio qualify for advanced standing. These students place out of the first year of the program and join the class in its third semester. AP students take their required history courses in the second year.

Master in Landscape Architecture II (MLA II)

MLA II students enter the landscape architecture program holding an accredited four- or five-year bachelor in landscape architecture. Because many enter the program with professional experience, MLA II students can provide valuable insight into both academic and professional pursuits in landscape architecture. The MLA II program lasts four semesters, with one core studio and the option of enrolling in thesis instead of studio during the final semester.

URBAN DESIGN

Urban design is offered at the GSD as a four-semester, post-professional, studio-based program that combines intense design instruction, extensive applied research, and knowledge of urban history and theory. Master of Architecture in Urban Design (MAUD) and Master of Landscape Architecture in Urban Design (MLAUD) candidates share a strong core curriculum in their first semester, which includes the "Elements of Urban Design Core Studio," the "Urban Design Proseminar," and the "Cities by Design" lecture course. The remaining three semesters offer a more flexible academic path that allows students to take advanced studios and elective courses across all three GSD departments. The curricular structure encourages advanced individual and collective research and the possibility to develop an elective thesis.

Master of Architecture in Urban Design (MAUD)

The program leading to the MAUD is intended for individuals who have completed a five-year undergraduate professional program in architecture, an MArch, or equivalent. After a one-semester core studio, students may opt to pursue option studios, thesis, or coursework (with approval) during their remaining semesters.

Master of Landscape Architecture in Urban Design (MLAUD)

Jointly administered with the Department of Landscape Architecture, the program leading to the MLAUD is intended for individuals who have completed a five-year undergraduate professional degree in landscape architecture, an MLA, or equivalent. Students begin with the same one-semester core studio as MAUD candidates and may opt to pursue option studios, thesis, or coursework (with approval) during their remaining semesters.

URBAN PLANNING

The Master in Urban Planning (MUP) professional degree program is focused on the understanding, analysis, and influence of the variety of forces that shape the built environment and affect the quality of human experience. The program is rooted in four fundamental themes: sustainable development, international planning, social and critical concerns, and urban design. In the first year, students enroll in a two-semester core studio. During the second year, students may pursue option studios, thesis, or coursework (with approval). Students must choose at least one concentration area or design their own concentration in consultation with the program director.

Concentration Areas:
Environmental Planning
History and Theory
Housing and Neighborhood Development
International Planning
Real Estate and Urban Development
Transportation and Infrastructure
Urban Design
Urban Analytics

DESIGN STUDIES

Master in Design Studies (MDes)

The MDes is a post-professional, project- and research-based program that uses novel and alternative methodologies in a collaborative, immersive, and multimedia environment of students, researchers, scholars, and practitioners. Students customize a cross-disciplinary course of study with a high level of specialization in addressing contemporary practices of design and modes of production that transcend disciplinary boundaries. Students often contribute to work performed in GSD research labs and initiatives. MDes is a three-semester program with an option to split the final semester. Advanced-placement status may be granted on rare occasions.

Concentration Areas:

Art, Design, and the Public Domain (ADPD)

seeks creative and ambitious individuals from all backgrounds and academic disciplines with a keen interest in contemporary issues of urban, historical, aesthetic, and technological culture, and with a predilection for intervention, exhibition, and public work. Of particular importance are the practices that seek to engage with the public and social realm with a view to shaping and transforming human action and historical experience. ADPD engages in forms of spatial practice that are defining the new and moving boundaries of the design disciplines.

Critical Conservation (CC)

applies issues of culture, history, and identity to design and development, transcending such outdated dialectics as past-future, traditional-modern, and us-them. Unlike preservation programs that presume the permanence of architecture and use top-down regulation to reinforce existing power structures, CC extends beyond issues of age, history, and aesthetics to offer a framework of theory and research tools encompassing social, political, and cultural meaning to offer students an understanding of the tensions between progress and tradition, the issues of permanence and obsolescence, and underlying forces often masked by the union of ideologies, preservation, and politics.

Energy and Environments (EE) allows students to examine material and energy issues—broadly defined, from the molecular to the territorial—across disciplines and scales, expanding the discourse on sustainable design to a more ambitious and totalizing praxis of energy and environments. How designers might better characterize the exchanges and coupling of matter and energy across multiple spatial and temporal scales is central to the pedagogy necessary for a more thermodynamically cogent design practice in the 21st century.

History and Philosophy of Design (HPD) is a platform for inquiry into the disciplines of architecture, urbanism, and landscape architecture, and their aligned aesthetic, technological, and spatial practices. The program provides students the opportunity for historical and philosophical explorations into the social, cultural, technical, and political contexts of design, and is directed toward individuals for whom advanced study can serve as preparation for future work in pursuit of a PhD degree, practice, and design pedagogy, as well as careers in journalism, film and digital media, or design curation related to the built environment.

Real Estate and the Built Environment (REBE) places design within the crucible of finance, examining the ways each can add value to the other. As part of a design discourse, financial analyses—feasibility studies, economic models, and investment strategies—acquire added social, cultural, and aesthetic dimensions. Mirroring the experience many graduates encounter in practice, students explore how form can have an impact on investment and value.

Risk and Resilience (RR) sets out to support novel approaches to sociospatial planning through design. Design as a discipline provides cities, communities, and individuals with tools to effectively prepare for, cope with, and anticipate rapid change within the spatial, social, and economic vulnerabilities it produces. The program prepares students to identify, articulate, and propose preemptive forms of practice.

Technology (Tech) advances innovative methods for making and understanding form and technologically driven design through technological experimentation. Students pursue a broad spectrum of inquiries, including design computation, digital fabrication, robotics, and the exploration of responsive environments. Cutting across scales, students engage subjects from the level of a single artifact or building to landscapes and urban systems.

Urbanism, Landscape, Ecology (ULE) invites an examination of contemporary practices of design and modes of production as they inform and manifest urbanism. Students pursue topics related to contemporary urbanism, landscape, geography, or territory within the broader contexts of the global, social, and natural environment, where longstanding disciplinary divides between the urban and the ecological have given way to more fluid, polyvalent, and potentially more productive relations.

DESIGN ENGINEERING

Master in Design Engineering (MDE)
The MDE is a unique collaborative program between the GSD and the John A. Paulson School of Engineering and Applied Sciences (SEAS). As our world faces increasingly complex, often unpredictable dilemmas of consequence to human lives and environments—including rapid urbanization, ecological changes, and resource scarcity, and their negative impact on sociocultural dynamics—these and other problems demand innovative, multifaceted solutions that transcend disciplines and scales. By training a new generation of innovators who operate both creatively and analytically, think strategically, and collaborate broadly, the MDE program develops graduates capable of leading change and advancing novel, real-world solutions. The integrated fields of design and engineering are uniquely positioned to address the world's toughest challenges and this two-year program prepares the next generation of leaders to create transformative solutions that positively impact society.

In the first year, students take a year-long interdisciplinary design studio along with elective courses complemented by a series of public lectures and intimate discussions with prominent innovators, designers, and thought leaders. During the second year, students complete an independent design engineering project on a topic of their choice. The MDE pedagogical model is geared toward enabling synergies that emerge through the collaboration of the interdisciplinary cohort. The instruction further emphasizes collaborative problem solving by bridging the gaps between academic fields and practical, real-world stakeholders, and fosters a design intelligence that engages quantitative and qualitative thinking, combining computational, visual, experimental, strategic, and aesthetic methods.

DOCTORAL STUDIES

Doctor of Design (DDes)

The DDes program focuses on applied research and emphasizes the advancement of knowledge in the design disciplines for students who already hold master's degrees. The typical DDes investigation involves the construction of a series of theoretical hypotheses validated through research and experimentation. After one year of coursework, students prepare for and take a general examination on their research subject and begin to prepare a dissertation proposal to be reviewed by their faculty advisor and another professor who wills it on their dissertation committee. Upon passing their generals, second-year candidates may act as teaching fellows responsible for leading course sections, discussing reading assignments with students, and grading papers. In the third year, candidates finish their research and prepare their dissertation for defense before a committee of three to four faculty members from the GSD and often from other institutions from around the world.

Doctor of Philosophy (PhD)

The PhD program in architecture, landscape architecture, and urban planning is cogoverened by the GSD and the Graduate School of Arts and Sciences (GSAS). It is intended for those who wish to enter teaching and advanced research careers in the history and theory of architecture, architectural technology, landscape architecture, and urban form from antiquity to the present; or the analysis and development of buildings, cities, landscapes, and regions with an emphasis on social, economic, technological, ecological, and infrastructural systems.

The PhD recently announced a new track in architectural technology. Doctoral research undertaken in this area will have the aim of advancing the state of knowledge in green building, and will typically include issues related to computation and simulation, environmental concerns, and energy performance. In addition to a highly interdisciplinary curriculum that includes the theoretical and empirical approaches, especially history and philosophy of technology, the student will be associated with the Harvard Center for Green Buildings and Cities, which will provide the intellectual context for the research.

Faculty 2017–2018

Iñaki Ábalos
Professor in Residence of
Architecture

Nadir Abdessemed
Lecturer in Landscape
Architecture

Volkan Alkanoglu
Lecturer in Architecture

Simon Allford
Design Critic in Architecture

Stefano Andreani
Research Associate in
Architecture

Alex Anmahian
Lecturer in Architecture

Frank Apeseche
Lecturer in Architecture and
Urban Planning and Design

Steven Apfelbaum
Lecturer in Landscape
Architecture

Andrew Atwood
Design Critic in Architecture

Bridget Baines
Peter Louis Hornbeck
Design Critic in Landscape
Architecture

Sai Balakrishnan
Assistant Professor of Urban
Planning

Martin Bechthold
Kumagai Professor of
Architectural Technology

Pierre Bélanger
Associate Professor of
Landscape Architecture

Francesca Benedetto
Design Critic in Landscape
Architecture

Silvia Benedito
Associate Professor of
Landscape Architecture

Anita Berrizbeitia
Professor of Landscape
Architecture

Eve Blau
Adjunct Professor of the
History and Theory of Urban
Form and Design

Heather Boesch
Design Critic in Architecture

Jennifer Bonner
Assistant Professor of
Architecture

Montserrat Bonvehi Rosich
Lecturer in Landscape
Architecture

Neil Brenner
Professor of Urban Theory

Jeffry Burchard
Assistant Professor in
Practice of Architecture

Joan Busquets
Martin Bucksbaum Professor
in Practice of Urban Planning
and Design

Claire Cahan
Instructor in Architecture

Sean Canty
Design Critic in Architecture

Peter Carl
Visiting Professor in
Architecture

Jose Castillo
Lecturer in Urban Planning
and Design

Manabu Chiba
Design Critic in Landscape
Architecture

Danielle Choi
Assistant Professor of
Landscape Architecture

Bryan Chou
Instructor in Landscape
Architecture

Emanuel Christ
Design Critic in Architecture

Elizabeth Christoforetti
Design Critic in Architecture

Preston Scott Cohen
Gerald M. McCue Professor
in Architecture

Felipe Correa
Associate Professor of Urban
Design

Salmaan Craig
Lecturer in Environmental
Technology

Daniel D'Oca
Associate Professor in
Practice of Urban Planning

Dilip da Cunha
Lecturer in Urban Planning
and Design

Diane E. Davis
Charles Dyer Norton
Professor of Regional
Planning and Urbanism

Reinier de Graaf
Design Critic in Architecture

Eric de Broche des Combes
Lecturer in Landscape
Architecture

Odile Decq
Design Critic in Architecture

Timothy Dekker
Lecturer in Landscape
Architecture

Tomás dePaor
Design Critic in Architecture

Jill Desimini
Associate Professor of
Landscape Architecture

Gareth Doherty
Assistant Professor of
Landscape Architecture and
Senior Research Associate

Craig Douglas
Lecturer in Landscape
Architecture

Sonja Dümpelmann
Associate Professor of
Landscape Architecture

Edward Eigen
Associate Professor of
Architecture and Landscape
Architecture

Rosetta S. Elkin
Assistant Professor of
Landscape Architecture

Natalia Escobar Castrillón
Instructor in Architecture

Teman Evans
Lecturer in Architecture

Teran Evans
Lecturer in Architecture

Billie Faircloth
Lecturer in Architecture

Ann Forsyth
Professor of Urban Planning

Kristin Frederickson
Design Critic in Landscape
Architecture

Jenny French
Design Critic in Architecture

David Gamble
Lecturer in Urban Planning
and Design

Jeanne Gang
Design Critic in Architecture

Christoph Gantenbein
Design Critic in Architecture

Jose Luis Garcia
del Castillo y López
Instructor in Architecture

Kersten Geers
Design Critic in Architecture

Ana Gelabert-Sanchez
Design Critic in Urban
Planning and Design

Jose Gomez-Ibanez
Derek Bok Professor of
Urban Planning and Public
Policy

Stephen Gray
Assistant Professor of Urban
Design

Toni L. Griffin
Professor in Practice of
Urban Planning

Allan Hamilton
Lecturer in Urban Planning
and Design

Helen Han
Teaching Associate in
Architecture

Steven Handel
Visiting Professor in
Landscape Architecture

Nicolas Hannequin
Design Critic in Architecture

Ewa Harabasz
Lecturer in Architecture,
Landscape Architecture, and
Urban Planning and Design

Michael Haroz
Lecturer in Urban Planning
and Design

K. Michael Hays
Eliot Noyes Professor of
Architectural Theory

Christopher Herbert
Lecturer in Urban Planning
and Design

Jock Herron
Instructor in Architecture

Gary Hilderbrand
Professor in Practice of
Landscape Architecture

Chuck Hoberman
Pierce Anderson Lecturer in
Design Engineering

Andrew Holder
Assistant Professor of
Architecture

Eelco Hooftman
Peter Louis Hornbeck
Design Critic in Landscape
Architecture

Michael Hooper
Associate Professor of Urban
Planning

Hiromi Hosoya
Design Critic in Urban
Planning and Design

Eric Höweler
Associate Professor of
Architecture

Florian Idenburg
Associate Professor in
Practice of Architecture

Catherine Ingraham
Lecturer in Architecture

Toyo Ito
Design Critic in Architecture

Karen Janosky
Lecturer in Landscape
Architecture

Mark R. Johnson
Lecturer in Architecture

Sharon Johnston
Design Critic in Architecture

Sawako Kaijima
Assistant Professor of
Architecture

Hanif Kara
Professor in Practice of
Architectural Technology

Jerold S. Kayden
Frank Backus Williams
Professor of Urban Planning
and Design

Zhang Ke
Design Critic in Architecture

Jesse M. Keenan
Lecturer in Architecture

Jungyoon Kim
Design Critic in Landscape
Architecture

Mikyoung Kim
Design Critic in Landscape
Architecture

Niall Kirkwood
Professor of Landscape
Architecture and Technology

Arthur Kohn
Lecturer in Urban Planning
and Design

Rem Koolhaas
John Portman Professor in
Practice of Architecture

Zeina Koreitem
Design Critic in Architecture

Alex Krieger
Professor in Practice of
Urban Design

Seng Kuan
Lecturer in Architecture

Jeannette Kuo
Assistant Professor In
Practice

Grace La
Professor of Architecture

Christopher Lee
Associate Professor in
Practice of Urban Design

Mark Lee
Design Critic in Architecture

George L. Legendre
Associate Professor in
Practice of Architecture

Sergio Lopez-Pineiro
Lecturer in Landscape
Architecture

James Lord
Design Critic in Landscape
Architecture

Jon Lott
Assistant Professor of
Architecture

Andrea Love
Lecturer in Architecture

Greg Lynn
Design Critic in Architecture

Niklas Maak
Lecturer in Architecture

Ali Malkawi
Professor of Architectural
Technology

Michael Manfredi
Design Critic in Urban
Planning and Design

Edward Marchant
Lecturer in Urban Planning
and Design

Sébastien Marot
Lecturer in Architecture

Christopher Matthews
Lecturer in Landscape
Architecture

John May
Assistant Professor of
Architecture

Patrick McCafferty
Lecturer in Architecture

Alistair McIntosh
Lecturer in Landscape
Architecture

Rahul Mehrotra
Professor of Urban Design
and Planning

Frederick Merrill
Design Critic in Urban
Planning and Design

Panagiotis Michalatos
Lecturer in Architecture

Toru Mitani
Design Critic in Landscape
Architecture

Kiel Moe
Associate Professor of
Architecture and Energy

Jennifer Molinsky
Lecturer in Urban Planning
and Design

Rosalea Monacella
Design Critic in Landscape
Architecture

Rafael Moneo
Josep Lluis Sert Professor in
Architecture

Toshiko Mori
Robert P. Hubbard
Professor in the Practice of
Architecture

Mohsen Mostafavi
Dean and Alexander and
Victoria Wiley Professor of
Design

Farshid Moussavi
Professor in Practice of
Architecture

Mark Mulligan
Associate Professor in
Practice of Architecture

Arancha Muñoz-Criado
Aga Khan Design Critic in
Landscape Architecture

Carles Muro
Associate Professor of
Architecture

Erika Naginski
Robert P. Hubbard Professor
of Architectural History

Paul Nakazawa
Associate Professor in
Practice of Architecture

Anna Neimark
Design Critic in Architecture

Nicholas Nelson
Lecturer in Landscape
Architecture

Yusuke Obuchi
Lecturer in Architecture

Rok Oman
Design Critic in Architecture

Kayoko Ota
Lecturer in Architecture

Dwayne Oyler
Design Critic in Architecture

Megan Panzano
Assistant Professor of
Architecture

Yoonjin Park
Design Critic in Landscape
Architecture

Eric Parry
Design Critic in Architecture

Katharine Parsons
Lecturer in Landscape
Architecture

Richard Peiser
Michael D. Spear Professor
of Real Estate Development

Pablo Pérez-Ramos
Instructor in Landscape
Architecture

John Peterson
Lecturer in Architecture

Antoine Picon
G. Ware Travelstead
Professor of the History of
Architecture and Technology

Robert Gerard Pietrusko
Assistant Professor of
Landscape Architecture and
Architecture

Michael Piscitello
Teaching Associate in
Architecture

Andrew Plumb
Design Critic in Architecture

Chris Reed
Professor in Practice of
Landscape Architecture

William Reisz
Lecturer in Architecture

Eva Respini
Lecturer in Architecture

Peter Rowe
Raymond Garbe Professor
of Architecture and Urban
Design and Harvard
University Distinguished
Service Professor

David Rubin
Design Critic in Architecture

Thomas Ryan
Lecturer in Landscape
Architecture

Frederick Salvucci
Lecturer in Urban Planning
and Design

Holly Samuelson
Assistant Professor of
Architecture

Allen Sayegh
Associate Professor in
Practice of Architectural
Technology

Markus Schaefer
Design Critic in Urban
Planning and Design

Patrik Schumacher
Design Critic in Architecture

Martha Schwartz
Professor in Practice of
Landscape Architecture

Mack Scogin
Kajima Professor in Practice
of Architecture

Richard Sennett
Visiting Professor in Urban
Planning and Design

Andres Sevtsuk
Assistant Professor of Urban
Planning

Shohei Shigematsu
Design Critic in Architecture

Malkit Shoshan
Lecturer in Urban Planning
and Design

Robert Silman
Lecturer in Architecture

Enrique Silva
Lecturer in Urban Planning
and Design

Jorge Silvetti
Nelson Robinson Jr.
Professor of Architecture

Christine Smith
Robert C. and Marian K.
Weinberg Professor of
Architectural History

Susan Snyder
Lecturer in Architecture

Laura Solano
Associate Professor in
Practice of Landscape
Architecture

Ricardo Solar
Instructor in Architecture

Lily Song
Lecturer in Urban Planning
and Design

Matthew Soules
Visiting Associate Professor
in Architecture

Kathy Spiegelman
Design Critic in Urban
Planning and Design

Abby Spinak
Lecturer in Urban Planning
and Design

Oana Stanescu
Design Critic in Architecture

John R. Stilgoe
Robert and Lois Orchard
Professor in the History of
Landscape Development

James Stockard
Lecturer in Urban Planning
and Design

Clayton Strange
Design Critic in Urban
Planning and Design

Marina Tabassum
Design Critic in Architecture

Claudia Taborda
Lecturer in Landscape
Architecture

Belinda Tato
Design Critic in Architecture

George Thomas
Lecturer in Architecture

Raymond Torto
Lecturer in Urban Planning
and Design

Matthew Urbanski
Associate Professor in
Practice of Landscape
Architecture

David Van Severen
Design Critic in Architecture

Michael Van Valkenburgh
Charles Eliot Professor
in Practice of Landscape
Architecture

Felipe Vera
Lecturer in Urban Planning
and Design

Špela Videčnik
Design Critic in Architecture

Charles Waldheim
John E. Irving Professor of
Landscape Architecture

Bing Wang
Associate Professor in
Practice of Real Estate and
the Built Environment

Emily Waugh
Lecturer in Landscape
Architecture

Emily Wettstein
Lecturer in Landscape
Architecture

Amy Whitesides
Design Critic in Landscape
Architecture

Elizabeth Whittaker
Associate Professor in
Practice of Architecture

Andrew Witt
Assistant Professor in
Practice of Architecture

Krzysztof Wodiczko
Professor in Residence of
Art, Design, and the Public
Domain

Cameron Wu
Associate Professor of
Architecture

Jenny Wu
Design Critic in Architecture

Roderick Wyllie
Design Critic in Landscape
Architecture

Pei Zhu
Design Critic in Architecture

Donald Zizzi
Lecturer in Urban Planning
and Design

Students
2017–2018

MASTER IN ARCHITECTURE I (MARCH I)

Mena Wasti Ahmed
Kofi Akakpo
Chantine Akiyama
Rana Aksoy
Cari Alcombright
Miriam Alexandroff
Ahmad Altahhan
Alice Armstrong
Emily Ashby
Rekha Auguste-Nelson
Peiying Ban
Esther Mira Bang
Sasha Bears
Willem Bogardus
Sandra Bonito
Calvin Boyd
Benjamin Bromberg Gaber
Jeffrey Burgess
Charles Burke
Nathan Buttel
Biru Cao
Antonio Casalduc
Stanislas Chaillou
Caroline Chao
Ching Him Chee
Peitong Chen
Shiyang Chen
Joanne Cheung
Sum In Sarah Cheung
Jeremy Chevis-Benson
Chieh Chih Chiang
Haanbee Choi
Seo Won Choi
Sukhwan Choi
Kevin Chong
Kai-hong Chu
Gina Ciancone
Taylor Cook
Amanda Darmosaputro
Elizabeth De Angelis
Cynthia Deng
Zixuan Deng
Marc Dessauvage
Claire Djang
Katherine Du
Stella Dwifaradewi
Panharith Ean
Elif Erez
Valeria Fantozzi
Zhixing Wanwan Fei
Martin Fernández
Ariel Flotte
Christopher Gallegos
Ya Gao
Angeliki Giannisi
Vladimir Gintoff
Nadege Giraudet
Marianna Gonzalez
Brayton Gregory
Jonathan Gregurick
Chris Grenga

Aria Griffin
Ian Grohsgal
Xiangyu Guo
Yuqiao Guo
Fabiola Guzman Rivera
Taylor Halamka
Myo Han
Rebecca Han
Won Jeong Han
Adrian Harrison
Douglas Harsevoort
Kenneth Hasegawa
Benjamin Hayes
Matthew Hayes
Chen He
Isa He
Christina Hefferan
Ashley Hickman
Konrad Holtsmark
Kira Horie
Hannah Hoyt
De Qian Huang
Jingyuan Huang
Shihao Huang
Yousef Hussein
Jihoon Hyun
Tomotsugu Ishida
Golnoush Jalali
Suthata Jiranuntarat
Young Eun Ju
Jia Jung
Anna Kaertner
Nyeonggeun Kang
Sarah Kantrowitz
Lina Karain Silwani
Danielle Kasner
Evan Kettler
Aryan Khalighy
Haram Kim
Mingyu Kim
Minyong Kim
Shaina Kim
Yuna Kim
Wyatt Komarin
Lindsey Krug
Ho In Kuong
Daniel Kwon
Hyojin Kwon
Hoi Ying Lam
Peteris Lazovskis
Brian Bo Ying Lee
Dohyun Lee
Ezra Lee
Jungwoo Lee
Madeline Eggink Lenaburg
Ethan Levine
Naomi Levine
Ruize Li
Jessica Lim
Keunyoung Lim
Shao Lun Lin
David Ling
Qinrong Liu
Yaxuan Liu
Anna Kalliopi Louloudis
Kaoru Lovett
Fan Lu
Kun Luo
Yan Ma
Radu-Remus Macovei
Caleb Marhoover
Glen Marquardt

Adam Maserow
Lauren Matrka
Naureen Mazumdar
Grace McEniry
Thomas McMurtrie
Marcus Mello
Steven Meyer
Farhad Mirza
Milos Mladenovic
Matthew Moffitt
Chit Yan Paul Mok
Yina Moore
Adam Moqrane
Khorshid Naderi-Azad
Paris Nelson
Andrew Ngure
Bryant Nguyen
Matthew Okazaki
Donald O'Keefe
Evan Orf
Bryan Ortega-Welch
Meric Ozgen
Mark Pantano
Andy Park
Francesca Perone
Yen Shan Phoaw
David Pilz
Luisa Piñeros Sánchez
Ethan Poh
Philip Poon
Alexander Searle Porter
Irene Preciado Arango
Luisa Respondek
Jihyun Ro
Cara Roberts
Julia Roberts
Matthew Rosen
Lane Raffaldini Rubin
Xianming Sang
Thomas Schaperkotter
Anne Schneider
Julia Schubach
Jennifer Shen
Adam Sherman
Gio Shin
Veronica Smith
David Solomon
Humbi Song
Anne Stack
Morgan Starkey
Isabel Strauss
Adam Strobel
Mahfuz Sultan
Xiaotang Tang
Noelle Tay
Lee Tammy Teng
Bijan Thornycroft
Tianze Tong
Y-Nhi Tran
Ho Cheung Tsui
Omar Valentin
Samantha Vasseur
Isabelle Verwaay
Khoa Vu
Son Vu
John Yau Chung Wang
Taylor MacKenzie Wasson
Madelyn Willey
Dixi Wu
Emerald Hanguang Wu
Siyuan Xi
Jialiang Xiang

Shaina Yang
Yuhou Yang
Jung Chan Yee
Tsun Hong Yeung
Carolyn Yi
Euipoom Estelle Yoon
Steven Young
Jessica Yuan
Hyunsuk Yun
Ailing Zhang
George Zhang
Huopu Zhang
Yiran Zhang
Sheng Zhao
Sylvia Zhao
Pengpeng Zheng
Eric Zuckerman
Brian Zug

MASTER IN ARCHITECTURE I AP (MARCH I AP)

William Adams
Andrew Bako
Aleksis Bertoni
Zoey Cai
Andres Camacho
Jing Chang
Beining Chen
Karen Duan
Christina Graydon
Jun Ho Han
Wilson Harkhono
Tsz Hung Hu
I-Yang Huang
Meng Jiang
Han Jin
Yungi Jung
Yeonmoon Kim
Yoonjin Kim
Joshua Kuhr
Zhixin Lin
Benoit Maranda
Zi Meng
Ian Miley
Alfred Chun Hin Pun
Yue Shao
Bradley Silling
Igsung So
Alexandru Vilcu
Mark Wang
Han Cheol Yi
Long Chuan James Zhang
Shaowen Zhang
Yubai Zhou

MASTER IN ARCHITECTURE II (MARCH II)

Nada AlQallaf
Danielle Aspitz
Tam Banh
Yotam Ben Hur
Jingyi Bi
Astrid Cam Aguinaga
Xinyu Cao
James Carrico
Gloria Chang
Sichuan Chen
Ningxin Cheng

Phakaphol Chinburi
Ece Comert
Aimilios Davlantis Lo
Fang Fan
Wei-Che Fu
Matthew Gehm
Anastasios Giannakopoulos
Beijia Gu
Jin Guo
Benjamin Hait
Xiao Han
Sungjoon Hong
Ran Huo
Sophie Juneau
Danielle Kemble
Jinwoo Kim
Julia Kim
Woo-Young Kim
Choonghyo Lee
Shen Li
Xinyun Li
Kai Liao
Elias Logan
Vy Mai
Eduardo Martinez-Mediero
    Rubio
Yumiko Matsubara
Michael Matthews
Hayden Minick
Liana Nourafshan
Jack Oliva-Rendler
Poap Panusittikorn
Juhee Park
Sampath Pediredla
Benjamin Pennell
Meaghan Pohl
Benjamin Pollak
Farnoosh Rafaie
Arlyn Ramirez-Diaz
Francisco Ramos
Dylan Rupar
Daniel Saenz
Huma Sahin
Juan Sala
Noam Saragosti
Stefan Sauter
Oorvi Sharma
Xichen Sheng
Poyao Shih
Sejung Song
Scarlet Ziwei Song
Alexandros Spentzaris
Yang Chun Su
Justin Tan
Şevki Topçu
Julio Torres Santana
Nicolas Turchi
Ya-shin Tzeng
Aime Vailes-Macarie
Cassidy Viser
John David Wagner
Chi-Hsuan Wang
Claire Watson
Zachary Weimer
Wei Xiao
Sonny Meng Qi Xu
Sol Yoon
Cheng Zeng
Jianing Zhang
Kun Zhang
Xi Zhang

Meng Zhao
Xin Zheng

MASTER IN
LANDSCAPE
ARCHITECTURE I
(MLA I)

Michael Ahn
Jungrok An
Jonathan Andrews
Dylan Anslow
Madeleine Aronson
Naoko Asano
Michelle Benoit
Xiao He Bi
Carson Booth
Yoni Angelo Carnice
Colin Chadderton
Hannah Chako
Jiawen Chen
Joan Chen
Su-Yeon Choi
Kelly Clifford
Kira Clingen
Helena Cohen
Emmanuel Coloma
Sydney Conaway
Anna Curtis-Heald
Qiaoqi Dai
Warwin Davis
Sarah Diamond
Yuru Ding
Alexandra Distefano
Emily Drury
Sophie Elias
Gideon Finck
Carson Fisk-Vittori
Isabella Frontado
Kara Gadecki
Ana Garcia
Samuel Gilbert
Melissa Green
Benjamin Hackenberger
Ernest Haines
Mark Heller
Caroline Hickey
Emily Hicks
Aaron Hill
Dana Hills
Zoe Holland
Jenjira Holmes
Xingyue Huang
Cecilia Huber
Jiyun Jeong
Diana Jih
Edyth Jostol
Jonathan Kuhr
Sirinya Laochinda
Yanick Lay
Charlotte Leib
Annie Liang
Christopher Liao
Matthew Liebel
Danica Liongson
Jiacheng Liu
Siyu Liu
Zeqi Liu
Ann Lynch
Nicholas Lynch
Hannah Lyons-Galante
Alison Malouf

Claire Malone Matson
McKenna Mitchell
Nathalie Mitchell
Isabel Preciado
Andrés Quinche
Estello-Cisdre Raganit
Eleanor Rochman
Ann Salerno
Elizabeth Savrann
Davi Parente Schoen
Sophia Sennett
Mengfan Sha
Evangeline Sheridan
Ciara Stein
Melody Stein
Zixuan Tai
Jena Tegeler
Connie Trinh
Hannah Van der Eb
Andreea Vasile Hoxha
Marisa Villarreal
Parawee Wachirabuntoon
Amanda Walker
Na Wang
Yifan Wang
Yujue Wang
Zhaodi Wang
Timothy Webster
Ahran Won
Matthew Wong
Yue Wu
Siwen Xie
Nan Yang
George Zhang
Haoyu Zhao
Xin Zhong
Xinyi Zhou

MASTER IN
LANDSCAPE
ARCHITECTURE I AP
(MLA I AP)

Mena Wasti Ahmed
Nada AlQallaf
Aiysha Alsane
Tam Banh
Camila Barbosa
Daniel Berdichevsky
Isabel Brostella
Shimin Cao
Meredith Chavez
Anne Chen
Lingya Chen
Kuzina Cheng
Nai Tzu Cheng
Oi Wai Charity Cheung
Mariel Collard
Carlos Espinoza
Luis Flores
Mengting Ge
Juan Grisales
Ran Gu
Kevin Jin He
Christin Hu
Siyu Jiang
Eunsu Kim
Nam Jung Kim
Andy Lee
Juhyuk Lee
Rose Lee
Sang Yoon Lee

Sunmee Lee
Wan Fung Lee
Hanying Li
Jianshuang Li
Mengfei Li
Ting Liang
Varat Limwibul
Maria De La Luz
    Lobos Martinez
Yanni Ma
Chenxiang Meng
Monica Miyagusuku
Melissa Naranjo
Kai Chi Ng
Stacy Passmore
Nadyeli Quiroz
Stefano Romagnoli
Lane Raffaldini Rubin
Greta Ruedisueli
Zephaniah Ruggles
Rhea Shah
Hye Rim Shin
Joshua Stevens
Amanda Ton
Zishen Wen
Ting Fung Wong
Shing Hin Bryan Woo
Cho-Hao Wu
Leilei Wu
Sonny Meng Qi Xu
Yiting Xi
Qiao Xu
Liu Yang
Zhenyu Yang
Ziwei Ye
Seok Min Yeo
Chengzhang Zhang
Tongtong Zhang
Xi Zhang
Xiaowei Zhang
Xiaoyuan Zhang
Chuanying Zheng

MASTER IN
LANDSCAPE
ARCHITECTURE II
(MLA II)

William Baumgardner
Zheng Cong
Hannah Cusick
Yuqing Dai
Xiaoyin Kuang
Peilin Li
Yinan Liu
Matthew Macchietto
Paul Fletcher Phillips
Peeraphol Sangthongjai
Xiwei Shen
Isaac Stein
Alfred Sus
Jianing Tao
Izgi Uygur
Mengze Xu
Boxiang Yu
Hui Yuan
Bailun Zhang
Chengzhe Zhang
Junbo Zhang

MASTER OF ARCHITECTURE IN URBAN DESIGN (MAUD)

Samuel Adkisson
Jannet Arevalo
Diane Athaide
Camila Barbosa
Foteini Bouliari
Maria Veronica
    Cardenas Vignes
Meredith Chavez
Difei Chen
Fengqian Chen
Hyungjoo Choi
Yoeun Chung
John Crowley
Aránzazu de Ariño Bello
Gustavo Diaz Paz
Maxime Faure
Rose Florian Rodriguez
Juan Pablo Fuentes
Chang Gao
Sebastián Gaviria Gómez
Maitao Guo
Camila Gutiérrez Plata
Olivia Hansberg
Tianhui Hou
Yunyan Hu
Yang Huang
Natalia Kagkou
Hiroki Kawashima
Theodore Kofman
Tatum Lau
Chen Li
Xu Li
Ting Liang
Xinwen Liu
Minzi Long
Lizbeth Lopez Lopez
Chenghao Lyu
Siwen Ma
Karen Mata
Robert Meyerson
Pojiang Nie
Mariana Paisana
Zhuo Pang
Yuzhou Peng
Maria Peroni
Loyiso Qaqane
Xin Qian
Jinpeng Qiao
Zhengyu Qin
Loren Rapport
Billy Schaefer
Sudeshna Sen
Hyeji Sheen
Evan Shieh
Ashutosh Singhal
Maoran Sun
Pengcheng Sun
Shining Sun
Luke Tan
Konstantina Tzemou
Shenting Wang
Xiyao Wang
Steven Ward
Hayden White
Carla Wijaya
Chaoran Wu
Weijia Wu

Eileen Xie
Zhile Xie
Zhou Xu
Zeming Yang
Xiaoyan Yin
Alexander Yuen
Miao Zhang
Ping Zhang
Renyi Zhang
Xiao Zhang
Yuchuan Zhang
Chenglong Zhao
Shuo Zhao
Xueyao Zhou
Yasong Zhou
Eduardo Zizumbo Colunga

MASTER OF LANDSCAPE ARCHITECTURE IN URBAN DESIGN (MLAUD)

Ruanlanming Du
Ruocan Fu
Linyu Liu
Charles Smith
Abbey Wallace
Boxiang Yu
Zhangkan Zhou

MASTER IN URBAN PLANNING (MUP)

Muniba Ahmad
Andrew Alesbury
Syed Ali
Carolyn Angius
Mariah Barber
Maura Barry-Garland
Daniel Becerra
Mark Bennett
Kimberly Bernardin
Roody Botros
Colleen Brady
Juan Caicedo
Astrid Cam Aguinaga
Paul Caporaso
Anna Carlsson
Cesar Castro
Gina Ciancone
Carissa Connelly
Matthew Coogan
Alyssa Curran
Cynthia Deng
Erick Diaz
McKayla Dunfey
Ross Eisenberg
Sidra Fatima
Lena Ferguson
José Carlos Fernández Salas
Amy Friedlander
Matthew Genova
Aubrey Germ
Kimberly Geronimo
Angela Gile
Vladimir Gintoff
Kathryn Gourley
Solomon Green-Eames
Mark Heller
Natasha Hicks

Alice Hintermann
Simone Hodgson
Takafumi Inoue
Asad Jan
Neha Joseph
Jia Jung
Jennifer Kaplan
Miriam Keller
James Kendall
Edward Lamson
Willow Latham
Caroline Lauer
Andy Lee
Malika Leiper
Yinan Li
Jessica Liss
Laura Lopez Cardenas
Radu-Remus Macovei
Eleni Macrakis
Emily Marsh
Catherine Mccandless
Marcus Mello
Amirah Ndam Njoya
Jonathan Ngige
Eamon O'Connor
Kyle Ofori
Daniel Padilla
Jeanette Pantoja
Nerali Patel
Emma Pattiz
Yakima Pena Perez
Mariana Pereira Guimarães
Yuki Perry
Casey Peterson
Emma Phillips
Joshua Pi
Leah Pickett
Jack Popper
Alifa Putri
Angelica Quicksey
Andrés Quinche
Aaron Ramirez
Gabriel Ramos
Alexander Rawding
Juan Reynoso
Alexander Rogala
Rian Rooney
Justin Rose
Chandra Rouse
Benjamin Sadkowski
Jillian Schmidt
Davi Parente Schoen
Matthew Schreiber
Sanjay Seth
Jorge Silva
Megan Slavish
Rodrigo Solé
Ciara Stein
Melanie Stern
Armando Sullivan
Claire Summers
Firas Suqi
Shanasia Sylman
Mayu Takeda
Donald Taylor-Patterson
Malia Teske
Stefan Trevisan
Finn Vigeland
Hung Vo
Chanel Williams
Katherine Wolf

MASTER IN DESIGN STUDIES, ART, DESIGN, AND THE PUBLIC DOMAIN (MDES ADPD)

Kathryn Abarbanel
Francisco Alarcon
Aránzazu de Ariño Bello
Inés Benitez
Sahej Bhatia
Isabella Frontado
Ming Guo
Jungmoon Ham
Keith Hartwig
Hanna Kim
Stella Kim
Kiyoto Koseki
Je Sung Lee
Shuang Liang
Eric Moed
Mallory Nezam
Ana Luiza Padilha Addor
Sunyoung Park
Penelope Phylactopoulos
Andrew Connor Scheinman
Malinda Seu
Daniel Shieh
Daniel Tompkins
Alicia Valencia
Mengfei Wang
Rudy Weissenberg
Natthida Wiwatwicha
Diana Zwetzich-Schachter

MASTER IN DESIGN STUDIES, CRITICAL CONSERVATION (MDES CC)

Luisa Brando Laserna
Yonghui Chen
Francisco Colom Jover
Haoming Fu
Carrie Gammell
Yanan He
Esesua Ikpefan
Isaac Kornblatt-Stier
Yiyi Liang
Xiaoxiao Liu
Prathima Muniyappa
Jacqueline Palavicino
Longyun Ren
Alok Shrivastava
Enrique Aureng Silva
Ranjani Srinivasan
Betzabe Valdés López
Zhoutong Wang
Yanhan Zhang

MASTER IN DESIGN STUDIES, ENERGY AND ENVIRONMENTS (MDES EE)

Seung-Hyeok Bae
Anteo Boschi
Pamela Cabrera
Kenner Carmody
Esteban Estrella Guillén

Margaret George
Iain Gordon
Jung Min Han
Tai-Hsin Hsu
Ching Che Huang
Anqi Huo
Aurora Jensen
Ao Li
Wenting Li
Peter Osborne
Zlatan Sehovic
Christine Voehringer
Xiaoran Wang
Xiaoshi Wang
Bohan Zhang

MASTER IN DESIGN STUDIES, HISTORY AND PHILOSOPHY OF DESIGN (MDES HPD)

Ryan Beitz
Carolyn Bly
Charles Burke
Zach Crocker
Elif Erez
Juan Garcia Mosqueda
Savina Hawkins
Charlotte Leib
Cody Pan
Yara Saqfalhait
Antonios Thodis
Samantha Vasseur

MASTER IN DESIGN STUDIES, REAL ESTATE AND THE BUILT ENVIRONMENT (MDES REBE)

Dalia Al Derzi
Patricia Alvarez
Jonathan Andrews
Georgios Avramides
Megan Berry
Luc Carpinelli
Stephanie Choe
Carissa Connelly
Andrey Drozdov
Romayh El Jurdi
Jordan Girard
Augustinas Indrasius
Ankita Jain
Jeremy James
Young Jee Jang
Andrew Kern
Jung Joon Kim
John Lee
Jong Hwa Lee
Siyu Long
Roger Mroczek
Rishad Netarwala
Van-Tuong Nguyen
Varzan Patel
Samuel Pun
Alaa Rafaat Abdelrazik
Utkarsh Rawal
Ana Daniela Rodriguez
Ambieca Saha
Yi Sha

Naman Srivastava
Yuanqi Sun
Masamichi Ueta
Betty Vuong
Andrew Wade
Yifan Wang
Zini Wang
Carlotta Weller
Wei Xiao
Yuanhui Xin
Hong Yang
Boxuan Zhang
Hao Zhang
Jibing Zhang
Nan Zhou
Mamun Uz Zoha

MASTER IN DESIGN STUDIES, RISK AND RESILIENCE (MDES RR)

Cesar Castro
Gloria Chang
Mariel Collard
Silvia Danielak
Michael de St Aubin
Natasha Hicks
Pablo Izaga Gonzalez
Yan Liu
Lizbeth Lopez Lopez
Samuel Matthew
Charles Newman
Susanna Pho
Maclean Sarbah
Hazal Seval
Isaac Stein
Natalie Wang
Naomi Woods

MASTER IN DESIGN STUDIES, TECHNOLOGY (MDES TECH)

Sulaiman Alothman
Difei Chen
Peitong Chen
Honghao Deng
Jingchen Gao
Olga Geletina
Christina Glover
Nicolas Hogan
Hyeon Ji Im
Mari Jo
Francisco Jung
Andrew Kim
Haeyoung Kim
Yonghwan Kim
Jiabao Li
Lubin Liu
James Moffet III
Yuan Mu
Nicolas Oueijan
Xiaobi Pan
Elissavet Pertigkiozoglou
Nathan Peters
Jasmine Roberts
Styliani Rossikopoulou Pappa
Johae Song
Sejung Song

Max Vanatta
Math Whittaker
Wenying Wu
Diana Yan
HyeJi Yang
Junran Yang
Xiao Zhang

MASTER IN DESIGN STUDIES, URBANISM, LANDSCAPE, AND ECOLOGY (MDES ULE)

Jungrok An
Xin Chen
Rajji Desai
Pablo Escudero
Juan Grisales
Pol Fité Matamoros
Siyang Jing
Natalia Kagkou
Danica Liongson
Samuel Maddox
Eduardo Pelaez
Nadyeli Quiroz
Margaret Tsang
Sofia Xanthakou
Erin Yook
Adelle York

MASTER IN DESIGN ENGINEERING (MDE)

Nicole Adler
Zeerak Ahmed
Nicole Bakker
Jeronimo Beccar Varela
Jeremy Burke
Humberto Ceballos
Ngoc Doan
Jenny Fan
Kun Fan
Ramon Gras Aloma
Chao Gu
Saif Haobsh
Brian Ho
Vivek Hv
Anesta Iwan
Julie Loiland
Chien-Min Lu
Erin McLean
Arjun Menon
Terra Moran
Santiago Mota
Neeti Nayak
Saad Rajan
Michael Raspuzzi
Carla Saad
Julian Siegelmann
Kenneth So
Katherine Spies
Vish Srivastava
Karen Su
Janet Sung
Kiran Wattamwar

DOCTOR OF DESIGN (DDES)

Spyridon Ampanavos
Nicole Beattie
Ignacio Cardona
Yujiao Chen
Michael Chieffalo
Somayeh Chitchian
Daniel Daou
Ali Fard
Wendy Fok
Yun Fu
Jose Luis Garcia del Castillo y López
Mariano Gomez-Luque
Boya Guo
Saira Hashmi
Yujie Hong
Vaughn Horn
Xiaokai Huang
Kristen Hunter
Daniel Ibañez
Aleksandra Jaeschke
Ghazal Jafari
Seung Kyum Kim
Jingping Liu
Miguel López Meléndez
Yingying Lu
Mojdeh Sadat Mahdavi Moghaddam
Jeffrey Nesbit
Xuanyi Nie
Sarah Norman
Pablo Pérez-Ramos
Carolina San Miguel
Andreina Seijas
Julia Smachylo
Jihoon Song
Lara Tomholt
Guy Trangos
Juan Pablo Ugarte
Hanne van den Berg
Bing Wang
Liang Wang
Jung Hyun Woo
Longfeng Wu
Dingliang Yang
Arta Yazdanseta
Nari Yoon
Jeongmin Yu
Jingyi Zhang

DOCTOR OF PHILOSOPHY (PHD)

Salma Abouelhossein
Matthew Allen
Amin Alsaden
Maria Atuesta
Katarzyna Balug
Aleksandr Bierig
Brett Michael Culbert
Taylor Davey
John Dean Davis
Phillip Denny
Igor Ekstajn
Samaa Elimam
Tamer Elshayal
Natalia Escobar Castrillón
Brandon Finn

Matthew Gin
Lisa Haber-Thomson
Thomas Hill
Jacobé Huet
Hannah Kaemmer
Diana Louise Lempel
Manuel Lopez Segura
Morgan Ng
Bryan Norwood
Sabrina Osmany
Sun Min Melany Park
Marianne Potvin
Etien Santiago
Peter Sealy
Christina Shivers
Justin Stern
Adam Tanaka
Gideon Unkeless
Rodanthi Vardouli|
Dimitra Vogiatzaki
Eldra Walker
Angela Wheeler
Wei Zhang

Staff

Whitney Airgood-Obrycki
Senior Research Analyst,
Joint Center for Housing
Studies

Afshaan Alter Burtram
Program Coordinator,
Architecture

Joseph Amato
Facilities Operations
Assistant, Building Services

Kathleen Anderson
Staff Assistant, Executive
Education and International
Programs

Alla Armstrong
Financial Manager, Academic
Finance

John Aslanian
Director of Recruitment,
Student Affairs, and Career
Development

Lauren Baccus
Assistant Dean of Human
Resources

Kermit Baker
Program Director for
Remodeling Studies, Joint
Center for Housing Studies

Pamela Baldwin
Assistant Dean for Faculty
Affairs

Lauren Beath
Payroll Coordinator, Finance
Office

Preston Belton
Web Developer, Computer
Resources

Jenna Bjorkman
Communications Specialist,
Harvard Center for Green
Buildings and Cities

Susan Boland-Kourdov
Web Administrator,
Computer Resources

Dan Borelli
Director of Exhibitions,
Communications

Renée Browne
Accounting Assistant,
Academic Finance

Kevin Cahill
Director of Facilities
Management, Building
Services

Bonnie Campbell
Executive Assistant,
Development and Alumni
Relations

James Chaknis
Communications and
Outreach Coordinator, Joint
Center for Housing Studies

Joseph Chart
Senior Major Gift Officer,
Development

Peter Christiansen
Staff Assistant, Computer
Resources

Lindsey Cimochowski
Associate Director of
Development Strategies and
Donor Services

Carra Clisby
Assistant Director
for Development
Communications and Donor
Relations

Satomi Collins
Assistant Director for
Global Programs, Web
and Marketing, Executive
Education

Sean Conlon
Registrar, Student Services

Anne Cowie
Senior Major Gift Officer,
Development

Kathryn Cox
Controller, Finance Office

Anne Creamer
Coordinator, Career Services

Travis Dagenais
Assistant Director of
Communications

Anna Devine
Communications Specialist,
Communications

Sarah Dickinson
Research Support Services
Librarian

Kerry Donahue
Associate Director of
Communications & External
Relations, Joint Center for
Housing Studies

Stephen Ervin
Assistant Dean for
Information Technology,
Computer Resources

Julia Falkoff
Special Projects Analyst,
Academic Services

Alaina Fernandes
Executive Coordinator,
Landscape Architecture and
Urban Planning and Design

Ernesto Fernandez
Development Information
Systems Manager

Jeffrey Fitton
Outreach and Events
Manager, Harvard Center for
Green Buildings and Cities

Angela Flynn
Center and Finance
Coordinator, Joint Center for
Housing Studies

Rena Fonseca
Director of Executive
Education and International
Programs

Nicole Freeman
Senior Major Gift Officer,
Development

Riordan Frost
Associate Research Analyst,
Joint Center for Housing
Studies

Jennifer Gala
Associate Director of
Executive Education and
International Programs

Heather Gallagher
Financial Associate, Finance
Office

Erica George
Coordinator of Student
Activities and Outreach,
Student Services

Keith Gnoza
Director of Financial
Assistance; Assistant
Director of Student Services

Mark Goble
Chief Financial Officer

Meryl Golden
Director of Career Services,
Student Services

Santiago Gomez
Admissions Assistant,
Student Services

Hal Gould
Manager of User Services,
Computer Resources

Lindsey Grant
Assistant Director of Events
and Special Projects,
Development

Arin Gregorian
Financial Associate,
Academic Finance

Linda Gregory
Staff Assistant,
Frances Loeb Library

Gail Gustafson
Director of Admissions and
Student Learning Resources
Manager, Student Services

Mark Hagen
Windows System
Administrator, Computer
Resources

Tessalina Halpern
Staff Assistant, Student
Services

Ryanne Hammerl
Staff Assistant, Student
Services

Christopher Hansen
Digital Fabrication Technical
Specialist, Fabrication Lab

Barry Harper
Staff Assistant, Building
Services

Christopher Herbert
Managing Director, Joint
Center for Housing Studies

Alexander Hermann
Associate Research Analyst,
Joint Center for Housing
Studies

Johann Hinds
Help Desk Technician,
Computer Resources

Ryan Hodgson
Academic Appointment
and Payroll Coordinator,
Academic Services

Timothy Hoffman
Faculty Planning
Administrator, Academic
Affairs

Taylor Horner
Department Administrator,
Architecture

Sarah Hutchinson
Program Coordinator,
Landscape Architecture and
Urban Planning and Design

Estefania Ibáñez Moreno
Executive Assistant,
Academic Services

Ryan Jacob
Academic Affairs
Administrator

Maggie Janik
Multimedia Producer,
Communications

William Jenkins
Facilities Operations
Supervisor

Paige Johnston
Public Programs Manager,
Communications

Beth Kass
Associate Director,
Development and Alumni
Communications

Johanna Kasubowski Abe
Materials and Media
Collections Librarian,
Frances Loeb Library

Jeffrey Klug
Director, Design Discovery

Nathaniel Koven
Program Manager, Executive
Education and International
Programs

Ardys Kozbial
Library Manager,
Frances Loeb Library

Beth Kramer
Associate Dean for
Development and Alumni
Relations

Elizabeth La Jeunesse
Senior Research Analyst,
Joint Center for Housing
Studies

Mary Lancaster
Associate Director for
Finance and Administration,
Joint Center for Housing
Studies

Ashley Lang
Associate Director of
Academic Programs
Administration

Amy Langridge
Finance Manager, Executive
Education

Pamela Larsen
Events Coordinator,
Development

Kevin Lau
Head of Instructional
Technology Group and
Library, Frances Loeb Library

Seah Lee
Recruitment Assistant,
Student Services

Burton LeGeyt
Digital Fabrication Technical
Specialist and Shop
Supervisor, Fabrication Lab

David Luberoff
Deputy Director, Joint Center
for Housing Studies

Anna Lyman
Director of External
Administration, Dean's Office

Robert Marino
Finance and Grant Manager,
Harvard Center for Green
Buildings and Cities

Edwin Martinez
Help Desk Technician,
Computer Resources

Kenneth Masse
Facilities Operations
Coordinator, Building
Services

Anne Mathew
Director of Research
Administration

Daniel McCue
Senior Research Associate,
Joint Center for Housing
Studies

Eiji Miura
Publications Coordinator,
Joint Center for Housing
Studies

Jennifer Molinsky
Senior Research Associate,
Joint Center for Housing
Studies

Margaret Moore De Chicojay
Programs Administrator,
Advanced Studies Program

Janina Mueller
GIS and Data Librarian,
Frances Loeb Library

Janessa Mulepati
Program Coordinator, Master
in Design Engineering,
Advanced Studies Program

Michelle Muliro
Human Resources and
Payroll Coordinator

Geri Nederhoff
Director of Admissions
and Diversity Recruitment
Manager, Student Services

Caroline Newton
Director of Internal
Administration, Dean's Office

Ketevan Ninua
Staff Assistant, Development

Alexander Nosnik
Financial Analyst, Finance
Office

Lauren O'Brien
Faculty Affairs Coordinator,
Academic Affairs

Christine O'Brien
Financial Associate,
Communications

Trevor O'Brien
Manager of Building Services

Barbara Perlo
Program Manager, Executive
Education

John Peterson
Curator, Loeb Fellowship

Jackie Piracini
Assistant Dean for Academic
Services

Lisa Plosker
Associate Director of Human
Resources

David Brad Quigley
Director of Alumni Relations
and Annual Giving

Nony Rai
Coordinator, Research
Administration

Pilar Raynor Jordan
Financial Associate,
Academic Finance

Alix Reiskind
Digital Initiatives Librarian,
Frances Loeb Library

Shannon Rieger
Associate Research Analyst,
Joint Center for Housing
Studies

Patricia Roberts
Executive Dean

Meghan Sandberg
Publications Coordinator,
Communications

Jocelyn Sanders
Senior Major Gift Officer,
Development

Madelin Santana
Assistant Director for
Global Programs, Executive
Education

Ronee Saroff
Assistant Director of Digital
Content and Strategy,
Communications

Jennifer Sigler
Editor in Chief, Publications
and *Harvard Design
Magazine*, Communications

James Skypeck
Development Coordinator

Robin Slavin
Career Services Counselor,
Student Services

Matthew Smith
Media Services Manager,
Computer Resources

Laura Snowdon
Dean of Students and Assistant
Dean for Enrollment Services

Jonathan Spader
Senior Research Associate,
Joint Center for Housing
Studies

Susan Spaulding
Building Services
Coordinator

Kelly Sprouse
Staff Assistant, Development
and Alumni Relations

Ken Stewart
Assistant Dean and Director
of Communications and
Public Programs

Whitney Stone
Assistant Director, Principal
Gift Prospect Management
and Strategy, Development

Amber Stout
Development and Leadership
Gift Coordinator

Rebeccah Stromberg
Executive Assistant to the
Dean, Dean's Office

Marielle Suba
Associate Editor,
Communications

Aimée Taberner
Director of Academic
Programs Administration

Ellen Tang
Assistant Director of
Financial Aid, Student
Services

Elizabeth Thorstenson
Program Coordinator,
Advanced Studies Program

Kathan Tracy
Director of Development,
Major and Principal Giving,
Development

Jennifer Vallone
Accounting Assistant,
Finance Office

Rachel Vroman
Manager of the Digital
Fabrication Lab

Elizabeth Walat
Director of Financial Planning
and Analysis, Finance Office

Courtney Ward
Assistant Director of
Leadership and Reunion
Gifts, Development

Ann Whiteside
Assistant Dean for
Information Services,
Frances Loeb Library

Sara Wilkinson
Director of Human
Resources

Abbe Will
Research Associate, Joint
Center for Housing Studies

Kelly Wisnaskas
Manager of Special
Programs, Student Services

Sally Young
Coordinator, Loeb Fellowship
Program

Ines Zalduendo
Special Collections Archivist
and Reference Librarian,
Frances Loeb Library

David Zimmerman-Stuart
Exhibitions Coordinator,
Communications

Courses Fall 2017

CORE STUDIOS

Architecture Core Studio I:
Project
Cameron Wu (coordinator),
Sean Canty, Jenny French,
Zeina Koreitem, Andrew
Plumb

Landscape Architecture Core
Studio I
Silvia Benedito and Danielle
Choi (co-coordinators),
Francesca Benedetto, Gareth
Doherty, Emily Wettstein,
Alistair McIntosh

Urban Planning Core Studio I
Sai Balakrishnan (coordi-
nator), David Gamble, Ana
Gelabert-Sanchez, Lily Song

Architecture Core Studio III:
Integrate
Eric Höweler and Jon Lott
(co-coordinators), John May,
Kiel Moe, Oana Stanescu,
Belinda Tato, with Robert
Silman (consultant)

Landscape Architecture Core
Studio III
Jill Desimini and Sergio
Lopez-Pineiro (co-coordi-
nators), Montserrat Bonvehi
Rosich, Craig Douglas,
Rosalea Monacella, Pablo
Pérez-Ramos

Elements of Urban Design
Felipe Correa (coordinator),
Anita Berrizbeitia, Stephen
Gray, Clayton Strange, with
Robert Gerard Pietrusko
(workshop), Michael Manfredi
(consultant), Richard Sennett
(consultant)

Collaborative Design
Engineering Studio I
(with SEAS)
Fawwaz Habbal, Andrew Witt,
Jock Herron, Peter Stark

OPTION STUDIOS

Entropy, History, Time.
Architectural Infrastructure
for a Gravel Pit in Spain
Iñaki Ábalos

Tibet Contemporary: Building
in the Himalayas
Zhang Ke

A Bank for Burbank and
Other L.A. Stories
Andrew Atwood, Anna
Neimark

People in Motion
Odile Decq with Nicolas
Hannequin

Northern Light
Toshiko Mori

Identity, Idiom, Id
Preston Scott Cohen

Rethinking Haussmann: The
Function of a 21st-Century
Multi-Story Residential
Building
Farshid Moussavi with
Ricardo Solar

The Monument
Emanuel Christ, Christoph
Gantenbein

$2,000 Home
Marina Tabassum

The Frugal Palazzo
Kersten Geers, David Van
Severen

Rotterdam Study Abroad
Option Studio: Countryside
Rem Koolhaas

Tokyo Study Abroad Option
Studio: Transforming
Omishima into a Beautiful
Japanese Garden
Toyo Ito

Retooling Metropolis II: L.A.!
Chris Reed

The Anatomy of an Island
Bridget Baines, Eelco
Hooftman

Excavating Space and
Nature in Tokyo
Toru Mitani with Manabu
Chiba

Civic Spaces in an Age of
Hyper-Complexity: From
Protest to Reverie
Mikyoung Kim with
Bryan Chou

The Unfinished City:
Envisioning 21st-Century
Urban Ideals in Tallinn's
Largest Soviet-Era Housing
District
Andres Sevtsuk

Refugees in the Rust Belt
Daniel D'Oca

Robots In and Out of Buildings
Greg Lynn, Jeffrey Schnapp

Phantom Coast:
Transforming San Francisco's
Eastern Waterfront
James Lord, Roderick Wyllie

VISUAL STUDIES AND COMMUNICATION

Architectural Representation:
Origins + Originality
Megan Panzano

Projective Representation in
Architecture
Cameron Wu

Spatial Analysis and the Built
Environment
Andres Sevtsuk

Landscape Representation I
Emily Wettstein

Landscape Representation
III: Landform and Ecological
Process
Craig Douglas, Rosalea
Monacella

Communication for
Designers
Emily Waugh

Paper or Plastic: Reinventing
Shelf-Life in the Supermarket
Landscape
Teman Evans, Teran Evans

Drawing for Designers:
Techniques of Expression,
Articulation, and
Representation
Ewa Harabasz

Immersive Landscape:
Representation through
Gaming Technology
Eric de Broche des Combes

Scalar Practices in
Landscape Architecture
Alistair McIntosh

Experiments in Computer
Graphics
Zeina Koreitem

Public Projection: Projection
as a Tool for Expression and
Communication in Public
Space
Krzysztof Wodiczko

Art, Design, and the Public
Domain Proseminar
Krzysztof Wodiczko

DESIGN THEORY

Theories of Landscape as
Urbanism, Landscape as
Infrastructure: Paradigms,
Practices, Prospects
Pierre Bélanger

Teaching Techniques
Preston Scott Cohen

Conservation of Older
Buildings: Techniques and
Technics
Robert Silman

Culture, Conservation, and
Design
Susan Snyder, George
Thomas

The Idea of Environment
Dilip da Cunha

Field Methods and Living
Collections
Rosetta S. Elkin

An Unsentimental Look at
Architecture and Social Craft
John Peterson

Material, Atmosphere, and
Ambience
Toshiko Mori

It's a Wild World: Future
Scenarios for Feral
Landscapes
Jill Desimini

Rotterdam Study Abroad
Seminar: The Invention of
the Countryside—A Critical
Iconography
Niklas Maak

Tokyo Study Abroad Seminar:
Tokyo—Catalysts for Change
Kayoko Ota

HISTORY AND THEORY

Studies of the Built North
American Environment:
1580 to the Present
John R. Stilgoe

History and Theory of Urban
Interventions
Neil Brenner

Buildings, Texts, and
Contexts I
K. Michael Hays, Erika
Naginski, Andrew Holder

Urbanization in the East
Asian Region
Peter Rowe

Histories of Landscape
Architecture I: Textuality and
the Practice of Landscape
Architecture
Edward Eigen

North American Seacoasts
and Landscapes: Discovery
Period to the Present
John R. Stilgoe

Authority and Invention:
Medieval Art and Architecture
Christine Smith

Structuring Urban
Experience: From the
Athenian Acropolis to the
Boston Common
Christine Smith

Signal, Image, Architecture
II: Automation, or the Politics
of Very Large Numbers
John May

Competing Visions of
Modernity in Japan
Seng Kuan

Practical Wisdom 2
Peter Carl

Forest, Grove, Tree: Planting
Urban Landscapes
Sonja Dümpelmann

Architecture and Its Texts
(1650–1800)
Erika Naginski

Rotterdam Study Abroad
Seminar: Designing and
Managing Worlds in the
Countryside
Sébastien Marot

SOCIOECONOMIC STUDIES

Real Estate Finance and
Development
Richard Peiser, David
Hamilton Jr.

Land Use and
Environmental Law
Jerold S. Kayden

Cities by Design I
Rahul Mehrotra and Peter
Rowe (coordinators) with Eve
Blau, Joan Busquets, Felipe
Correa, Jerold S. Kayden,
Alex Krieger

Field Studies in Real
Estate, Planning, and Urban
Design: Seattle, WA, and
Framingham, MA
Richard Peiser

Policy Making in Urban
Settings (at Harvard Kennedy
School)
James Carras

Analytic Methods of Urban
Planning: Quantitative
Michael Hooper

Analytic Methods: Qualitative
Ann Forsyth

Transportation Policy and
Planning
José Gómez-Ibáñez

Housing and Urbanization in
the United States
Jennifer Molinsky, James
Stockard

Healthy Places
Ann Forsyth

Contemporary Developing
Countries: Entrepreneurial
Solutions to Intractable
Problems (at Harvard
Business School)
Tarun Khanna with Satchit
Balsari, Rahul Mehrotra,
Krzysztof Gajos, Doris
Sommer

Urban Economic Concepts
for Real Economic
Development
Donald Zizzi

Sustainable Real Estate
Jesse M. Keenan

Environment, Politics, and
Action
Abby Spinak

Global Leadership in
Real Estate and Design:
Barcelona, Spain, and
Seaport District, Boston, MA
Bing Wang, A. Eugene Kohn

The Spatial Politics of Land:
A Comparative Perspective
Sai Balakrishnan

The Gentrification Debates:
Perceptions and Realities of
Neighborhood Change
Toni L. Griffin

Real Estate Finance and
Development Fundamentals
for Public and Private
Participants (at Harvard
Kennedy School)
Edward Marchant

Public Space
Jerold S. Kayden

SCIENCE AND TECHNOLOGY

Environmental Systems 1
Ali Malkawi

Environmental Systems 2
Andrea Love

Construction Systems
Billie Faircloth

Ecologies, Techniques, Technologies I
Rosetta S. Elkin, Matthew Urbanski

Structural Design 2
Martin Bechthold

Ecologies, Techniques, Technologies III: Ecology and the Design World
Steven Handel, Christopher Matthews

The Innovator's Practice: Finding, Building, and Leading Good Ideas with Others (at SEAS)
Beth Altringer

Innovation in Science and Engineering: Conference Course (at SEAS)
David Weitz

Water Engineering (at SEAS)
Chad Vecitis

Computer Vision (at SEAS)
Todd Zickler

Material Practice as Research: Digital Design and Fabrication
Martin Bechthold

Changing Natural and Built Coastal Environments
Steven Apfelbaum, Katharine Parsons

Introduction to Computational Design
Sawako Kaijima, Panagiotis Michalatos

Mapping II: Geosimulation
Robert Gerard Pietrusko

Forms of Energy: Nonmodern
Kiel Moe

Hybrid Formations I: In Pursuit of Novel Form
Volkan Alkanoglu

Visualization (at SEAS)
Johanna Beyer

Deployable Surfaces: Dynamic Performance through Multi-Material Architectures
Chuck Hoberman with Jonathan Grinham

Nano, Micro, Macro: Adaptive Material Laboratory
Salmaan Craig, Joanna Aizenberg

Tokyo Study Abroad Seminar on Structure and Material in Japan
Mits Kanada

PROFESSIONAL PRACTICE

Foundations of Practice
Jeffry Burchard, Jesse M. Keenan

Integrative Frameworks for Technology, Environment, and Society I
Woodward Yang with Martin Bechthold, Diane E. Davis, Chuck Hoberman, and Robert Silman

Frameworks of Contemporary Practice
Paul Nakazawa

Innovation in Project Delivery
Mark R. Johnson

PROPAEDEUTIC AND ADVANCED RESEARCH

Aggregate Effects: Re-tooling the Small City for Environmental and Social Impact at Multiple Scales
Anita Berrizbeitia

Real Estate and City Making in China
Bing Wang

Ecology, Infrastructure, Power
Pierre Bélanger

Emergent Urbanism: Design Visions for the City of Hermosillo, Mexico (Project-based class)
Diane E. Davis, Felipe Vera

Preparation for Independent Thesis Proposal for MUP, MAUD, or MLAUD
Michael Hooper

Independent Thesis in Satisfaction of Degree MArch
Andrew Holder

MDes Open Projects 1
John May

Preparation for MLA Design Thesis
Charles Waldheim

Independent Design Engineering Project I
Martin Bechthold, Woodward Yang

MArch II Proseminar
Jennifer Bonner, Jorge Silvetti

Urban Design Proseminar
Eve Blau

Proseminar in Urbanism, Landscape, Ecology
Charles Waldheim

Doctoral Program Proseminar
Peter Rowe

Spring 2018

CORE STUDIOS

Architecture Core Studio II: Situate
Jeffry Burchard, Tomás dePaor (co-coordinators), Elizabeth Christoforetti, Jenny French, Sean Canty, Patrick McCafferty

Landscape Architecture Core Studio II
Silvia Benedito (coordinator), Montserrat Bonhevi Rosich, Kristin Frederickson, Belinda Tato, Eric de Broche des Combes (workshop), Nadir Abdessemed (workshop)

Urban Planning Core Studio II
Daniel D'Oca (coordinator), Stephen Gray, Kathy Spiegelman, Frederick Merrill (consultant), Richard Peiser (consultant)

Architecture Core Studio IV: Relate
Jeannette Kuo (coordinator), Jennifer Bonner, Andrew Holder, Grace La, Matthew Soules, Elizabeth Whittaker

Landscape Architecture Core Studio IV
Pierre Bélanger (coordinator), Francesca Benedetto, Danielle Choi, Sergio

Lopez-Pineiro, Rosalea Monacella, Robert Gerard Pietrusko, Amy Whitesides (consultant)

Collaborative Design Engineering Studio II
Chuck Hoberman, Fawwaz Habbal, Heather Boesch, Jock Herron, Peter Stark

OPTION STUDIOS

,Tri,3,Tre
Mack Scogin

Model as Building—Building as Model
George L. Legendre

After the Storm: Restructuring an Island Ecosystem
Jeanne Gang with Claire Cahan

ROOT: Rediscovery of Jingdezhen Contemporary
Zhu Pei

Agent-Based Parametric Semiology—The Design of Information-Rich Environments
Patrik Schumacher

In the Details: The Space between God and the Devil
Dwayne Oyler, Jenny Wu

Museum Island
Sharon Johnston, Mark Lee

Study Abroad Option Studio: Making London
Simon Allford, Hanif Kara

Rotterdam Study Abroad Option Studio: Countryside II
Rem Koolhaas

Broadway Shuffle II: Performance/Space
Gary Hilderbrand

Korea Remade: Alternate Nature, DMZ, and Hinterlands
Jungyoon Kim, Niall Kirkwood, Yoonjin Park

Ecology, Culture, and Identity: Revitalizing the Cultural Landscape of the Huerta of Valencia, Spain
Arancha Muñoz-Criado

Quito and the Elasticity of the Spanish-American Block
Felipe Correa

Zhengzhou: Designing Critical Nodes for the "Urban Grids"
Joan Busquets

The Industrious City: Rethinking Urban Industry in the Digital Age
Hiromi Hosoya, Markus Schaefer

Extreme Urbanism V: Exploring Hybrid Housing Typologies, Elphinstone Estate, Mumbai
Rahul Mehrotra

Urban Disobedience: 99 Provocations to Disrupt Injustice in St. Louis
Toni L. Griffin

Manila: Future Habitations
Rok Oman, David Rubin, Špela Videčnik

Between Earth and Sky: A Building for the HafenCity, Hamburg
Eric Parry

Phantom Urbanism
Reinier de Graaf with Ricardo Solar

VISUAL STUDIES AND COMMUNICATION

Digital Media I
Allen Sayegh

Digital Media II
Andrew Witt

Responsive Environments: The Future of Shopping
Allen Sayegh with Stefano Andreani

Constructing Visual Narratives of Place
Francesca Benedetto

Curatorial Practice
Eva Respini

Near Drawing
Volkan Alkanoglu

New Natures: Constructing a Brief of Coextensive Networks
Rosalea Monacella

Painting for Designers: Techniques, Methods, and Concepts
Ewa Harabasz

Interdisciplinary Art and Design Practices
Silvia Benedito

DESIGN THEORY

The Nature of Difference: Theories and Practices of

Landscape Architecture
Anita Berrizbeitia, Claudia Taborda

Designing the American City: Civic Aspirations and Urban Form
Alex Krieger

Urban Form: Transition as Condition
Eve Blau

Advanced Seminar in City Form: Future of Streets
Andres Sevtsuk

Experiments in Public Freedom
Sergio Lopez-Pineiro

Spaces of Solidarity
Malkit Shoshan

Robots In and Out of Buildings
Greg Lynn, Jeffrey Schnapp

Philosophy of Technology
Robert Silman

Urban Grids: Open Form for City Design 2
Joan Busquets

Rotterdam Study Abroad Seminar: World Without Work: A Rural Utopia?
Niklas Maak

London Study Abroad Seminar: London: Past, Present, and Emerging
Simon Allford, Hanif Kara

London Study Abroad Seminar: Architecture After Neoliberalism
Irénée Scalbert

HISTORY AND THEORY

Buildings, Texts, and Contexts II
Erika Naginski, Antoine Picon

Film Theory, Visual Thinking
Giuliana Bruno

Histories of Landscape Architecture II: Design, Representation, and Use
Sonja Dümpelmann

Modernization in the Visual United States Environment
John R. Stilgoe

Adventure and Fantasy Simulation, 1871–2036
John R. Stilgoe

Modern Architecture and Urbanism in China
Peter Rowe

Super Landscapes, Super Sports
Sonja Dümpelmann

Making Sacred Space
Christine Smith

Bavarian Rococo: Heterotopias
Andrew Holder

Cities, Infrastructures, and Politics: From Renaissance to Smart Technologies
Antoine Picon

Bramante is Better than Alberti . . .
Jorge Silvetti

Andrea Palladio: Innovative Learning Experience
Guido Beltramini, Howard Burns

Urban Tactics on the Arabian Peninsula
Todd Reisz

Materiality, Visual Culture, and Media (atthe Department of Visual and Environmental Studies)
Giuliana Bruno

Architecture and Landscape Before and After Watergate
Edward Eigen

Conservation, Destruction, and Curating Impermanence
Natalia Escobar Castrillón

Power and Place: Culture and Conflict in the Built Environment
Susan Snyder, George Thomas

Rotterdam Study Abroad Seminar: Architecture, Urbanism, and Agriculture
Sébastien Marot

The Texts of the Modern: In Search of a New Narrative Canon
Rafael Moneo

SOCIOECONOMIC STUDIES

Public and Private Development
Jerold S. Kayden

Urban Politics and Planning (at Harvard Kennedy School)
Quinton Mayne

Cities by Design II: Projects, Processes, and Outcomes
Stephen Gray

Advanced Real Estate Finance
Frank Apeseche

Building and Leading Real Estate Enterprises and Entrepreneurship
Frank Apeseche

Housing and Urbanization in Global Cities
Alexander von Hoffman

Urbanization and International Development
Sai Balakrishnan

Towns and Settlements in Metropolitan Regions
Peter Rowe

U.S. Housing Markets, Problems, and Policies
Christopher Herbert

Climate Change Resistance and Adaptation
Jesse M. Keenan

Environment, Economics, and Enterprise
Holly Samuelson, Frank Apeseche

Planning for Climate Change: Scarcity, Abundance, and the Idea of the Future
Abby Spinak

Energetics of Urbanization
Neil Brenner, Kiel Moe

Community Development: Past, Present, Future
Lily Song

Urban Transportation Planning and Implementation
Frederick Salvucci

Urban Design for Planners
David Gamble

International Humanitarian Response (at Harvard T. H. Chan School of Public Health)
Stephanie Kayden

Creating Real Estate Ventures: A Legal Perspective
Michael Haroz

Affordable and Mixed-Income Housing Development, Finance, and Management
Edward Marchant

Market Analysis and Urban Economics
Ray Torto

Urban Governance and the Politics of Planning in the Developing World
Enrique Silva

SCIENCE AND TECHNOLOGY

Building Simulation
Ali Malkawi, Holly Samuelson

Materials
Alex Anmahian

Ecologies, Techniques, Technologies II
Laura Solano, with Karen Janosky

Structural Design I
Patrick McCafferty

Cases in Contemporary Construction
Eric Höweler

Ecologies, Techniques, Technologies IV
Jill Desimini, Alistair McIntosh

Design Survivor: Experimental Lessons in Designing for Desirability
Beth Altringer

Survey of Energy Technology (at SEAS)
Michael Aziz

Innovative Construction in Japan
Mark Mulligan

Urban and Town Ecology
Richard T. T. Forman

Mapping: Geographic Representation and Speculation
Robert Gerard Pietrusko

Water, Land-Water Linkages, and Aquatic Ecology
Timothy Dekker, Nicholas Nelson

Urban Restoration Ecology
Steven Handel

Analytic Geometries, Descriptive Geometries: Thinking and Making
George L. Legendre, Cameron Wu

Interface Design: Integrating Material Perceptions
Sawako Kaijima

Quantitative Aesthetics: Design as Signal
Panagiotis Michalatos

Structures in Landscape Architecture
Alistair McIntosh

Planted Form and Re-Formation: Past Futures and Antecedent Inventions
Danielle Choi

Optimizing Facade Performance: A Deep Dive on Design Decisions
Andrea Love

PROFESSIONAL PRACTICE

Integrative Frameworks for Technology, Environment, and Society II
Woodward Yang with lectures by Sai Balakrishnan, Diane E. Davis, Ali Malkawi, Antoine Picon

Practices of Landscape Architecture
Niall Kirkwood, Karen Janosky, Thomas Ryan

Scenes of Design, Development, and Disaster
Todd Reisz

Non-Professional Practice
Oana Stanescu

PROPAEDEUTIC AND ADVANCED RESEARCH

Housing Tropes and the Role of Design
Rahul Mehrotra

Beyond Reconstruction: Mexico and the 2017 Earthquakes
Jose Castillo, Diane E. Davis

Miami Resilience: Health and Affordability
Jesse M. Keenan

Independent Design Engineering Project II
Martin Bechthold, Woodward Yang

Independent Thesis in Satisfaction of the Degree MArch
Andrew Holder

Independent Thesis in Satisfaction of the Degree MAUD, MLAUD, or MUP
Michael Hooper

MDes Open Project II
John May

Independent Thesis in Satisfaction of the Degree MLA
Charles Waldheim

Research Methods in Landscape Architecture
Edward Eigen

What is a Thesis? Conversations on Means and Methods of the Thesis Project
Jon Lott

Methods of Research in Art and Design: A Workshop-Tutorial
Krzysztof Wodiczko

Discourse and Methods II
K. Michael Hays, Catherine Ingraham

Fellowships and Prizes

Wheelwright Prize
Aude-Line Dulière
(Brussels, Belgium)

Veronica Rudge Green Prize in Urban Design
The High Line

2017–2018 LOEB FELLOWS

Samuel Bonnet
International Development and Crisis Response
(Geneva, Switzerland)

Andrew Freear
Architecture and Education
(Hale County, AL)

Johanna Gilligan
Urban Agriculture and Youth Development
(New Orleans, LA)

Matthew Mazzotta
Art and Community
(Canton, NY)

Shaney Peña-Gómez
Urban Planning and Design in Border Communities (Santo Domingo, Dominican Republic)

Surella Segu
Urban Planning and Design, Housing (Mexico City, Mexico)

James Shen
Architecture, Historic Preservation, and Adaptive Reuse (Beijing, China)

Tau Tavengwa
Journalism, Publication, and Convening (Cape Town, South Africa)

Eric Williams
Performance, Visual Arts, and Economic Development (Chicago, IL)

RICHARD ROGERS FELLOWSHIP

Aleksandr Bierig
(Cambridge, MA)

Peter Buš
(Zurich, Switzerland)

Irina Davidovici
(Zurich, Switzerland)

Alexis Kalagas
(Zurich, Switzerland)

Cathy Smith
(Newcastle, Australia)

Kaz Yoneda
(MArch '11; Tokyo, Japan)

STUDENT FELLOWSHIPS, PRIZES, AND TRAVEL PROGRAMS

Araldo A. Cossutta Annual Prize for Design Excellence
Kenneth Hasegawa (MArch I)

Clifford Wong Prize in Housing Design
Isabelle Verwaay (MArch I)

ETH Zurich Exchange Program
Elif Erez (MArch I), Khoa Vu (MArch I)

KPF Fellowship
Eduardo Martinez-Mediero Rubio (MArch II)

Peter Rice Prize
Nicole Bakker (MDE), Peter Osborne (MDes EE), Spyros Ampanavos (DDes)

Takenaka Summer Internship
Vita Chi-Hsuan Wang (MArch II)

Digital Design Prize
Alexander Searle Porter (MArch I)

Plimpton Poorvu Prize
1st Prize: Georgios Avramides (MDes REBE), Jong Hwa Lee (MDes REBE), John Jeong-Bum Lee (MDes REBE), Emily Megan Marsh (MUP), Alexander James Rawding (MUP); 2nd Prize: Dalia Al Derzi (MDes REBE), Alaa Raafat Abdelrazik (MDes REBE), Carlotta Weller (MDes REBE)

Best Paper on Housing
Caroline Lauer (MUP)

AIA Henry Adams Medal
Alexander Searle Porter (MArch I)

AIA Henry Adams Certificate
Shaowen Zhang (MArch I AP)

Alpha Rho Chi Medal
Rekha Auguste-Nelson (MArch I)

James Templeton Kelley Thesis Prize
Scarlet Ziwei Song (MArch II)

Julia Amory Appleton Traveling Fellowship in Architecture
Elias Logan (MArch II)

Department of Architecture Faculty Design Award
Isabelle Verwaay (MArch I), Beijia Gu (MArch II)

Kevin V. Kieran Prize
Elias Logan (MArch II)

Charles Eliot Traveling Fellowship in Landscape Architecture
Stacy Passmore (MLA I AP)

Charles Eliot Traveling Fellowship in Landscape Architecture (Alternate)
Tam Banh (MLA I AP, MArch II)

Jacob Weidenmann Prize
Daniel Berdichevsky (MLA I AP)

Peter Walker & Partners Fellowship for Landscape Architecture
Sonny Meng Qi Xu (MArch II, MLA I AP)

ASLA Certificate of Honor
Tam Banh (MLA I AP, MArch II), Greta Ruedisueli (MLA I AP), Peeraphol Sangthongjai (MLA II)

ASLA Certificate of Merit
William Baumgardner (MLA II), Nathalie Mitchell (MLA I), Elizabeth Savrann (MLA I)

Norman T. Newton Prize
Matthew Wong (MLA I)

Landscape Architecture Thesis Prize
Ernest Haines (MLA I), Seok Min Yeo (MLA I AP)

Award for Outstanding Leadership in Urban Planning
Miriam Keller (MUP) and Mayu Takeda (MUP)

Award for Outstanding Leadership in Urban Design
Theodore Kofman (MAUD)

Award for Academic Excellence in Urban Planning
Caroline Lauer (MUP)

Award for Academic Excellence in Urban Design
Konstantina Tzemou (MAUD)

Ferdinand Colloredo-Mansfeld Prize for Superior Achievement in Real Estate Studies
John Jeong-Bum Lee (MDes REBE)

Druker Traveling Fellowship
Maxime Faure (MAUD)

Urban Planning and Design Thesis Prize in Urban Design
Alexander Yuen (MAUD)

Urban Planning and Design Thesis Prize in Urban Planning
Colleen Brady (MUP)

The Award for Excellence in Project-Based Urban Planning
Lena Ferguson (MUP)

The Award for Excellence in Urban Design
Alexander Yuen (MAUD)

AICP Outstanding Student Award
Jeanette Pantoja (MUP)

Outstanding Leadership in Real Estate Award
Van-Tuong Ngo Nguyen (MDes REBE), Andrew Wade (MDes REBE)

The Project Prize in Design Studies
Jiabao Li (MDes Tech), Enrique Aureng Silva (MDes CC)

Dimitris Pikionis Award
Pol Fité Matamoros (MDes Tech)

The Daniel L. Schodek Award for Technology and Sustainability
Keith Hartwig (MDes ADPD) and Xiaoshi Wang (MDes EE)

Overall Academic Performance in Design Engineering
Zeerak Ahmed (MDE)

Outstanding Independent Design Engineering Project
Julie Loiland (MDE), Michael Raspuzzi (MDE)

Leadership and Community in Design Engineering
Brian Ho (MDE)

Student Groups

Taylor Halamka (MArch I)
President

Igsung So (MArch I AP)
Academic Chair

Mena Wasti Ahmed (MArch I, MLA I AP)
Diversity and Inclusion Chair

Samuel Matthew (MDes RR)
Student Groups Chair

William Baumgardner (MLA II)
Professional Development Chair

Esther Mira Bang (MArch I)
Social Events Chair

Bryan Ortega-Welch (MArch I)
Resources Chair

ORGANIZATIONS
African American Student Union (AASU)
ChinaGSD
Harvard Urban Planning Organization (HUPO)
GSD MEdiNA
LatinGSD
The Real Estate Development (RED) Club
Queers in Design
Women in Design

CLUBS
Achronology
AfricaGSD
AR/VR Club
Asia Real Estate Association
Beer and Dogs
Brazil GSD
CareerXplorer
Climate Governance Initiative
Code Without Frontiers
Design Research Forum (DRF)
EuropeGSD
GARLIC GSD
Greece GSD
gsBees
GSD Arts Group
GSD Christian Fellowship
GSD Music Band
GSD Soccer
GSD Urban Mobility
GSD/HKS Community Development Project (CDP)
GSD Veterans
GSDJ
Harvard Student Blockchain Group
Harvard Student East Asia Urban Forum
The Harvard Real Estate Review
Harvard Student Chapter of the American Society of Landscape Architects (ASLA)
HCI @ GSD
Healthy Places
India GSD
Italian GSD
Japan GSD
JewSD
Korea GSD (KGSD)
Masks (formerly GSD Theory)
Newswall
Open Letters
OpenMDE
Other Pedagogies
POP^UP
Project Link
Rowing Club
Southeast Asia GSD
Spain GSD
Sustainable Architecture for Inequality
Time Matters
Travel GSD
Urban GSD
xDesign
YogaGSD

Research

The Office for Urbanization

Director: Charles Waldheim, John E. Irving
Professor of Landscape Architecture

The Office for Urbanization draws upon the School's history of design innovation to address societal and cultural conditions associated with contemporary urbanization. It develops speculative and projective urban scenarios through sponsored design research projects.

RESEARCH CENTERS

Harvard Center for Green Buildings and Cities (CGBC)

Founding Director: Ali Malkawi, Professor of Architectural Technology

The Harvard CGBC aims to transform the building industry through a commitment to design-centric strategy that directly links research outcomes to the development of new processes, systems, and products.

Harvard Joint Center for Housing Studies

Managing Director: Christopher Herbert, Lecturer in Urban Planning and Design

The Harvard Joint Center for Housing Studies advances understanding of housing issues and informs policy through research, education, and public outreach programs.

DESIGN LABS

City Form Lab

Director: Andres Sevtsuk, Assistant Professor of Urban Planning

The City Form Lab investigates how urban form affects the quality of life in 21st-century cities. It develops new analytic software tools for urban designers and planners and researches the effects of city design decisions on social, economic, and environmental well-being.

Computational Geometry Lab

Directors: Preston Scott Cohen, Gerald M. McCue Professor in Architecture; Andrew Witt, Assistant Professor in Practice of Architecture; Cameron Wu, Associate Professor of Architecture

The Computational Geometry Lab studies the intersection of design and science of shape and form, aided by computational tools and design intuition. The lab combines computational, formal, architectural, and historical research into a heterogeneous yet synthetic agenda.

Healthy Places Design Lab

Directors: Ann Forsyth, Professor of Urban Planning; Jennifer Molinsky, Lecturer in Urban Planning and Design

The Healthy Places Design Lab asks how health is related to place, and how we can make places healthier—questions of wide current concern in the United States and globally. This lab links faculty and students at the GSD to others within the School and beyond.

The Just City Lab

Director: Toni L. Griffin, Professor in Practice of Urban Planning

The Just City Lab investigates the definition of urban justice and the just city, and examines how design and planning contribute to the conditions of justice and injustice in cities, neighborhoods, and the public realm.

Material Processes and Systems Group (MaP+S)

Director: Martin Bechthold, Kumagai Professor of Architectural Technology

MaP+S understands, develops, and deploys innovative technologies in the promotion of design as an agent of change in the quest for a better future.

Responsive Environments & Artifacts Lab (REAL)

Director: Allen Sayegh, Associate Professor in Practice of Architectural Technology

REAL pursues the design of digital, virtual, and physical worlds as an indivisible whole. It recognizes the all-pervasive nature of digital information and interaction in the realms of architectural, urban, and landscape design.

Social Agency Lab

Director: Michael Hooper, Associate Professor of Urban Planning

The Social Agency Lab studies the ways in which individuals, institutions, and organizations shape social outcomes in cities.

Exhibitions 2017–2018

DRUKER DESIGN GALLERY

In recognition of a $15-million gift from Ronald M. Druker (Loeb Fellow '76), the main exhibition gallery at the GSD has been named the Druker Design Gallery.

The Druker Design Gallery features the work of faculty, students, and researchers and scholars from across the design fields. Located at Gund Hall, the gallery serves as a site for experimentation and explication of ideas and plays a fundamental role in the pedagogical life of the school. The gallery is open to the public, and has a long and rich history of exhibitions that engage the historical and contemporary conditions of design discourse across physical, digital, and spatial media.

Soft Thresholds: Projects of RMA Architects, Mumbai

> August 21–October 15, 2017
> Curator: Rahul Mehrotra, Professor of Urban Design and Planning

This exhibition on the works of RMA Architects, Mumbai + Boston, represents the compulsive drive of the practice to construct *soft thresholds*—through research, engagement with the city, and making of architecture.

Soft Thresholds: Projects of RMA Architects, Mumbai

Landscape: Fabric of Details

> October 30–December 21, 2017
> Curator: Toru Mitani

This exhibition of a selection of projects by Toru Mitani and his practice, Studio on Site, is about how small things have a significant, perceptual impact on diffuse landscapes. The title itself is an incitement to connect ideas that operate at vastly different scales. "Fabric," when coupled with the word "landscape," elicits notions of system, underlying structure, grain, orientation, or texture of the continuous ground. "Details" are things in themselves, discreet and contingent, requiring a shift in focus to dissect and scrutinize technique, dimension, and materials. A second definition of "fabric" from the Latin *fabrica* is to make, to fabricate, and faber the craftsmen. In other words, fabric is both system and craft.

Landscape: Fabric of Details

Inscriptions: Architecture Before Speech

> January 22–March 11, 2018
> Curators: K. Michael Hays, Eliot Noyes Professor of Architectural Theory; Andrew Holder, Assistant Professor of Architecture

If recent theory has highlighted architecture's turn to evident resemblance and signification, we argue this tendency has also produced its other: The landscape of contemporary practice is filled with work whose motivating interests are anterior to meaning and averse to thematization; they are, in a way, pre-speech. Projects in this mode are born of the original human postulate to claim a place in the world, to confirm having been there, to make and mark a difference. *Inscriptions* is a broad survey of work that problematizes, resists, and exceeds signification by appealing to other kinds of cultural engagements, agreements, and fantasies of architecture's origins. Projects by GSD faculty spanning over 35 years of practice are interspersed as conceptual keystones among works from emerging architects across the American academy, offering a theory of the structural relationships that bind and organize the apparent delirium of the contemporary field.

Live Feed: Platform 10

>March 26–May 11, 2018
>Curators: John May, Assistant Professor
>of Architecture; Jon Lott, Assistant
>Professor of Architecture; Design Team:
>Justin Gallagher (MArch '17), Grace
>McEniry (MArch I), Scott March Smith
>(MArch '17), Emerald Hanguang Wu
>(MArch I), Sofia Balters (MArch '17),
>Benjamin Halpern (MArch '17), Hyojin
>Kwon (MArch I)

Among the most significant changes in everyday life over the past half-century are those that originate in the relatively recent emergence of so-called "real-time" technologies: electronic currency markets, embedded reporting, social media, reality television, traffic monitoring, security networks. In every instance, the implicit claim made by these technologies is the same: by collapsing the distance between life and its representations, real-time techniques offer a more accurate (and therefore a more objective) depiction of our lives. Indeed, the *New Oxford American Dictionary* states that "real time" is "the actual time during which a process or event occurs"—a not-so-subtle tautology that hardly separates it from time itself.

Live Feed: Platform 10

Commencement 2018

>May 23–July 29, 2018

Each year, the Commencement exhibition showcases work from graduating students, offering a glimpse into what they have created during their time at the Harvard GSD. All featured work is selected by students themselves, and displayed in poster form alongside postcard versions for visitors to take. Prize-winning projects from across departments are also on display in Frances Loeb Library.

Transformations + Connections: Harvard Undergraduate Architecture Studies studio projects

>August 25–September 28, 2017
>Curators: Megan Panzano, Assistant
>Professor of Architecture; Lisa
>Haber-Thomson (PhD)

The two studio-based courses offered in the Harvard Undergraduate Architecture Studies track—*Transformations* and *Connections*—explore architectural means and methods of design. Each begins from a different scale of inquiry, but converge at a similar end. This exhibition combines the output from the two studios conducted during the Spring 2017 semester.

Real Talk

>October 5–December 21, 2017
>Curators: African American Student Union

Real Talk collects photographic portraits and personal reflections of participants in the GSD's second Black in Design Conference, entitled "Designing Resistance, Building Coalitions," to reveal how their stories relate to identity, design, resistance, and coalition building. This exhibition is a part of a larger movement to reclaim the histories of underrepresented groups, utilizing visual narratives to assert their agency. Amid an increasingly complicated, fragmented, and noisy media landscape, *Real Talk* is a space for black designers and their allies to present their own candid narratives.

Baroque Machinations (2012–2017)

> January 22–March 11, 2018
> Curator: <u>Cameron Wu</u>, Associate Professor
> of Architecture; Teams: (2017) <u>Iman
> Fayyad</u> (MArch '16); (2014) <u>Iman Fayyad</u>;
> (2012) <u>W. Gavin Robb</u> (MArch '14).
> 2017 CAB Presentation: <u>Hyojin Kwon</u>
> (MArch I), <u>Milos Mladenovic</u> (MArch I)

Plans of three Baroque churches (Sant'Ivo alla
Sapienza by Francesco Borromini; San Carlo alle
Quattro Fontane by Francesco Borromini; Unnamed
Church by Guarino Guarini) serve as subjects for
close reading and formal analysis in this exhibition.
Through drawing and animation, each investigation
offers a wide range of architectural characteristics
produced using a single rule set of descriptive
geometric construction. These divergent characteristics designate architectural opposites in terms of
type, spatial organization, and projective relationships—radial/rectilinear, figure/field, quadrilateral/
hexagonal, centralized/axial.

ULSAN REMADE: Manufacturing the Modern Industrial City

> March 18–May 11, 2018
> Curators: <u>Niall Kirkwood</u>, Professor of
> Landscape Architecture and Technology;
> <u>Sang Yong Cho</u> (MLA '14)

Kirkwood's studio reconsidered the City of Ulsan,
Republic of Korea's prime industrial and manufacturing center as part of a more livable and
sustainable metropolitan industrial landscape and
a locale of shifting local and global economies
and inventive domestic and civic environments of
energy, waste, and metabolism.

FRANCES LOEB LIBRARY

Portman's America & Other Speculations

> August 28–October 25, 2017

Combining the talents of an architect, artist, and
developer, John Portman was able to embark on a
series of large-scale building projects—megastructures—that radically redefined the relationship of
architecture to the city and its citizens. Iwan Baan's
new photographs of Portman's work, commissioned for the recent book *Portman's America
& Other Speculations* (edited by Dean Mohsen
Mostafavi), document Portman's work in bare,
candid fashion. This exhibition presents a curated
selection of these photographs, offering a complex
and nuanced reading of both John Portman the
architect and his architecture.

Border Ecologies

> November 1–December 21, 2017
> Curator: <u>Malkit Shoshan</u>, Lecturer in
> Urban Planning and Design

Borders shape and consolidate relations between
states, people, jurisdictions, political entities, and
territories. While some borders are stable, others
are in a constant flow. The demarcation of borders
is a body politic. It regulates economic relations and
people's access to places, resources, and rights.
Borders are powerful instruments that determine
the way our surroundings are organized, inhabited,
and controlled, and the ways communities relate to
one another—while some break through borders to
survive, others fence themselves off.

Border Ecologies

Design and the Just City

> March 26–May 11, 2018
> Curator: <u>Toni L. Griffin</u>, Professor in
> Practice of Urban Planning; Research
> Assistants: <u>Caroline Lauer</u>, <u>Milan Outlaw</u>,
> <u>Meghan Venable-Thomas</u>, <u>Natasha Hicks</u>,
> <u>Emily Marsh</u>, <u>Nerali Patel</u>, <u>Chandra Rouse</u>,
> <u>Mayu Takeda</u>

The Just City Lab investigates the concept of the
"Just City," and how design and planning contribute
to the conditions of justice and injustice in cities,
neighborhoods, and the public realm. This exhibition presents an interrogation of whether design
can have an impact on correcting urban injustice,
inequality, and disparity. Together with the Just City
Index, four project case studies, and video conversations with prominent voices, this exhibition asks
us all to contemplate the intention and effective-
ness of design practice to address issues of social
and spatial justice, and examine our own values for
a Just City.

Feminine Power and the Making of Modern Architectural History

January 29–March 18, 2018
Curators: Women in Design

Drawing on a range of archival materials, "Feminine Power and the Making of Modern Architectural History" juxtaposes Jaqueline Tyrwhitt (1905–1983) and Alison Smithson (1928–1993), two women at the center of the transnational network of theoreticians and practitioners who shaped the post-war architecture and urbanism movement. Through writings, photographs, and drawings, this exhibition celebrates women's underrecognized voices in the making of modern architectural history in order to cultivate new perspectives on gender and power within the Harvard GSD community and beyond.

Feminine Power and the Making of Modern Architectural History

"A Spoon" and "Client ID: NSyuO-fJxYI4DTUf7zWa-osilclb5E7-qmEzyjuu"

Curators: Youngjin Song (MDes '17);
Tanuja Mishra (MDes '17)

In Youngjin Song's *A Spoon*, viewers are invited to choreograph improvisational movements with the spoons presented in front of them; a spoon is animated by two people and vice versa, while the two subjects are animated by the object. The project presents an attempt to experiment how a very personal yet ordinary tool could contribute to a shared eating experience and to help build relationships between and among people.

In Tanuja Mishra's *Client ID: NSyuO-fJxYI4DTUf7zWa-osilclb5E7-qmEzyjuu*, the artist has alienated herself from her work and looked at it from the eyes of artificial intelligence. The resultant artwork has been developed in collaboration with the algorithm, where she has allowed it to generate insights on her work.

"286 South" and the Essential Role of Architects

Curator: Benjamin Halpern (MArch '17)
2016–2017 Clifford Wong Prize in Housing Design

This project is not about universal housing or good-for-society housing—the types that typically win such awards as the Clifford Wong Prize. This project is about super-luxury housing. Yet this project is also about "the essential role of architects"—to design with creative agency for housing of any type. And thus, this project should be judged not only by what it does for the specific inhabitant, but also by what it does for the discipline of architecture.

Global Energy Landscapes: Evolutionary Process of Infrastructures in New Territories: The Patagonia Case

January 22–March 4, 2018
Author: Stefano Romagnoli (MLA I AP)

This is an essay on the new capabilities and responsibilities of man-made logistics to intervene with the planet's resources in the new century. It is an interdisciplinary study of the environmental, territorial, economic, and social impact of the new infrastructures that profess to enhance the resources of the planet, exploring the levels of appropriation of the world's great natural reserves or "global gardens," antagonistic to the growth and urban concentrations in globalized, hyperdense cities.

Inhabiting the Limbo

March 12–May 11, 2018
Author: Zahra Safaverdi (MArch '17),
Irving Innovation Fellow

In recent history, the distinction between the product of imagination, the physical manifestation of the image, and that which belongs to the reality of quotidian life is clear. This clarity and emphasis on keeping the realm of the real discernible from the realm of the imagery is the product of modernity. With the progression of digital technology, however, the boundaries between real and imagery is once again blurred in the world at large. With the virtual world bleeding into our daily life and an ambiguous definition of what is actually considered real and what is not, the current definition of space, with an emphasis on separating reality from imagery, needs a revision.

GUND HALL EXTERIOR

PULSUS

September 1–December 15, 2017
Curator: Allen Sayegh, Associate
Professor in Practice of Architectural
Technology

The city is an electrifying fray, a maddening web of cacophony that connects every one of us to every one of others. How can we find solace in a world that doesn't stop?

PULSUS is an ambient, interactive, and experimental installation, part of a collaborative project between INVIVIA and the GSD's Responsive Environments & Artifacts Lab. Molded and folded from concrete, the same material that gives the city her gravity-defying forms, *PULSUS* collects real-time data from the city and reinterprets this dynamic information into interactive soundscapes. As it hums and mists to every small fluctuation in urban activity, these concrete blankets encourage visitors to relax, cool off, and tune in to the dynamic pulses of the city's communication frenzy.

PULSUS

KIRKLAND GALLERY

Kirkland Gallery is a student organization dedicated to supporting the Harvard GSD community and its emerging artists and designers.

2017–2018 Curators: Ana Luiza Padilha Addor (MDes ADPD), Kathryn Abarbanel (MDes ADPD), Inés Benitez (MDes ADPD), Luisa Brando Laserna (MDes CC), Eric Moed (MDes ADPD), Sampath Pediredla (MArch II), Malinda Seu (MDes ADPD), Alicia Valencia (MDes ADPD)

Toolmaking

Aimilios Davlantis Lo (MArch II)

Echo Chamber

James Moffet III (MDes Tech), Morgan Starkey (MArch I)

Cosas Más Extrañas

Biquini Wax EPS
Co-hosted by Kirkland Gallery, the GSD Arts Committee, Latin GSD, and the Signet Society

Do You Want to Share an Uber?

Anonymous

In:Vision

Keith Hartwig (MDes ADPD), Matthew Battles, Associate Director of metaLAB

Eating-X-Breathing

Melody Stein (MLA I); Benjamin Hackenberger (MLA I) and Kira Clingen (MLA I)

Coastal Imaginary

Kahira Ngige (MUP), Loyiso Qaqane (MAUD), Nerali Patel (MUP)

To Draw a Line

Katarina Burin, Shadi Harouni, Lucy Siyao Liu, Daniela Rivera, Keijaun Thomas

Everyone Here is Faking It.

Samuel Maddox (MDes ULE)

Ouroboros

Shuang Liang (MDes ADPD)

Publications
2017–2018

HARVARD DESIGN MAGAZINE

Harvard Design Magazine 44: "Seventeen." Edited by <u>Jennifer Sigler</u> and <u>Leah Whitman-Salkin</u>. Fall/Winter 2017.

Harvard Design Magazine 45: "Into the Woods." Edited by <u>Jennifer Sigler</u> and <u>Leah Whitman-Salkin</u>. Spring/Summer 2018.

Atelier Bow-Wow. *Architectural Ethnography.* Copublished with Sternberg Press, 2017.

Peter Rowe. *Design Thinking in the Digital Age.* Copublished with Sternberg Press, 2018.

Virgil Abloh. *"Insert Complicated Title Here."* Copublished with Sternberg Press, 2018.

PLATFORM

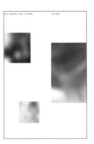

Platform 10: Live Feed. Edited by <u>John May</u> and Jon Lott, with <u>Sofia Balters</u> (MArch '17), <u>Benjamin Halpern</u> (MArch '17), <u>Justin Gallagher</u> (MArch '17), and <u>Grace McEniry</u> (MArch I). Copublished with Actar, 2017.

Chris Reed. *Retooling Metropolis: Working Landscapes, Emergent Urbanism.* 2017.

<u>Rok Oman</u>, <u>David Rubin</u>, and <u>Špela Videčnik</u>. *Kuala Lumpur: Designing the Public Realm.* 2017.

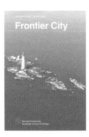

Florian Idenberg. *Work Environments: Space Work.* 2017.

<u>Adriaan Geuze</u> and <u>Daniel Vasini</u>. *Frontier City: Strategies for Boston Harbor.* 2018.

Portman's America: & Other Speculations. Edited by <u>Mohsen Mostafavi</u>. Copublished with Lars Müller, 2017.

Ethics of the Urban: The City and the Spaces of the Political. Edited by <u>Mohsen Mostafavi</u>. Copublished with Lars Müller, 2017.

STUDENT PUBLICATIONS

Harvard Real Estate Review 6. Edited by <u>John Lee</u> (MDes REBE), with <u>Patricia Alvarez</u> (MDes REBE), <u>Van-Tuong Nguyen</u> (MDes REBE), <u>Naman Srivastava</u> (MDes REBE), <u>Andrew Wade</u> (MDes REBE), <u>Carson Booth</u> (MLA I), and <u>Carla Wijaya</u> (MAUD).

New Geographies 09: Posthuman. Edited by <u>Mariano Gomez-Luque</u> (DDes) and <u>Ghazal Jafari</u> (DDes). Copublished with Actar, 2017.

OBL/QUE, vol. 2. Edited by <u>Natalia Escobar Castrillón</u> (PhD).

Open Letters, issues 52–64. Edited by <u>Zach Crocker</u> (MDes HPD), <u>Vladimir Gintoff</u> (MArch I, MUP), <u>Jessica Lim</u> (MArch I), <u>Elias Logan</u> (MArch II), <u>Milos Mladenovic</u> (MArch I), and <u>Enrique Aureng Silva</u> (MDes CC).

Public Programs 2017–2018

Luisa Lambri with Mark Lee
Rouse Visiting
Artist Lecture
August 31, 2017

REM (2016)
Film screening, with
discussion by director
Tomas Koolhaas
September 5, 2017

Rahul Mehrotra
Exhibition Lecture
September 6, 2017

Meet the Loeb Fellows
2017–2018 Fellows:
Samuel Bonnet, Andrew
Freear, Johanna Gilligan,
Matthew Mazzotta,
Shaney Peña-Gómez,
James Shen, Surella
Segu, Tau Tavengwa,
Eric Williams
September 11–14, 2017

Loeb Fellows (left to
right): Matthew Mazzotta,
Eric Williams, Surella
Segu, James Shen,
Andrew Freear, Shaney
Peña-Gómez, Samuel
Bonnet, Tau Tavengwa, and
Johanna Gilligan.

Iwan Baan
Rouse Visiting
Artist Lecture
September 12, 2017

Simon Allford
"Constructing the Idea:
The Essential and the
ExtraOrdinary"
September 18, 2017

Clare Lyster and Mason
White GSD Talks
"Third Coast Atlas: Prelude
to a Plan"
Book discussion
moderated by Charles
Waldheim, in panel
with contributors Pierre
Bélanger, Rosetta S.
Elkin, Rania Ghosn, and
Daniel Ibañez
October 3, 2017

Teresa Moller
"A Moment of Silence"
Sylvester Baxter Lecture
October 5, 2017

"Black in Design Conference
2017: Designing Resistance,
Building Coalitions"
Keynote speakers: Hamza
Walker, DeRay Mckesson
Speakers: Antionette D.
Carroll, Brandon Breaux,
Ceasar McDowell,
Courtney D. Cogburn,
Diane Jones Allen, the
Just City Lab, Ingrid
LaFleur, K. Wyking
Garrett, Leslie Salmon
Jones, Mabel O. Wilson,
Mario Gooden, Michelle
Joan Wilkinson, Nailah
Randall-Bellinger, Roger
Bonair-Agard, Sekou
Cooke, Sharon Egretta
Sutton, Stephen Gray, Tau
Tavengwa, Toni L. Griffin,
Walter Hood, Wyoma
Organized by the Harvard
GSD African American
Student Union
October 6–8, 2017

"Rethinking Pei: A Centenary
Symposium"
Speakers: Daniel M.
Abramson, André
Bideau, Edward Eigen,
Annette Fierro, K.
Michael Hays, Eric
Höweler, Seng Kuan,
Grace La, Delin
Lai, Stuart Leslie,
William Pedersen, Li
Chung (Sandi) Pei,
Leslie Robertson,
Cole Roskam, Brett
Schneider, Shohei
Shigematsu, Janet
Adams Strong, Shirley
Surya, Yvonne Szeto,
Kellogg Wong
Organized by the
Harvard GSD with
M+ and the Faculty of
Architecture
at the University
of Hong Kong
October 12–13, 2017

Timothy Greer
"Why Tear Down the Oldest
Building on 5th Avenue?"
Organized by the
GSD Alumni Insights
and Real Estate
Development Club
October 16, 2017

Liam Gillick
Rouse Visiting
Artist Lecture
October 16, 2017

Richard Sennett
"The Open City"
GSD Talks
October 17, 2017

Kenneth Frampton
"Megaform as Urban
Landscape"
Senior Loeb
Scholar Lecture
October 23, 2017

Silvia Kolbowski
"This Monument Which
is Not One"
Senior Loeb
Scholar Lecture
October 24, 2017

Silvia Kolbowski

Virgil Abloh
"Insert Complicated
Title Here"
Core Studio
Public Lecture
October 26, 2017

Odile Decq
"Architecture Thinking"
October 27, 2017

Anna Neimark and
Andrew Atwood
"Working Buildings"
GSD Talks
October 30, 2017

Toru Mitani
Daniel Urban
Kiley Lecture
October 31, 2017

Patricia Urquiola
Margaret McCurry
Lectureship in the
Design Arts
Open House Lecture
November 2, 2017

Malkit Shoshan
"Border Ecologies"
GSD Talks
November 6, 2017

Michelle Chang
"Songs You Know by Heart"
GSD Talks
November 7, 2017

Jorge Silvetti
"TYPE: Architecture's
Elusive Obsession and the
Rituals of an Impasse"
Eduard Sekler
Memorial Lecture
November 7, 2017

Erik L'Heureux
"Hot & Wet"
Wheelwright
Prize Lecture
November 8, 2017

James Welling
"Pathological Color"
Rouse Visiting
Artist Lecture
November 13, 2017

Ronald Rael
"Borderwall as Architecture"
GSD Talks
November 15, 2017

Michael Jakob
"Landscape Architecture and
the 'New Generic'"
November 16, 2017

Harry West
"Servant or Svengali: Design,
AI, and CX"
November 27, 2017

Junya Ishigami
November 29, 2017

K. Michael Hays and
Andrew Holder
"Architecture Before Speech:
A Conversation"
Exhibition Lecture
January 23, 2018

Rosa Sheng
"Why Equity Matters for
Everyone: A New Value
Proposition for Design"
January 25, 2018

Ken Yeang
"Ecoarchitecture and
Ecomasterplanning: The
Work of Ken Yeang"
January 26, 2018

Annabelle Selldorf
January 30, 2018

Sarah Oppenheimer
"FE_20180201"
    Rouse Visiting
    Artist Lecture
    February 1, 2018

Gerard & Kelly
"On Modern Living"
    February 2, 2018

Danielle Choi
    Kiley Fellow Lecture
    February 9, 2018

Mayor Rahm Emanuel
    Cosponsored by the
    Harvard Joint Center
    for Housing Studies
    and the Office of
    Communications
    February 20, 2018

Kahlil Joseph
"Gamma"
    Rouse Visiting
    Artist Lecture
    February 22, 2018

"On Monuments: Place,
Time, and Memory"
    Speakers: Drew Gilpin
    Faust, Mohsen Mostafavi,
    Robin Kelsey, Sarah
    Lewis, Jennifer Roberts,
    Krzysztof Wodiczko, Homi
    K. Bhabha, Erika Naginski
    Co-organized by the
    Harvard GSD, the
    Harvard University
    Committee on the
    Arts, and the Harvard
    University Faculty of Arts
    and Sciences
    February 27, 2018

Aaron Sachs
"'A Common Treasury for
All': Toward a Deeper History
of Environmental Justice"
    Frederick Law
    Olmsted Lecture
    March 1, 2018

Mark Joseph and Amy Khare
"Succeeding Where
Mixed-Income Transformation
Falls Short: A Path to Equity
and Inclusion in Our Cities"
    Cosponsored by the
    Harvard Joint Center for
    Housing Studies
    March 2, 2018

Wheelwright Prize Finalist
Presentations
    2018 Finalists:
    Aude-line Dulière,
    José Esparza Chong
    Cuy, Gustavo Utrabo,
    Catty Dan Zhang
    March 5, 2018

Zhuang Weimin
"Lever Social Change in
China Through Design—
Teaching, Research,
and Practice"
    March 6, 2018

Otobong Nkanga
    Rouse Visiting
    Artist Lecture
    March 8, 2018

Samia Henni
"Designing for the 'milie
féminin': France's Attempts
to Keep Algerian Women
Away from Islamic Customs"
    Aga Khan
    Program Lecture
    March 9, 2019

Suad Amiry
"Reclaiming Space: Riwaq's
50 Village Project in Rural
Palestine"
    Aga Khan
    Program Lecture
    March 20, 2018

Thomas Phifer
"Recent Work"
    March 22, 2018

Jeannette Sordi, Luis
Valenzuela, and Felipe Vera
"The Camp and the City:
Territories of Extraction"
    Book discussion, in
    panel with contrib-
    utors Maria Ignacia
    Arrasate, Sourav Kumar
    Biswas, and Agustina
    Gonzáles Cid
    March 27, 2018

Beatriz Colomina
"The Secret Life of Modern
Architecture or We Don't
Need Another Hero"
    Organized by
    Women in Design
    March 28, 2018

Reinier de Graaf
"Phantom Urbanism"
    March 29, 2018

David Mizan Hashim
"Experiments in Global
Design Practice: The
VERITAS Adventure"
    GSD Alumni
    Insights Lecture
    March 30, 2018

Peter Märkli
"My Profession, The Art
of Building"
    April 2, 2018

"Harvard HouseZero
Typology Symposium"
    Speakers: Preston Scott
    Cohen, Ali Malkawi, K.
    Michael Hays, Antoine
    Picon, Erika Naginski,
    Stephen Gray, Gary
    Hilderbrand
    Moderator: Grace La
    April 3, 2018

Left to right: Mohsen
Mostafavi, Min Chen, Drew
Gilpin Faust, Ali Malkawi, and
Alan Garber.

Jeanne Gang
"Thinking Through Practice
and Research"
    Open House Lecture
    April 5, 2018

Amanda Levete
    April 9, 2018

"Territorializing the Urban,
Urbanizing the Territory: New
Research" Colloquium
    Speakers: Samaa
    Elimam, Tommy Hill,
    Maria Atuesta, Tamer
    Elshayal; with Eve
    Blau, Neil Brenner, and
    Antoine Picon
    Co-organized by the
    Urban Theory Lab, the
    History/Theory Platform,
    and the PhD Program in
    Architecture, Landscape
    Architecture, and
    Urban Planning
    April 10, 2018

Raphael W. Bostic
"Fair Housing in the U.S.:
Past, Present, and Future?"
    John T. Dunlop Lecture
    April 10, 2018

Eric Parry
"Webs, Plates, Fists, and
Gloves: Designing with
Metals in Architecture"
    April 12, 2018

"Reframing Housing
Development: How Changes
in Design, Construction, and
Regulation Could Reduce the
Cost of Housing"
    Speakers: Chris
    Herbert, Andrew
    Freear, Brian Phillips,
    Michael Thomas, Katie
    Swenson, Randy Miller,
    James Shen, Fritz
    Wolff, Frank Anton,
    Jesse Kanson Benanav,
    Adhi Nagraj, Harriet
    Tregoning, Shekar
    Narasimhan, Marc
    Norman, Surella Segu,
    Christopher Herbert
    Copresented by the
    Harvard Joint Center
    for Housing Studies,
    the Loeb Fellowship,
    and the Office of
    Communications
    April 13, 2018

Henry N. Cobb, Peter
Eisenman, and Rafael Moneo
"How Will Architecture Be
Conceived?"
    April 17, 2018

Yvonne Cagle
    April 19, 2018

Raf Simons and Sterling
Ruby with Jessica Morgan
    Rouse Visiting Artists
    April 23, 2018

Left to right: Jessica
Morgan, Sterling Ruby, and
Raf Simons

Stig L. Andersson
"After Nature"
    April 24, 2018

Paola Antonelli
    Class Day Address
    May 23, 2018

Setting
the Table
Index

Published by the Harvard University Graduate School of Design and Actar.

Printed in Germany by PieReg, Berlin

ISBN 978-1-948765-10-7

Library of Congress Control Number: 2018946960

This book is typeset in Vendôme, Akzidenz Grotesk Old Face, and Nimbus Monospace.

The Harvard University Graduate School of Design is a leading center for education, information, and technical expertise on the built environment. Its Departments of Architecture, Landscape Architecture, Urban Planning and Design, Design Studies, and Design Engineering offer master and doctoral degree programs, and provide the foundation for the school's Advanced Studies and Executive Education Programs.

Actar
440 Park Avenue South
17th Floor
New York, NY 10016
actar.com

Harvard University
Graduate School of Design
48 Quincy Street
Cambridge, MA 02138
gsd.harvard.edu

HARVARD UNIVERSITY GRADUATE SCHOOL OF DESIGN

Mohsen Mostafavi
Dean and Alexander and Victoria Wiley Professor of Design

Ken Stewart
Assistant Dean and Director of Communications and Public Programs

Jennifer Sigler
Editor in Chief

Marielle Suba
Associate Editor

Meghan Sandberg
Production Manager

Travis Dagenais
Editorial Support

COLLECTION TEAM

Dan Borelli
Director of Exhibitions

David Zimmerman-Stuart
Exhibitions Coordinator

Ann Whiteside
Assistant Dean for Information Services

Janina Mueller
GIS and Data Librarian

Kevin Lau
Head of Instructional Technology Group and Library

Ardys Kozbial
Library Manager

Anita Kan
Model Coordinator

Ray Coffey
Model Coordination Assistant

GSD PHOTOGRAPHY

Anita Kan
Zara Tsanev
Justin Knight

PLATFORM 11: SETTING THE TABLE EDITORIAL TEAM

Esther Mira Bang
Lane Raffaldini Rubin
Enrique Aureng Silva
Editors

PLATFORM ADVISORY TEAM

Michael Hooper
Faculty Advisor
Urban Planning and Design

Megan Panzano
Faculty Advisor
Architecture

Robert Gerard Pietrusko
Faculty Advisor
Landscape Architecture

BOOK DESIGN

Neil Donnelly
Ben Fehrman-Lee
Designers

SETTING THE TABLE PHOTOGRAPHY

Adam DeTour
Photographer

Robyn Maguire
Photography Assistant

IMAGE CREDITS

97
Photos: Iwan Baan

140
Photo: Allan Buxton

61
Photo: Serge Hasenböhler, courtesy Sarah Oppenheimer

136, 138
Parawee Wachirabuntoon (MLA I)

121
Caroline Chao (MArch I)

180
Mies van der Rohe Archive, Museum of Modern Art, New York. © 2018 Artists Rights Society (ARS) New York / VG Bild-Kunst, Bonn

212
Image adapted from photo by Cheongwadae / Blue House

277
© Gran Fury

ACKNOWLEDGMENTS

The editors would like to thank the GSD for giving us the reins for this project and having faith that students should lead this effort. We would especially like to thank Marielle Suba for her dedication and patience. This book—and the newly imagined *Platform* series—would not be possible without her. We owe special thanks to Adam DeTour, who was an artistic partner to our project and whose photography lends the book its visual atmosphere. Thanks to Ken Stewart, Dan Borelli, Jennifer Sigler, Meghan Sandberg, David Zimmerman-Stuart, Maggie Janik, and the Office of Communications for supporting us throughout the duration of the project. Thanks to Michael Hooper, Megan Panzano, and Robert Gerard Pietrusko for sharing their insights, perspective, and experience with us along the way. Thanks to Susan Spaulding, Trevor O'Brien, Joseph Amato, and the Building Services staff for allowing us to occupy the entirety of Gund Hall to write the poems and setup the photos seen in this book. Thanks to Afshaan Alter Burtram, Alaina Fernandes, Taylor Horner, Sarah Hutchinson, Ashley Lang, Janessa Mulepati, and Aimée Taberner for providing the information necessary to contextualize hundreds of courses and projects. Thanks to Anita Kan and Ray Coffey, as well as Ann Whiteside, Kevin Lau, Janina Mueller, and the Frances Loeb Library Staff for supporting the collection of hundreds of models and digital project submissions. Additional thanks go to Martin Bechthold, Silvia Benedito, Rosetta S. Elkin, Zeina Koreitem, Burton LeGeyt, Caroline Newton, and Rachel Vroman for their help. We thank Mohsen Mostafavi for his continued support—intellectual and otherwise—and trust in us to capture a year of work at the GSD. Finally, we thank our colleagues, the students of the GSD, for their work, which made this book possible.